# Development through Liberation

Development through Liberation

# Development through Liberation

## Third World Problems and Solutions

### Gerald J. Kruijer

*Translated by Arnold Pomerans*

HUMANITIES PRESS INTERNATIONAL, INC.
Atlantic Highlands, NJ

First published in 1987 in the United States of America by
HUMANITIES PRESS INTERNATIONAL, INC.,
Atlantic Highlands, NJ 07716

© Gerald J. Kruijer, 1987

ISBN 0–391–03538–X
ISBN 0–391–03539–8 (Pbk.)                    LC 86–3915

Printed in Hong Kong

# Contents

v

# Foreword

It is not uncommon for sociologists to write about the poor and the oppressed. I sometimes think that our profession makes a good living out of it. But is rare to find us writing *for* the poor. To be sure, many of us write with a genuine sympathy and a concern to better the lot of the wretched of the earth. But such concern is often made subservient to the overriding need to stay within the rigorous parameters of scientific discourse. But how can a social science that is committed to value freedom and objectivity serve the needs of those who are oppressed by prevailing values and truths? How can the language of academia acquired through university education be used by those who never even finish school?

This dilemma is the key to Gerald Kruijer's lifelong work and this, his final, contribution to the struggle for liberation. The dilemma is not new, but the conviction and the passion with which it is resolved is.

Social science, Kruijer believed, will only serve the liberation of the poor if it liberates itself. It must liberate itself from the fruitless search for abstract concepts and timeless generalisations; from the neutering quest for unbiased objectivity and from its self-imposed sterile jargon.

Kruijer's science of liberation is about taking sides: that is, taking sides with the poor. Its starting-point is the real-life experiences of the poor, and it then proceeds to uncover, layer by layer, the debilitating structures of inequality and power which oppress the poor. The objective is to point to organizational, institutional and practical steps that can be taken – and indeed to point to those that frequently have been taken – to free the oppressed from their bondage.

Some readers may find the emotive language of this book an irritant. But the language is chosen to be a language that will reflect the experience of pain and struggle. For example, Kruijer argues that it is wrong to seek unemotional terms like 'unequal exchange' when laden terms like 'exploitation' convey so much better the experience of an indebted peasant suffering at the hands of a ruthless landowner or middleman. He argues that the liberation scientist should purposefully select a term or description that makes his/her viewpoint of anger or disapproval abundantly clear. This is the reason why the author shuns Marxist terminology with the same determination as with which he rejects the academic language of the bourgeois liberal tradition. Throughout he prefers the commonsense language of daily practice. The excellent translation from the Dutch by Arnold Pomerans has ensured that this objective has been wholly achieved.

Not everyone, not even some of those who share Kruijer's commitment and political conviction in broad outline, will agree with every detail of the substance of this work. Some, myself included, will recoil at the uncritical treatment of state socialist societies, particularly, for instance, the case of North Korea. Also, Kruijer's ahistorical and generalising perspective of the Third World, as a rather homogeneous group of nations in which economic and social development cannot take place as long as the umbilical cord with international capitalism has not been broken, is a perspective which I along with many others no longer regard as adequate in the restructured global political economy of the 1980s. Nevertheless the excellent descriptions of life in the Third World, covering all continents and gathered through personal travel and study, will deepen our understanding of the structures and processes that still dominate the lives of the *masses* of the population of the Third World, in whatever country, be it Brazil, South Korea or Ethiopia.

Kruijer died on 13 March 1986. He had only just put the finishing touches to this revised English version of *Bevrijdingswetenschap. Een partijdige visie op de Derde Wereld*, first published in the Netherlands in 1983.

From his student days in the war-torn city of Amsterdam, where he was actively involved in the resistance to German occupation, to his polemical and strident work as writer and speaker for Third World campaign groups in retirement – as well as during his long and prolific career as an 'academic' professor in between – Kruijer has always consistently and passionately fought alongside and for the oppressed. A stimulating debater, a generous and encouraging friend, he will be missed by all who knew him well and whose lives and ideas he enriched.

*Sheffield University*                                ANKIE M.M. HOOGVELT

# Introduction

The world in which we live can be viewed and judged in different ways, depending on our values and interests. This book is an attempt to view the problem of development from the standpoint and concerns of the poor in the Third World. That approach introduces a methodological question which must be answered: the author's attitude to his subject. Such themes as poverty and misery and opposition to them can be treated in a neutral, detached manner, but that is not my way. I shall not try to sham objectivity, but shall deliberately present the case of the poor; I shall take sides.

In serious studies, all conclusions must be supported by carefully collected data and correct reasoning. However, the collection of the data, and hence the conclusions, are unavoidably influenced by the researcher's interests, by the particular phenomena to which he directs his attention. Since I am aware of this selective process, I feel that I should mention my personal motives, and in that way clarify my approach.

I take a political stand on poverty, and all the misery connected with it: I treat it in the spirit of the Atlantic Charter framed by Roosevelt and Churchill in 1941 when their countries were threatened by their competitors, Germany and Japan. The Atlantic Charter states that the United States and Great Britain intend to work for a peaceful world in which all human beings can enjoy freedom from fear or want. This conception of freedom is also a central part of this book: freedom, to me, is first and foremost the elimination of those conditions that constrict life. Such freedom comes in the wake of struggle. In 1968, on a walk through Havana, my attention was attracted by the noise of crackling and banging. My curiosity aroused, I walked towards it and came upon an exhibition hall with the inscription 'Third World' above the entrance. Inside was a collection of pictures

1

and objects artistically portraying the problems. At the end came the solution: huge photographs covering the entire walls of a hall showed *guerrilleros* in the act of throwing hand grenades and firing machine guns with sound effects to match. I agreed with the analysis. Poverty is mainly caused by interhuman relationships and must be eliminated by peaceful means if possible. But if this is not possible, it must be eradicated by armed struggle against the forces at home responsible for it, as well as against powerful groups outside. I intend to make what contribution I can to that struggle. This is unlikely to please everybody. Both on the right and on the left there is strong opposition to what is described as interference in the affairs of another country. I beg to differ. To me, the world is one, a single network of governments, social groups (conservative and progressive) of enterprises and organisations playing an international role, and I cannot see why I must refrain from passing judgement or from involvement if there are abuses outside my own country.

The somewhat derisory dismissal of Europeans who, far from the heat of the struggle, present their ideas from comfortable armchairs, is another matter. Though not entirely unjust, this criticism must nevertheless be rejected. Every attitude that weakens the liberation struggle is something I condemn. Emancipation is not advanced in any way when feminists make derogatory remarks about men who support the women's movement, when workers reject intellectuals who take up their cause, when the freedom fighters in the Third World reject help from Europeans. And so I participate in the struggle that is being waged in the Third World, and do so with growing commitment. In step with the radicalisation of social relationships in the Third World, my thoughts about these relationships have grown more radical. I tend increasingly to side with the liberation movements and what I now practise in my own profession is what I call liberation science, a scientific approach whose aim is to make a contribution to the process by which the socially oppressed put an end to relationships that impede their progress. Those who speak out on this subject are speaking out for a committed science.

They are committed to children who try to play but cannot do so because of malnutrition. They are committed to the men and women who are paid starvation wages, and to the peasants whose produce earns them a pittance. They are committed to the many

who have no work at all or too little work and who try to live
from the crumbs of welfare that fall from the tables of the rich.
For the rickshaw boys; for the men and women who go in search
of loads with a rope round their neck; for the women who must
give themselves for money to loathsome men, and for those who
are oppressed and violated by their own menfolk. They are
committed to the homeless children scavenging for food in the
refuse bins of Santiago and immortalised in the verses of Victor
Jara, who sang not so long ago, until his mouth was smashed by
the rifle-butt of a Chilean soldier. They are committed to the
*guerrilleros* who have taken up arms against the oppressors of the
poor.

Liberation science must serve the liberation struggle and make
a contribution to it, to a process that involves a leap forward of
consciousness, organisation and activity, and that leads to a
society based on liberty, fraternity and equality, as defined in the
section in Chapter 8 headed *The picture of the future*.

Throughout this book, when I refer to the problems of workers,
peasants and so on, I am of course referring to the problems of
men and women alike. I would have liked to make this point
explicit on all occasions but am prevented for reasons of style. I
apologise to those women readers who object to this omission,
and whose views on the subject I fully share.

Though this book is confined to the problems of the poor in the
Third World, it can also be applied to other liberation processes
because it is also a methodological study (which shows how those
who use this approach set to work).

As far as the Third World is concerned, my work at the
University of Amsterdam has taught me that amongst those
young people who are interested in its problems only a few are
able to take a Third World point of view. Conservative students
do not wish to do so and progressive students are impeded by
spectacles whose lenses have been distorted by critical focusing
on their own society. Disillusioned by the (side) effects of the
giddy heights to which the capitalist economy has climbed in the
rich countries, they believe that the poor countries must act
differently. Dreams of a healthy life in a small community with a
small-scale technology in which traditional culture is held in high
regard sway their thoughts and prevent them from seeing reality,
and the balance of power in particular, in sharp perspective. It is

the aim of this book to show why the Third World does so little dreaming and relies instead on actions that are often of a violent kind.

There are many studies of the Third World, and quite a few proposed solutions. My study is different because it is based consistently on the case of the poor, of the oppressed. Not that the oppressed are the main subject of the study; while it examines the oppressed it also analyses the oppressor, and in particular looks at the system of oppression. One of my books on Surinam (South America) is a systematic application of that approach.[1] Liberation science not only helps the oppressed to identify their problems, it also helps them to set up and run resistance movements.

In Chapter 1 I discuss the problem that constitutes the starting point of this study: the poverty or the great majority of men and women in the Third World. I go on to show why this problem can only be tackled satisfactorily with a certain approach. This is described in Chapter 2 (Liberation Science) in which the reader will discover, among other things, that those who practise this science have liberated themselves from neocolonial bonds and are antagonistic to the (social) science of the oppressor states. They feel it is essential to develop an independent Third World science and question those Marxist theories that apply more particularly to European conditions. I hasten to add, however, that, starting from the position of the oppressed, I often arrive at conclusions that are similar to those of Marxism–Leninism or have a great affinity with them. Admittedly, my book dispenses with one awkward aspect of many Marxist studies, namely a vocabulary that can only be understood by a small (elitist?) group of initiates. In other words, there is no Marxist–Leninist jargon.

But the oppressed are not the only subject of the study. As in other branches of applied science, the concepts and theories of liberation science are largely determined by an approach that links the present to the future. The liberation scientist has a picture of the present constellation of society and keeps a picture of the future before his mind's eye. An essential fact of the present constellation is inequality, while the picture of the future is based on the principle of equality.

The present-day world is described in Chapters 3, 4 and 5. It is a world in which the powerful oppress the powerless. The world of the future, which informs all the actions and policies of the liberation scientist is a world in which it is not easy to oppress others. This attractive future is described in Chapter 8. The two views of the world are very closely connected; the one is inconceivable without the other. It is almost impossible to describe and analyse the problems of the poor without a picture of a better world; conversely it is almost impossible to conceive of a better society without identifying the shortcomings of the present-day world. Alas, a better world is not yet within the grasp of the Third World. I believe that in the immediate future and for many decades to come, the struggle against international capitalism will dominate world politics, and that this struggle will be hard fought.

Chapter 6 is devoted to liberation theory. The theory entails certain solutions: the transformation of the balance of power in the poor countries as well as on the international scene. This will only come about if the oppressed succeed in smashing the power of their enemies, starting in their own countries. For that reason Chapter 7 is devoted to the liberation struggle. When that struggle has been won and power has been transferred to men and women who represent the interests of the people, then a liberation strategy based on equality can be developed and implemented. The last two chapters are devoted to this subject.

It goes without saying that a book covering so many subjects cannot be comprehensive: neither in respect of the factual material presented in it nor in respect of its argumentation. The book simply records my own experiences in the Third World, amplified by a number of quotations. It also presents a view that still needs closer examination, but in my opinion can already contribute to the discussion. This view entails a particular approach so that this book may be treated as a methodological study. It points the way for those who wish to study the problems of the Third World from the point of view of the interests of the poor. I suspect that some critics will dismiss my work as superficial. I myself prefer a friendlier term, namely global. But that does not mean that my presentation is over-generalised and abstract. This book includes many accounts of concrete situations; scenes of village life in Asia, Africa and America are described in some detail. In this respect, as well as in others, it is in the

Amsterdam sociographic tradition with its concrete descriptions of social life as a basis for more general reflections and, in particular, for the solution of social problems.

As an explanation of the tone in which this book is written, I would like to say just one thing about ways of describing the lot of the oppressed. In dealing with that subject it is sometimes necessary to report hard realities in strong words. A neutral, detached approach to writing about oppression and the struggle against it would have a camouflaging effect. The liberation scientist describes the dispossession and consequent pauperisation of independent peasants through the eyes of the victims, that is, in a highly emotional way. He studies the level of consciousness and the (potential) resistance of the oppressed, and if there is occasion to do so he allows his descriptions to resound with the social commitment of the freedom fighters.

The writer of this book does not claim to be presenting anything completely new. The Columbian sociologist, Orlando Fals Borda, used the term 'liberation sociology' some time ago, and the Nigerian scientist, Omafume Onoge, advocates liberation anthropology as an answer to cultural anthropology that holds the West up as an example and refuses to condemn capitalism.[2]

Nor is it new to side with the poor and oppressed. The number of writers who have done so and whose writings reflect a moral and political commitment is by no means small. Ankie M.M. Hoogvelt, a sociologist at the University of Sheffield, is one of them. She was kind enough to go through the longer Dutch version of this book and to suggest cuts and additions to the original.

Whether the material in this book is new, old, or new in part only is not particularly relevant. What matters is the need to bear in mind at all times the importance of using the most rigorous approach possible towards a phenomenon that is far from new but persists, namely the oppression of the majority of mankind. Much as so many priests have found it necessary to develop a liberation theology, so a liberation science had to emerge.

[And now for the central problem.]

# 1  Poverty

This book deals with hundreds of millions of people who suffer from the way the world is being run. But I shall begin with a single victim, with Carolina Maria de Jesus, a woman alone looking after herself and her three children. When people visited her in her *favela*, one of the slum districts of São Paulo (Brazil), they would exclaim in dismay: 'My God, imagine living somewhere like this, it's only good enough for pigs!' Carolina wrote this down in her diary, and I shall be quoting more from it to help to convey some impression of how the poor live.[1]

At the time that Carolina was keeping her diary, she spent her days searching through the dustbins of São Paulo for paper, scrap iron and rags, which she could then sell. 'After a day scavenging, my feet hurt so much that I can't walk another step.' But now and then she was lucky: 'Today I made rice and beans with fried eggs. What a joy!' Mostly, however, she had cause for little but complaint: 'I got hold of a whole lot of greens but it's no use to me without any fat. The children are frantic because there's nothing to eat.' 'My children are always hungry.'

In the past she used to sing, but 'I have forgotten how, for all joy has gone.' 'My life has been nothing but black up to now. My skin is black, and so is the place where I live.' 'If I find anything in a dustbin that I can eat, I eat it. I haven't got the courage to do away with myself.' 'I haven't done any washing for two weeks because I haven't been able to buy any soap. The bedding is so dirty, it turns your stomach.'

One day she came back to find the pillows filthy and her children reeking because a neighbour had poured the contents of her chamber pot over them. There is a lot of jealousy in the *favela*. While she was writing her diary, a six-year old girl said to her: 'What are you writing, you dirty nigger?' The child's mother heard her, but didn't tell her off.

There is very little mutual aid. 'I . . . wasn't feeling very well. The people in the *favela* knew that I was sick, but no one did anything for me.' 'Everyone who lives round here tries to keep himself to himself.' Fellow men are feared. When she was out picking up paper she worked quickly, for, as she wrote: 'I was afraid those monsters might break into my hovel and hurt my children. I worked in fear and trembling.'

In this slum, alcohol is a common sight. 'They drink to celebrate and they drink to drown their sorrow. Drink is balm for despair.' Time and again Carolina wrote about fights: 'They were fighting again. I have been living in the *favela* these eleven years and I am revolted by scenes like that.' 'They fight without knowing why.'

Carolina distrusts men. In a queue of waiting women, she wrote, she heard men being compared to animals. 'Mine is wild like a bull, and nasty too.' 'And mine is a donkey. The bastard.' 'All my life, men have given me nothing but trouble. And children, that they leave me to bring up.' 'I've had nothing but bitter experiences as far as men are concerned.' Carolina made several entries about women being beaten up by their husbands and fleeing into the streets, sometimes naked or half-dressed.

There is little interest in elections: 'The people don't pay any attention to the elections, they're like a Trojan horse trotted out every four years. The big shots only put in an appearance at election time.' Now and then a rebellious tone creeps in, for instance when she thinks of Father Luíz, who told her and her neighbours to be humble. 'I thought to myself, if Father Luíz was married with children and earned a pittance, I wonder just how humble he would be. He tells us that God only appreciates suffering when it's borne with resignation. If Father Luíz saw his own children eating rotten food that had been left over by vultures and rats, he'd probably rise up in revolt himself.' Another priest came along in a motor car and encouraged the people to have children. 'I thought to myself,' wrote Carolina, 'why do poor people have to have children? The children of poor people will never be anything more than labourers.'

In her dreams she saw a better life. 'A dream is the most wonderful thing there is.' 'I dreamt I lived in another house. I had everything I needed. Sacks and sacks of beans. I looked at the sacks and laughed, and I said to João [her son]: "Now we can kick poverty right out of the door." And I called out: "Out you go, poverty!".' 'I dreamt that I was an angel. My robe fell about me in rich folds. It had long pink sleeves. I rose straight up from the earth to heaven.' And her conclusion: 'The people of Brazil are only happy when they sleep.'

Throughout this book I shall refer to actual cases, before entering into a general discussion. As a result the reader should always be able to tell what I am talking about. Some of these cases I was able to observe for myself. I have come face to face with poverty on more than one occasion, in Peru, for instance, in 1974, in a tea-growing area. The district governor addressed the Netherlands Aid Mission of which I was a member and barely managed to master his emotions when he spoke of the worries that weighed down his people. Soon afterwards I saw for myself that he had not exaggerated. There was much malnutrition – especially among the children of large families – due mainly to lack of certain proteins and fresh vegetables. The adults stilled their hunger by chewing coca leaves and drinking maize or sugar-cane spirits. Diseases were common, the people had parasites (from polluted water), skin disorders (from the ubiquitous dirt), intestinal infections (from eating unwashed and poorly cooked foods), anaemia (from malnutrition), tuberculosis and many other afflictions. Housing conditions were abominable. In towns and villages, as well as in the countryside, I came across whole areas in which not a single home appeared adequate. Most houses were in a lamentable state. As a rule there was a single room to a family, at most two.

As elsewhere in Peru, there was a great deal of illiteracy among the inhabitants of this tea-growing area. Human relations were shaped and dominated by frustration, by migration to far-away labour markets, by poor organisation and by unstable male–female bonds. Poverty spells social disorganisation.

I feel justified in using the word poverty and speaking of the poor, because the people whose life I describe refer to themselves as poor people.

## The pattern of poverty

This picture of poverty, described as it was in a small valley, will be expanded in this section with particular stress on the psychological and social aspects, the intellectual and spiritual needs of the poor and the general dislocation of human relationships.

The pattern of poverty is one of frustration, of constant failure to reach any worthwhile objective. The poor are unable to realise their ambitions, however modest these may be. They turn away from their fellows and from society; an individualistic attitude predominates. The building of organisations does not strike them as a solution to their problems and is, in any case, obstructed by their circumstances, mental attitude and, last but not least, their enemies.

This pattern is characteristic of most capitalist societies in the Third World. It can also be found in quite a few prosperous capitalist countries, for instance in the slums of North America,[2] but here I shall confine myself to poverty in the Third World. Nor shall I discuss poverty and deprivation in the socialist countries.

Because the pattern of poverty is an adaptation and a reaction to a dependent form of capitalism, it assumes various degrees, depending on the extent to which capitalism has succeeded in affecting the great majority, and, of course, on how long it has been doing so. I came across it to a very pronounced extent in Jamaica, a country whose population was torn from Africa and has been affected by capitalism for a very long time. The pattern is just as clear in parts of Mexico, Puerto Rico and Peru.[3] It is less clearly developed, but nevertheless emphatically present, in Surinam. Special circumstances explain why the pattern of poverty in this ex-colony, now a neocolonial country, is less pronounced than in Jamaica.[4] In Jakarta, again, a sociologist did discover some aspects of the culture of poverty (a term coined by Oscar Lewis which is related to the pattern of poverty) but not all.[5] The most fatal feature is the disruption capitalism brings to those regions in which it is most deeply rooted; to mining and plantation areas, for instance, and to the vast urban slum districts. We may consider the pattern of poverty as a kind of index; in some countries it leaves more traces than in others. In those with few traces, more can be expected to emerge as soon as the capitalist grip on society becomes stronger. One think I wish to make clear, however: the presence of poverty is not necessarily bound up with the presence of the pattern of poverty described below – that pattern is part and parcel of a particular social structure.

I prefer not to use Oscar Lewis's term 'culture of poverty' because it raises certain difficulties. Culture – ideas about values, norms, and so on – is handed down from parents to children. Perhaps that applies to some aspects of the pattern as well, but the pattern itself is moulded in the main by the social experiences of those it affects.

Hence no culture of poverty, although it should be said that I greatly admire Lewis and do not agree with many of his critics.[6] The fact that he allows the people he studies to speak for themselves is something I particularly value. People tell him their life stories and he writes them down. He strives by this method to avoid describing the life of the poor from a middle-class standpoint, from that of the anthropologist.

Of considerable importance, too, is the fact that in his work Lewis paid great attention to the position of women. Life on the fringes of a dependent capitalist society spells martyrdom for men and women, but a woman's life is particularly arduous. She is oppressed in the productive no less than in the reproductive process. Reproduction means maintaining or increasing the means of production, including the class of wage labourers. In the capitalist mode of production it is women above all who have the task, for the most part unpaid, of feeding the workers and caring for them, and also of producing and rearing the future generation of workers.

The position of women in the productive process does not always find expression in the statistics. Unnoticed by the statistician, women join the black economy in the fields, in trade and in sweated outwork done in the home. They are paid much less than men, have fewer chances of promotion, are sexually abused (maidservants in particular) and in some cases – for instance when mechanisation is introduced – are displaced in their jobs by men. When they come home they still have to do their domestic chores, and here, too, they are oppressed. Oscar Lewis points out that in the slums of Mexico City men believe firmly that women should work for them unpaid.

It is not unusual for an African woman to work a sixteen-hour day. She gets up before sunrise, fetches water, looks after the children, cleans the home and the yard and prepares some food if there is any. Then she walks to the fields, her smallest child on her back, her tools on her head and in her hands. For hours she works on the land, keeping a constant watch over the children she has brought along with her. Then she gathers fuel, fetches more water, prepares and cooks food in a time-consuming and labour-intensive way, serves up the meal, tends the children, etc.[7]

Molara Ogundipe-Leslie, quoting Mao Tse-tung, says that the African woman carries six mountains on her back: the first and second are her oppression by neocolonialism and traditional structures, the third is her backwardness, the fourth is a man, the fifth is her colour or race, and the sixth, not the least important, is she herself: women are shackled by their own negative self-image, by centuries of internalising the ideologies of patriarchy and gender hierarchy.[8]

Before the colonial period women were involved in politics in various parts of Africa, but what power or influence they had was undone by the colonial rulers.[9] These rulers believed that the place of African women was in the home, as dependent wives and mothers.

In capitalist society, conceptions of the position of women are adapted, moreover, to the needs of production. This has been stressed by the Trinidadian sociologist, Rhoda Reddock. When slave ships carried enough cheap labour to the Caribbean it was not necessary for slave women to produce descendants. Instead, they were expected, just like the men, to work on their master's farm or estate. But as soon as the slave trade came to an end, everything changed: the workers themselves had to ensure the maintenance and preservation of their class. Family life was encouraged. But whenever necessary, women were brought back into the production process as cheap and submissive work units. Today in the so-called free trade zones, industrial areas in which foreigners are allowed considerable freedom, 70 per cent of all workers in foreign-owned industries are women. They often work much longer hours than men – an example is South Korea. In addition, their earnings are roughly half those of their male colleagues.[10] This is true not only of industry but also of work on the land, as we find in India.[11]

But let us return to the problems that afflict men and women alike. The analysis of poverty which follows is based in part on my own studies in Peru, in Surinam and in Jamaica. In the last, I was assisted by the Jamaican sociologist Pearl A. Gammon and the Surinamese sociologist U. Waldo Heilbron. We interviewed 248 mothers in Jamaica from the so-called lower class and, for amplification, we also put questions to two categories of the male population.[12]

If a strategy of change is to be developed then it becomes essential to study the pattern of poverty. In a later chapter, entitled The Liberation Struggle, I shall be dealing with the possibilities for change and with the means to be employed to that end. Here we shall merely examine a number of psychological and social factors that must be considered as a coherent whole. These factors are: hoped-for improvements but poor prospects; uncertainty and fear; individualism; an underdeveloped organisational life; reactions to frustration.

## Psychological and social factors

### *Hoped-for improvements but poor prospects*

Despite their disadvantaged position in the socio-economic fabric, the poor maintain hope for a betterment of their situation. It is true that the fulfilling of their daily needs takes up most of their attention – their straitened material circumstances make great demands on them and malnutrition undermines their resolve – but they do want a secure and successful life.

Some social forces kindle their hopes or desires. Education is one of these. An inquiry conducted by my institute showed that Surinamese children have hopes in a good future. Politics, too, is a force that arouses hope in some countries. At election time, politicians arouse expectations by telling the poor that if only they will unite (under their leadership), they will be strong enough to enforce improvements.

And so the flame of hope is kindled time and again, only to be snuffed out again soon afterwards. For the present is hard and the future anything but rosy. A large percentage of those interviewed in Jamaica thought that ordinary men and women are becoming worse off. Many felt that it was irresponsible to bring children into the world. Most of the poor are pessimistic; they see no hope of progress. Nowadays Jamaicans have to work almost as many hours as the slaves of old and, moreover, for inordinately low wages. Poverty and misery have been their lot for generations.

*Uncertainty and fear*

The poor are in so weak a negotiating position that they are forced to accept work that gives them very little security. Indeed, they are victims of exploitation and sometimes they even have to pay to get work. They have no, or very little, access to sources and channels of information. Their self-confidence and self-respect are low.[13]

Even those who are not too badly off are under constant threat. In the southern Italian village studied by Banfield under the fictitious name of Montegrano, the people were in dread of sliding down the social ladder.[14] Elsewhere, too, such feelings of anxiety are common. The poor are in no position to build up reserves against bad times. Even many Surinamese schoolchildren were found to be filled with anxieties. When asked to react to the statement 'I'm afraid of what will happen to me when I leave school', 39 per cent agreed with it, and only one-third said that they were not afraid of the future.

Women have even more reason for fear than the men. They are exploited more blatantly and live in continuous fear of being violated by their husbands, 'friends' or employers, on top of which they run the risk of bearing unwanted children.

*Individualism*

Anxiety, uncertainty and poor prospects would be reasons enough for uniting, but in a dependent capitalist system which offers few opportunities for advancement everyone looks upon his neighbour as a competitor. The poor in Ibadan (Nigeria) – wrote the British sociologist Gutkind – have set their hopes on climbing the social ladder as individuals. They do not cooperate. Each hopes that some rich person will turn up to help him or her personally.[15]

In 'Montegrano' people withdraw into their families – they have an egoistic family fixation; but elsewhere egoism is often purely individualistic. Thus many Caribbean women try to manage by themselves as best they can. They sell produce, keep some livestock and work smallholdings by themselves. They want to be as independent as possible. The word 'independent', which is so commonly used in the Caribbean, has the additional meaning of not wanting much to do with other people. From our enquiries in Jamaica and Surinam, it appeared that many people live without any strong ties to their fellow men; many seem to have few friends.

Without doubt, most accept the duty to help family members, but if their poverty is too great this duty cannot be fulfilled. Enquiries in Jamaica and Surinam have shown that only a few expect help from their family, least of all poor Jamaican women. People are even more pessimistic about help from their neighbours.

In Caribbean folk tales, the concept of 'every man for himself' is a very strong one. The cunning spider Anancy (symbol of the powerless black man) gets the better of the powerful noisy tiger by guile. (In Surinam people refer to felines such as the jaguar as 'tigri'.)

Poverty not only fosters egoism, it also breeds hostility towards those who are better off. The ethnographer Pechuël-Loesche came across this reference to envy in West Africa years ago: 'However high a bird may fly, to earth it must return.'[16] In Jamaica, where, as we know, most of the population is of West African descent, there is an almost identical saying: 'Independent John Crow fly high, but nebber min', one day him fedder will drop,' while the negroid bush dwellers of Surinam say: 'The bird flies, but its head is bound to end up on the ground.'[17] People who are well off or aim for riches (the high fliers) are disliked: public opinion is against them and wants them to live just like the rest of the poor (to come back to earth). John Crow is a great black bird who hovers for hours in the air.

It goes without saying that not every poor person is a hyper-individualist. There is a wide spectrum ranging from extreme individualism to complete self-denial, an utter dedication to the interests of society as a whole. But poverty forces most people to keep fairly close to the individualistic extreme.

## Underdeveloped organisational life

Life at the limits of subsistence offers few chances of building up organisations, the less so as that activity is often very dangerous for the oppressed.

Reports from all parts of the Third World refer to a low level of organisation. Thus the agricultural workers in the Kosi district in the Indian state of Bihar are reported to be so unorganised that they are unable to obtain better wages and working conditions. Without outside help, the researcher concludes, these workers will be quite unable to oppose the employers' determination to nip any such organisation in the bud.[18] In Ibadan, the unemployed even seemed unable to fit into the traditional friend and family groups.[19] And in a Tanzanian village the disposition of villagers to work together declined after the land ceased to be communally owned. The North American couple, the Keurs, who noted the absence of organised life among the poor in the Windward Islands, in the Netherlands Antilles, associated this lack with the existence of fierce class conflicts.[20]

Those who scan the Third World with an optimistic bias, young social scientists who have not been there before, see all sorts of hopeful developments even in the organisational field: groups saving together, making brooms together, selling things together and so on, but on closer investigation it all turns out to be very disappointing, for nearly all such organisations are short-lived. In some cases, they are backed by charitable middle-class people who use them to boost their own importance or the interests of their own class.

Now there are very good reasons why these organisations should be so poorly developed. People are afraid. They can expect strong opposition whenever they try to further their material interests in a way that clashes with the interests of others, their exploiters. To illustrate this point I would ask the reader to follow me down a river in Guyana. On the banks of this river, the Mahaicony, live stockfarmers, large and small, whose milk used to be transported daily by two prosperous farmers, who also acted as moneylenders, to the village of Mahaicony. Thanks to their monopoly, these two could raise transport prices almost at will while providing a minimal service. The government decided to help the stockbreeders and to set up a cooperative. Not everyone accepted that help. Some hesitated to do so because they owed money to the two rich men or because – more generally – they were afraid of them. And so they compromised, selling some of their milk through the cooperative and the rest through one of the two independent individuals. What happened may be imagined. There was a fierce struggle between the cooperative and the private entrepreneurs who threatened, in their capacity as shopkeepers, to withhold credit. Nor was that all. One morning those who had joined the cooperative found that their cows had had their tongues cut out, causing the animals to die of hunger. Later the boat belonging to the cooperative was sunk. But the cooperative stood fast. The government produced a new boat and prominent figures in the region came out in support of the cooperative. Thus there was a happy ending, in Mahaicony, although in many cases there is not.

In India peasants who join an association can expect fierce competition from private traders and moneylenders.[21] And in Latin America things are worse still. Here peasant associations and similar organisations are opposed by force. In 1980, thousands of people were killed in Guatemala, most for being members of social, religious and labour organisations or for having contacts with political parties. Guatemalans were only allowed to be members of such organisations as were under strict government control.[22] Even in countries where they have less cause to be afraid, the poor are generally weakly organised, and if they are members of organisations they participate less in the life of these organisations than do the privileged few.

The conclusion must be that those sections of the population who are worst off have little or no organisational power to change anything in the system. The poor have neither time nor energy to form organisations, besides which they are afraid to stick their necks out.

## Reactions to frustration

The reader will by now have gathered that it is almost impossible for the poor to satisfy their needs. They feel frustrated; they see almost insuperable obstacles placed before them.

The most immediate cause of their frustration is clearly their lack of an adequate income coupled to uncertainty about the future. Frustration involves hopelessness and a lack of prospects, and leads to a lack of self-respect. It is reported from one region in Mexico that the women there first began to despise themselves when they were no longer able to maintain themselves or to help their families. When the district in which they were born was integrated into the national economy of Mexico, their job opportunities shrank dramatically and they were forced to accept menial positions (as servants or prostitutes) with a consequent sense of inferiority.[23]

Frustrations are the result of a social situation that sociologists refer to as anomie, a state in which many people are prevented from attaining socially desirable ends by socially acceptable means and cease to care about the rules that define what may or may not be done.[24]

I shall now discuss various reactions to frustration, that is, to anomie: all-out effort; hoping for a miracle; keeping up appearances; escape; theft and violence; apathy and other reactions. I shall go on to examine the economic and political attitudes of people who live on the fringes of an underdeveloped capitalist society.

### All-out effort

Some poor people make an all-out, almost superhuman, effort to earn money. In Jamaica peasant women cover large distances in mountainous terrain on foot in order to sell small quantities of fruit in distant markets – veritable hunger marches!

Peasants in underdeveloped countries toil through the long hours of the day under the hot sun. Small shopkeepers and small tradesmen, too, stretch themselves to the limit to earn a mere pittance.

### Hoping for a miracle

If an all-out effort does not succeed, these marginal people hope to have a windfall. This explains why people in poverty-stricken countries are so obsessed with lotteries; the very poor join in whenever they are able to put together a few pennies. The dream of becoming rich at a stroke may be found in every walk of life, but for the poor it may seem the only way out, one for those who are convinced that they can only survive by luck, by a miracle.

## Keeping up appearances

Some people go out of their way to keep up the appearances of a 'decent bourgeois life'. They are the 'quiet poor', recognisable by their efforts to present a dignified demeanour through their dress, the furnishings of their homes and their speech. People who react in this way have not yet lost all hope, but believe they can improve their lot by imitating the behaviour of the upper classes. Perhaps they will be noticed, perhaps it will all pay off.

## Escape

Yet another response or adaptation is to take refuge, to retreat: into thoughts (daydreams, for instance), into ecstatic forms of religious worship or by leaving one's district or country (migration).

Throughout the Caribbean, you will meet groups of people who, at religious meetings, turn their thoughts away from the grey reality of daily life to linger in a better world. In the dark or by lamplight they – lost in profound reverie – dance to the rhythm of the drums. Jamaica, for one, is studded with small meeting houses, buildings made of planks and covered with thatch in which preachers lead the people in prayer. There is much Christian preaching and hymn-singing spiced with African ritual. Through clapping, drumming, rattling, praying aloud, reading from the Bible and shouts of approval the congregation displays its feelings and its convictions. Some of the faithful even become ecstatic, to the delight and encouragement of the rest. It needs no stressing that other religions, too, offer opportunities for escape, or that religion has many more aspects than the ones just mentioned. Politics, too, is a means of directing the mind to a better world, here on earth in this case. But not everyone believes in its efficacy.

A spectacular form of escape is migration. Many people in the poor world pack their bags and leave for the nearest big city or, if they have the chance, for another country. Thus 200000 girls have left rural Thailand for Bangkok, many to work in bars, teahouses, hotels or in the flesh trade as massage girls. With the money they earn they are able to support their families back home in their village, but they themselves live a miserable existence, seeking oblivion in drink and drugs.[25]

In West Africa, many people made for oil-rich Nigeria; from India and Egypt they went to Saudi Arabia; from the former British Caribbean to the United Kingdom and from Surinam to the Netherlands.

From data collected in Surinam it appears clear that emigration is a direct reaction to want. Few of those who went to the Netherlands did so for pleasure. Most of the old and young who were interviewed expressed a clear preference for living in Surinam.

## Theft and violence

Theft is a commonly-used means of acquiring some of the material pleasures normally reserved for the better-off. Violence, too, is a common reaction to hopelessness.

It is a central tenet of this book that poverty and oppression go hand in hand. The connection is most blatant in South Africa, where many forms of what the whites call criminal behaviour are also found. 'For me,' a black social worker in South Africa declared, 'there is no doubt that the main cause of the violence all round is the frustration of our people, a direct result of a system that reminds them every minute of the day that they are inferior.' Nor is it merely discrimination to which they react. In 1973, six out of every ten black people who broke the laws of the whites were unemployed.[26]

In South Africa, violence, that is the aggression of the oppressed, is also directed at fellow victims of the system, and much the same thing happens in Jamaica. There, people pay good money to consult an *obeahman* (sorcerer) on how to play a trick on a neighbour, how to make him sick, crippled or dead. The motive of such practices is often envy. A more up-to-date means of inflicting injury upon a hated neighbour is to employ a lawyer as soon as there is the slightest reason to do so.

## Apathy

Another way of coming to terms with poverty is to depress the level of ambition. Those who do so have given up striving after a better life. A proportion of these become utterly indifferent and fall into apathy. This is what happened, according to one researcher, among the peasants in central and southern Tunisia under French dominion. Poverty brought about a state of indifference. Since there were no prospects, people simply stopped being concerned about what the morrow might bring.[27]

Feeling hopeless and helpless, those under subjugation reconcile themselves to it by the delusion that nothing can be done. 'Our misery,' I heard people say near Cuzco (Peru), 'has been decreed by fate. We have been born to be dupes. Our lot has been cast, and if the spirits fail us things can only get worse.' The acceptance of frustrating social conditions as unalterable is common. In the Sudan, where social relations used to be patriarchal, people seemed quite resigned to the oppressive government, for as one of their proverbs puts it: 'The master of the sword is also master of the country.'[28]

*Some other reactions*

There are many more reactions to frustration than those we have mentioned. Some are totally ineffective: foolish things done out of sheer desperation. A popular means resorted to in the Caribbean for working towards the one fine day when one has a slightly larger amount of money to spend, the day when one is 'rich' for a moment, is by joining a savings club. The members make a regular – say a weekly – contribution they can ill afford to one of their club. In return, every member gets a turn at collecting the entire bank less the organiser's expenses. On the happy day, the winner is indeed quite 'rich', but he then has to pay off all the debts he has incurred during the laborious saving period.

Yet another way of acquiring money – if it cannot be gained by work – is to beg. This may be done either by holding out your hand in the street or by knocking at the door of the authorities. *Lanti-sa-pai*, the country can pay, this is called in Surinam.

**Economic attitudes**

The economic attitude of the poor is one of great caution.

Because a poor man has many enemies, and because his sources of support are so small, the peasant dare not take any risks. He arranges his affairs in such a way that the chances of losing everything are as small as possible. And in addition, he prefers quick-growing crops that will give him quick returns. He is also very keen on planting food for his own consumption, for that spells greater security. The need for quick returns and security is not confined to peasants. In Surinam, I noticed that the field labourers on the banana plantations expected quick results from trade union action. When these did not materialise, they saw no reason for paying their dues.

If a peasant notices that others profit excessively from his work, he withdraws and practises a kind of passive resistance, something that Gören Hydén, a political scientist with a great deal of experience in Tanzania, considers a plausible response. If the peasant holds the authorities responsible for his misfortunes, then he will resist the government and its officials, and if his position in the market economy gives him too little profit and security, he will refuse to be absorbed into the market economy.[29]

It struck me time and again that agricultural extension officers fail to appreciate the attitude of the impoverished peasant. They look upon him as a small entrepreneur, that is, someone who is prepared to invest his land, money and labour in those economic activities that produce the maximum financial returns. They are not completely wrong, but they are not completely right either. It is obvious that the peasant should want to make as large a profit as possible, but that is not the only factor that determines his behaviour. Security is another criterion and that is why he prefers a number of small, scattered fields to a large piece of land. It cuts his risks. The agricultural officer fails to grasp this fact, for to him efficiency is the paramount principle, and one large field is, of course, much easier to work.

The rather passive economic attitude of peasants and agricultural labourers everywhere, or at least of many of them, has been and continues to be a matter of record. However, it should be noted that in the socio-economic context in which these studies are made, a different, more active attitude would bring the peasants and workers very little benefit. The observations are confined to capitalist systems with a high degree of exploitation and peasants wielding little power.

## Political attitudes

None of the reactions to frustration we have mentioned leads to tangible changes in the structure and the cultural life of society. They only serve as safety valves, contain popular dissatisfaction, and so help to maintain the status quo. However, there are always some people who react with rebellion, and this could be a highly significant attitude if their rebellion led to the creation of a freedom movement. But very often rebellion, too, is no more than a safety valve. In the Caribbean there have been many rebellions. History during and following the period of slavery is full of revolts, but these were seldom aimed at fundamental social changes, and, in any case, had little success. At best, they led to minor changes or to the acceleration of developments that had already been started. It is a fact of life that people in capitalist Third World systems prefer rising into a higher class to social change. Only when the chances of advancement look utterly hopeless and when blame for this deadlock is placed on the prevailing social structure, is there a clamour for incisive social change.

There was and continues to be impressive resistance, as we shall see in Chapter 7, but for the most part people dare not resist. The poor peasant is threatened by dangers of all kinds: plant and animal diseases; hurricanes and floods; price fluctuations; trade restrictions; unemployment (inasmuch as he needs additional work), and most of all by his powerful fellows.

The Dutch social psychologist, Gerrit Huizer, who has a good eye for the (potential) spirit of resistance among the people, discovered in 1955 that the peasants in El Salvador stood in terror of their lords and masters.[30] The same is true of workers in the Third World. They feel impotent, and they consider it only common sense to bow to the inevitable, to adapt. And to justify this attitude they blame their misery on fate, on the accident of birth or colour, as well as on personal shortcomings. But that attitude can change. The germs for change are there, since resignation does not necessarily exclude political consciousness. This can be seen among the poor in Ibadan (Nigeria). Political consciousness is an insight into power relationships at the regional and national level, and into its effects upon the lives of various groups of people. This insight may be seen very clearly to be

present in the slum districts of Ibadan. The two hundred poor
people who were interviewed made a clear distinction between
'we, the poor' and 'they, the rich'.[31] I found much the same in
Jamaica and (to a somewhat lesser extent) in Surinam. Yet the
poor of Ibadan, conscious though they were of their lowly class
position, did not hold radical views. What they wanted was to rise
into the middle classes. This is also true of peasants: their political
struggles tend to centre round the demand for more land rather
than round broader political objectives, long-term concepts and
ideologies, a view reported by T. Shanin.[32] The lack of political
commitment among the poor has been remarked upon by many
writers. The poor are said to be more interested in changes in
their immediate environment – better houses, better schools,
etc. – than in broader political objectives. In elections, they do
not like to vote for 'left' parties which they think have little
chance of victory and cannot fulfil their promises, or so we are told
by Peter Lloyd, a British social anthropologist with a great deal
of experience in Nigeria.[33] The parties on the left often lack
appeal because of the many splinter groups that make it impossible
to create a truly effective force. The oppressed object to the
divisiveness of the left, and often feel suspicious of those who
present themselves as leaders. In Ibadan the general impression
of the *mekunnu* (the common people, or those without money) is
that political leaders look after their own interests at the expense
of the poor, and this feeling is shared in many parts of the world.

We must not, however, leave it at simply noting these facts; we
must also interpret them. And if we do, we cannot but repeat
what has already been said several times: the poor are afraid.
They dare not organise properly, let alone attack dangerous
enemies. However, as soon as they feel stronger or as soon as the
position of their enemies weakens, the picture changes and there
is no guarantee that they will not seize their opportunity.

Should the power of the oppressors waver, or should the
authorities close an eye to a certain degree of resistance, then
bottled-up resentment may be discharged. This can be gathered
from an incident I was told about by a former estate owner in
Peru. Her estate had been distributed among the farm workers
but she, of course, continued to be a well-known personage
throughout a wide area. One day, when she took friends to the
market in Puno and paused for a moment, a peasant woman who

had previously been her serf squatted down in front of her, pulled up her skirt and defecated as testimony to her hatred. This happened during the early years of the revolution led by the army, in about 1970, when many Peruvians were misled into thinking that a new age was dawning for them.

In many cases the oppressors are strong and give no quarter, so it is not at all surprising that many psychologists should have remarked upon the passive behaviour of the poor in oppressed countries. But it would be quite wrong to assume that poverty always goes hand-in-hand with passivity. Oscar Lewis, who has stressed the passive aspect of the so-called culture of poverty, has also rejected that misconception. If the poor organise themselves, in trade unions for instance, they have, according to Lewis, turned their backs on the culture of poverty. And that has happened, and continues to happen in many parts of the world. Organised peasants in North Korea, Vietnam, Indonesia, Guinea-Bissau, Zimbabwe, Nicaragua, El Salvador and other countries have taken up arms against their oppressors. And struggle in other forms can also be seen on all sides. Thus, in July 1976, barricades went up in the poorer districts of Lima, where there is rarely any active opposition to the authorities.[34] Two years later, a large proportion of the inhabitants of these *barriadas* voted for parties on the left, whereupon the radical wings of these parties launched an armed struggle in various parts of the country. They were encouraged to do so by the success of Sendero Luminosa, whose *guerrilleros* had defied the might of the authorities in the departments round Ayacucho in the *sierra*.

Elsewhere, too, the oppressed are no longer prepared to suffer in silence. South Africa has had a passive proletariat for decades, but during the last few years there has been active resistance, and in South Africa's neighbour, Namibia, the mine workers have a long history of struggle – they first went on strike as early as 1893. At the end of 1971 they declared a strike, which lasted over a month, in support of demands for economic and social improvements for all the country's workers.[35] And in India, according to Jan Breman, a Rotterdam development expert, the number of incidents that are presented as caste conflicts but are in fact class struggles are clearly on the increase. Breman was struck by the hatred and bitterness of the oppressed Indian people.[36]

One observer of peasant life in southern Iran said prophetically before the departure of the Shah that it would not be long before the kind of peasant described in textbooks by social anthropologists would have ceased to exist. Passive, conservative peasants, meekly hoping for a turn in their fortune and devoid of any real initiative, would be relics of the past.

**Poverty and inequality**

This chapter is devoted to poverty, but it has already quickly become plain that the problem of poverty is closely bound up with wealth.

Differences in income are certainly not confined to the Third World, but the differences there are very great indeed. The poor in the Third World are much poorer than the poor in the rich countries, a fact reflected in national averages. Thus the consumption of cereal per head of population in the prosperous countries (North America, Eastern and Western Europe) is five times as great as it is in Africa and India. At the same time, the energy consumption of the rich countries is much higher, and so is the demand for minerals, the prosperous capitalist countries consuming forty times as much aluminium as the poor countries, and a hundred times as much copper.[37] (By 'poor countries' I refer to countries in which the poverty of the masses is not merely a conspicuous phenomenon but must also be considered the most pressing problem.)

The difference in prosperity can be gauged by various criteria, such as satisfaction of basic needs, welfare provisions, employment, ownership of property or the means of production, and obviously also of (monetary) income. As an example of this last, we can take the case of Kenya, where around 1970 those with the highest incomes (the top 20 per cent) received 68 per cent of all incomes, while the poorest 40 per cent received 10 per cent. In the statistics of capitalist countries the income differences are to a large degree hidden by the quotation of figures for the top 20 per cent put together. It would be more revealing to contrast the rest with the top 5 per cent, when it would immediately become clear how great the differences really are.

Differences in income, far from diminishing, are increasing, above all in the countryside where poverty is growing. That is the conclusion of number of studies made in Asia.[38] What development there is, is largely confined to the towns and provides little extra employment. In the Third World, too, there is capital-intensive development on a large scale. Although the commission which examined this phenomenon had fewer data about Africa and South America than about Asia, it nevertheless gained the firm impression that in these continents, too, poverty was increasing with economic growth.[39] Another study, devoted to Mexico, Malaysia and Chile, confirmed that poverty is largely concentrated in the rural areas.[40]

In this global survey of inequality throughout the world, I have made use of data collected on a national scale. There was no alternative, but I should like to point out that as a rule I find working with the concept of countries unhelpful. In every country there are both oppressors and oppressed, an important distinction that is lost when we deal with whole countries. Moreover, it is quite false to speak of relationships between oppressing and oppressed countries. There are no countries that oppress others; the oppressing is done by big businesses or governments, that is by organisations. If we think in terms of countries, we thus simply distort the real situation. In this book I shall repeatedly reject all terms that distort social reality or veil it behind a smokescreen, and point out that all such distortions are exclusively in the interest of the ruling class. Still, it is unavoidable to speak of countries now and then, as witness my previous remarks about the consumption of alumium. Moreover, in order to avoid repetitive use of the term 'poor countries', I shall also be referring to the Third World. This is a term that many members of the United Nations apply to themselves whenever they want to distinguish themselves from the highly industrialised, and especially from the capitalist, countries which constitute the 'First World'. There are a number of reasons for objecting to the term 'Third World', a term that suggests third choice, third quality, and moreover conveys a false impression of unity, of the existence of an international pressure group with a common objective. However, the term has entered our language, and I can see no real objection to it. The 'Second World' is made up of those countries having a highly-developed socialist mode of production.

It is possible to criticise my emphasis of poverty. This calls for a

world of explanation. I consider poverty *the* central problem of
the great majority of mankind, because many of the other
problems that plague us – personal problems, sickness and wars –
are closely bound up with poverty. Should poverty disappear,
many other problems (but not all!) would be solved at one
stroke. People complain that poverty is too static a concept, but I
am forced to work with a static concept because the problems of
the people with whom I am concerned seem never to change:
their grandparents suffered poverty, their parents suffered poverty
and they now suffer poverty in turn. It is probable that their
children will be in no better a position.

The concept of poverty may be considered a relative concept,
both in relation to one's own needs and to the income of others.
In the second case, someone will consider himself poor if he feels
that he has to go short while others do not. I prefer a sociological
definition, however, one that is not confined to the purely
material aspects. The poor are poor not only in material but also
in social respects. Their income is so low that they are largely or
wholly debarred from the social life of society as a whole, of the
local community or of their family.

Having considered poverty in this chapter, I shall now proffer
an account of the social system of which poverty is an integral
part. I call it a poverty-and-wealth system. But first a word on
how the problems of the poor can be examined most effectively.

# 2 Liberation Science

## Introduction

This chapter is a plea for a consistent defence of the interests of the subjugated and oppressed; for a science in the service of the liberation movement. This approach differs in various respects from that of western social science. One essential distinction is the explicit acknowledgment of the political nature of the work. When I introduced my book on Surinam[1] at a gathering of colleagues, my opening words were: 'This is a political book. It reflects a political vision and helps me to pursue a political objective which, however, does not prevent it from being a "scientific" book!' By 'scientific' I mean that the facts are gathered and recorded as carefully as possible while all the arguments are based on the rules of logic. The political nature of the Surinam book was reflected in the formulation of the problem: how is it that so many Surinamese are poor and that they remain poor? And it also appeared from the criterion for judging the policy used to develop Surinam: was it to be indigenous and self-reliant, i.e. was it intended to develop the country's own resources by the Surinamese for the benefit of all Surinamese?

There have been many arguments about the effect of values on scientific research. The upshot has been that professional circles now generally accept that political attitudes do play a role in it. These political attitudes determine the investigator's sphere of interest and the type of phenomenon to which he directs his particular attention. I remember a discussion with a colleague in Amsterdam who claimed that it was possible to study social phenomena quite objectively, without value judgements. As an example he mentioned the fact that the Pinochet regime in Chile had suspended all civil liberties. This view of the South American scene is – however correct – nevertheless affected by value judgements, for whenever I think of the Chilean dictatorship I cannot help recalling that the workers in that country are being exploited more than they were before.

A well-known example of how one and the same subject can be viewed in two distinct ways is the Redfield–Lewis controversy. Redfield found that the people in the Mexican village he was studying lived harmoniously and that village society was characterised by homogeneity. Lewis, for his part, was struck by the marked differences: more than half the population was without land and lived in poverty. He observed a lack of cooperation and encountered a great deal of individualism among the villagers. Confronted with Lewis's interpretation, Redfield justified himself by saying that he had directed his attention at aspects that interested him personally and that he found attractive. And in so doing he made a profound philosophic remark, for every investigator does indeed make a personal choice from among the multitude of observable phenomena. This personal choice, this bias, determines the sphere of interest towards which the investigator directs his attention. A conservative investigator feels no need to discover to what extent industrialists enrich themselves through the labour power of peasants and workers. He is much more interested in the contribution industry makes to the national product, or in the extent to which industrialists have climbed the social ladder.

Because the choice an investigator makes from among the available facts is a consequence of his political views or philosophy of life, the social scientist must make his political and philosophical axioms explicit. Right-wing social scientists are not as a rule inclined to do so and hence, other things being equal, produce work of less scientific quality than that of their progressive colleagues who say quite openly where they stand. The traditional scientist prefers to give the impression that he does his work objectively and that he is equally concerned with all social groups, including the poor. The methodology of liberation science must reject this approach as untenable.

The reader of a scientific study ought to be told from what observed facts and value judgements the conclusions are derived. The result is 'valid' science – valid not least because of its social importance. Anyone who tries desperately to suppress or hide his value judgments runs the risk of losing his power of fathoming social reality. The result is the dehuminsation of learning. It so happens that people adopt a more evaluative attitude to society than the one they adopt to natural phenomena. The regime of a country, be it Cuba or Chile, can be more readily adjudged good or evil than such phenomena as the Bay of Santiago or the Cordillera de los Andes.

Not that every value judgement deserves a place in a scientific study. The acceptability of a value judgement must first be demonstrated with convincing factual material.

For scientific purposes it is desirable, whenever possible, to render the values contained in concepts explicit in the definitions. It is wrong to use terms that hide the author's political involvement. That is why I prefer the term 'exploitation' to, say, 'profiting from' or 'accumulation' because 'exploitation' reflects revulsion at those who take advantage of the oppressed. Shekhar Mukherji, too, uses the term exploitation – exploitation in the dirt and filth of the slums of Indian cities – when referring to rickshaw pullers and other low-grade opeartives who have been uprooted from the countryside and have come to eke out a miserable living in the towns. These people keep returning to their villages, which makes them circular migrants, according to Mukherji 'an insipid term for such an agonising process.'[2]

A scientist who refers to social status or class (e.g. the landed nobility) in the normal way, without showing his sympathy or revulsion, accepts the values held, consciously or unconsciously, by those he addresses. I refuse to do so. I want my readers to know where I stand, and that is why I speak of people I dislike in terms that leave no doubt as to my feelings. My opponents do precisely the same. When they talk of Eastern Europe they speak of communist countries and wield this term as a kind of insult. I take a less negative attitude to these countries and therefore call them what they call themselves: socialist countries.

Although every scientist knows that the terms he uses cannot be value-free, the effort to use value-free terms continues unabated. Thus some Amsterdam political scientists have declared that they intend to give a neutral significance to the term 'power', but I do not care for this idea. In my opinion power is wrong, and has to be opposed (in the section headed *Central concepts* I shall explain what I mean by 'power').

In short, I stand for a science that allows for approval and disapproval. An Amsterdam professor in 1968 did not agree with that approach. He argued, in particular, that social science cannot determine whether the gulf between poor and rich countries should be reduced. I think that such value-*free* science is nothing short of value-*less* science. If you exclude value judgements then you must confine yourself to superficial observations and cannot tackle the major problems of our day.

Dispensing with judgements about philosophically determined objectives leads to sterile scientific work. However a distinction must be made between reasoned judgements and observations. In making reasoned judgements, in drawing conclusions, we start from explicit value judgements, but when making observations, when gathering data, we must be as open-minded as possible, as were the Cuban sociologists who attempted to determine as accurately as they could what made their compatriots want to emigrate to the United States. I was told about this project when I visited Havana in 1968: a fine piece of scientific research.

## Solidarity groups

A cornerstone of the ideas developed in this book is the fact that class antagonism is responsible for the suffering of the great majority of the poor. There are also other conflicts – between ethnic groups, between men and women – and these will be mentioned as well. But the emphasis will be placed on class conflict, because my whole approach is based on treating poverty against the background of wealth.

Looking at problems from the viewpoint of the poor does not mean an uncritical acceptance of the attitudes they hold. That is, in any case, impossible since these attitudes differ a great deal; the poor have many divergent ideas and various solutions to their problems. Moreover, I reserve the right to point them towards solutions they themselves ignore or even reject. In fact, I see eye to eye with only some of the poor (and their leaders), namely with those whose ideals apply to all mankind. For while my solidarity group is the solidarity group of the poor, my objective is the attainment of progress for all. The ultimate objective of progress is not confined to some part of mankind but involves mankind as a whole. And the animal and plant kingdoms are involved too, indeed even non-living matter must benefit from a better world, and from those people who approach everything that exists with reverence, maintaining it as best they can. Seen in this light, everything that exists is part of my solidarity group, but for a strategy of progress I must first of all turn to, and make common cause with, that part of humanity which, by virtue of its social position, is opposed to brutal oppression – the part made up of the victims of exploitative systems in the Third World. Accordingly, I shall tackle the problems of the Third World from their social standpoint.

Starting out from the interests of a solidarity group has far-reaching methodological consequences: it means posing questions concerning the causes of oppression. That approach differs markedly from the usual abstract approach in which problems are viewed in a national perspective. Thus the problem of peasant farmers is usually viewed in the light of demographic factors and such macro-economic details as exports and imports. Peasants are there to fill mouths (for the birth rate is high) and they must earn foreign currency, so the argument goes – foreign currency for machinery from which the chief beneficiaries are, not the peasants, but entrepreneurs and the military, who belong to a different social class. And it is that class which is most interested in a national approach to problems. Liberation science does not start from the interests of a particular country, country being a misleading concept, but from the interests of the oppressed peasants. It paints a completely different picture, leads to quite different conclusions, and calls for a different explanatory theory. A theory that puts the interests of the poor first shows that poverty flows from oppression, which means that the solution is the elimination of all relationships based on subordination and dependence. That can only be achieved by a strong organisation and by struggle. All those who base their views of the peasant problem on national considerations subscribe to the theory that the underdevelopment of agriculture is due first and foremost to the incompetence of the peasantry and to shortcomings in their immediate environment. Their theories entail manipulation: peasants must be enjoined to work harder for the nation. Social reconstruction experts deliver inspired speeches calling for greater all-round commitment, and agricultural extension officers encourage the peasants to shoulder obligations and tie them down with subsidies and loans.

Liberation science rejects this approach: its starting points are not the problems of the country as a whole, of the whole population or of similarly vague sociological concepts, but of the solidarity group. Liberation scientists are so many servants of the solidarity group. Their studies are intended to make a contribution to the discussion of tactics and strategy, to increase social awareness, and so on.

To be as open as possible, the scholar presenting his findings must also state his epistemological assumptions, i.e. his approach to science, his view of man and nature and his view of society.

## The approach to science

How should the solidarity groups be studied? Can it be done in a scientific way? No unequivocal answers to these questions have been given. Philosophers claim that it is impossible to have satisfactory knowledge of social reality, and that no one is justified in proffering practical advice. Liberation science has no use for this type of philosophising, for those who wish to make a contribution to the struggle of the oppressed take the view that social phenomena are created by human beings, based on human relationships, and can therefore be grasped by human beings. When they discover that a large landowner oppresses his workers and enriches himself through their work, they conclude that they are entitled to trust their findings.

Liberation scientists believe that their work is scientifically valid if they examine the problems of the oppressed and everything connected with these problems in the most scrupulous way, if they collect their data by the best available methods and if they argue as correctly as possible from the standpoint of a clearly expressed vision of society. If they work in that way they assume that the phenomena they observe really exist and that their concepts and propositions are valid, i.e. grounded in reality. This is the approach of philosophical realism, which assumes that the objects of human cognition actually exist and that it is possible, by observation and rational thought, to depict them correctly.

In addition to concepts and propositions there is theory. Liberation theory is rooted in the practice of struggle. It is a coherent whole of meaningful concepts and pronouncements about social reality, from which it draws the correct conclusions. The theory is useful if it befits the liberation struggle.

In Western Europe and the United States, disciplines concerned with the Third World tend to be overspecialised. This renders them comparatively powerless and encourages the status quo. It is far more in the interests of the oppressed that their problems be studied in an interdisciplinary manner, that all the relevant economic, technological, cultural and political aspects be expounded fully, something that is also required for the formulation of a good, that is an integral, development programme.

It was in the university city of Arequipa (Peru) that I came across projects to study social problems in an integral manner.

**The view of man**

Social science directed at the improvement of human society must be based on an image of man. The necessary struggle cannot otherwise be conducted effectively, nor can the future be mouled in a satisfactory way.

It is, however, unnecessary to delve into the essence of human existence outside the social context in which people operate. That is what philosophical anthropology does, and it does not find it easy to cull that essence from the many differences between human beings now and in the past, with the result that its speculations on the innate, immutable nature of man carries little conviction. No one can pronounce on the subject with complete certainty. As far as liberation science is concerned this type of philosophy is expendable. It is enough to concentrate attention on the behaviour of people involved in capitalist relationships (which have to be changed) and to ask oneself what people must do to create and run a society that tends more towards equality and fraternity (which is the objective). During the transitional phase it is important to determine to what extent people moulded by capitalism can meet the demands of a fairer society. On that problem we can even gather some information in capitalist society, because not all relationships in that type of society are determined by the capitalist mode of production. Cases in point may be found in the behaviour of people in voluntary associations, family ties and friendships.

It seems reasonable to assume that people began to cooperate at an early phase of history. Through cooperation, through joining forces, they were able to reach their personal objectives more easily. This implies that people are mainly guided by self interest. I start from the premise that many people will do what they feel will do the greatest justice to their personality. That may mean doing what they like to do (achieving something in life, for instance), or to be what they like to be (a good mother, beautiful, etc.). In either case the aim is self-fulfilment.

In the main, therefore, people lead their own lives (or wish to do so). However, relating to others is another essential aspect of human existence, for without it man would never have become the powerful species he is. The need for cooperation has become an ethical imperative. Human beings have developed social systems that enable them not only to pursue their own self-interest but also to consider the interests of others. This entails a readiness to devote oneself to others and many people do indeed seek social justice for all. Still, it must not be overlooked that the relationship between human beings is also antagonistic, that they fight and exploit one another, and will use others for their own advantage.

We have just called man powerful, and that is true. He undoubtedly has a highly developed capacity to subordinate nature, to subject it to himself. He usually does so in collaboration with others, by working with them. Work is essential both for the pursuit of self-interest (self-fulfilment) and also for the social existence of human beings. However, it is a striking fact that some human beings prefer not to work, indeed hold a high position in society because they do no work at all. They merely consume, or at best give things away now and then. Here we have an essential human characteristic: the tendency to let others work for oneself, for one's own profit, is a strongly developed human trait, particularly under a capitalist system. Man's relationship to nature is of a similar kind; here, too, there is enrichment, in this case at nature's cost.

Enriching oneself at the expense of others has far-reaching consequences, because it involves gaining power over people. There has been much philosophising about the selfish tendencies of (most) people, and this raises the question of whether such selfishness is part and parcel of man's nature or whether it is created by social circumstances. I feel no need to enter into this kind of dicussion, but merely observe that the hereditary or non-hereditary nature of character is difficult to establish, and I assume further that social circumstances exert a great influence on human behaviour.

By analogy with 'working definition' and 'working hypothesis',[3] I shall be using a 'working picture' of man and – for reasons of social planning – I shall include egoism in this picture.

This picture accordingly has four essential features:

– profiting from others (if power relationships allow);
– cooperating with others for mutual advantage (if there is a power equilibrium);
– committing oneself to one's fellows (if social or, exceptionally, personal circumstances lead one to do so);
– self-fulfilment.

Liberation science wants to tilt the balance in favour of the last two features, by helping politicians to create social structures that impede the development of egoism and encourage self-fulfilment (inasmuch as it does not obstruct the self-fulfilment of others). I start from the premise that this shift in emphasis is in accord with human nature, that human beings can live together in peace and allow each other sufficient room for self-fulfilment. This picture of man is connected with my social picture: society too, I believe, is capable of change, because society is not something that stands against, beside or above the individual. Society consists of relationships between human beings. When human beings behave socially, the organisation of society will differ from that of a society based on selfishness. Conversely, the structure of society has an influence on the behaviour of human beings.

**The social picture: a dialectical view**

In the thinking of the liberation scientist, changes play an essential role. This distinguishes his thinking from that of the defenders of the status quo who believe that social reality should be in a permanent state of equilibrium and, during disturbances of that equilibrium, think (or hope?) that the balance will be restored sooner or later. Their approach does allow for changes, but only for those that take place gradually and without essentially transforming social relationships.

Social changes are usually thought to be caused by opposite forces inherent in a given social context. (I am about to explain what I understand by dialectical relations and dialectical processes.) Dialectical relations are conflictual relations between elements, between parts of a whole, that cannot exist without one another. In industry, for instance, we have management and we have workers. Both categories are needed if the industry is to function. They belong together and need each other, but at the same time they are opposed to each other, have distinct interests.

Another relationship full of tensions is that between man and society; between man as an individual and man as a social being. The individual has a great need for freedom, for self-fulfilment, but that freedom must to some extent be contained by social structures. This reflects a social necessity: man has to live with others, but this necessity restricts his freedom of movement, something he resents.

For dialectics, a whole is made up of opposing elements. The whole can only be known by knowledge of the interdependence of its parts, of the relationship between the elements that constitute it. In the dialectical approach to human behaviour, the parts are seen to be opposed to one another on the basis of oppositions of interests that lead to conflict and struggle.

In addition to dialectical relationships, we must also consider dialectical processes. Conflictual situations contain factors, or may have factors introduced, that can lead to the solution of the conflict by destruction of one of the conflictual elements, or by reconciliation of the elements with the consequent creation of a new situation. Inasmuch as dialectical thought is optimistic it expects progress rather than retrogression from these processes.

Society is intimately affected by dialectical processes because men can conceive of alternatives to what they see in front of them. Dialectical thought entails the view that the world, human beings and nature itself can be different. The dialectical approach is not only relevant to the description of social reality, it is also illuminating and helpful when it comes to predicting new developments or to mobilising the population.

In the *description* of a concrete social situation it appears that the most fundamental opposition is the one between productive forces (everything that is needed to produce) and productive relationships (the relationship of human beings to the means of production). If the productive relationships impede the development of the productive forces then there are tensions, and the same happens if the development of the productive forces leads to a situation in which the prevailing productive relationships are no longer satisfactory. Examples of the first state of affairs could be found in Peru and Cuba. The plantation system with its big landowners and servile peasants or underpaid agricultural labourers constituted a system of productive relationships that gravely impeded the development of the productive forces and the efficient use of the land. An example of the second state of affairs can be found in the present in both the highly developed and also in the underdeveloped countries. Technology has been making giant strides, with the result that more work can be done using fewer people. This development tends to undermine the system in which the captains of industry employ a fixed number of people to do a full day's work while an army of unemployed are kept idle. If more and more can be produced by the work of fewer and fewer hands, then it is obvious that the growing number of unemployed will insist forcibly that the means of production are transferred to common ownership and that work and profits are distributed as fairly as possible among all human beings. The result is a change in productive relationships.

Future social relationships in Surinam were not too difficult to predict before the military coup of 1980. In my book on that country I anticipated what would happen if the productive forces developed the way the authorities wanted. In that case, social contrasts were bound to increase. Mining and agriculture would become big modern industries with limited job opportunities, and a great deal of economic power would finish up in the hands of a few people.

In order to *mobilise* the people in support of a progressive system of development, social contrasts must first be drastically reduced. Moreover, to ensure appreciable growth and the fairest possible distribution, the consumption (of luxury goods) must be severely restricted, so that a considerable share of the national income can be saved and invested. But if the population is expected to make extra exertions and sacrifices, then this investment must indeed be made in the interests of all. The special advantages of the privileged social classes must be abolished and the sacrifices equally shared.[4]

Crucial to the dialectical approach is the idea of dynamic opposites; dynamic because they lead to changes. It is a view stressing conflict and struggle. The Norwegian peace researcher, Johan Galtung, agrees with this, but believes that the dialectical approach as such is not enough; we must also take stability and predictable continuity into account. For some time at least most systems are in a state of equilibrium. Perhaps their equilibrium is the calm before the storm, but it is wrong to deny or ignore this phenomenon.[5]

Galtung further claims that dialectical thought is holistic. Holism means that everything has to be considered as being part of a whole, but in the dialectical view the whole is a whole made up of contrasts that can only be known from the interdependence of the parts, from the relationships between the elements constituting the whole.

From the table of contents of this book, the reader might conclude that it has more of an analytical than of a holistic character: many parts and aspects are treated one at a time. Unfortunately there is no alternative. But because the book is full of references to the links between the parts and because a great deal of attention is paid to conflicts, it may indeed be said to use a holistic approach in the dialectical sense. It is the combination of a structural-analytic with a dialectical approach that enables one to study society and to interpret it as it is: a relatively unchangeable and yet changing phenomenon.

## Applied research

The social scientist is often accused of being opinionated when he points out how existing conditions can be changed. But he is also accused of the opposite: of being unable to state what has to be done in practice to achieve results. It has been said that an economist is someone who knows *tomorrow* from studies he has done *today* about what ought to have been done *yesterday*, while the sociologist is said to keep his own counsel on the matter. And quite a few sociologists do indeed feel that it is not their business to give practical advice. Liberation science, by contrast, is deeply concerned to discover how solidarity groups can be helped to hasten emancipation.

Liberation science is not afraid of giving advice; it is a form of applied research, that is, a science deliberately aimed at social effects. But it is indeed unassuming, because it realizes that social changes are not based on scientific studies but on the clash of social forces. All it can hope to do is to advise those groups which it believes play a valuable part in this social confrontation. Its advice is meant for policy makers, for the leadership of political parties, for groups within political parties, for progressive governments.

Applied research does not use methods of proof that differ essentially from those of pure research. The latter includes problem formulation (the question to be answered), orientation, the framing of hypotheses (preliminary answers to the questions posed, which give direction to the research), a research plan, the collection of data, the elaboration of the data (the testing of the hypotheses) and the drawing of conclusions.

Applied research, too, uses hypotheses, but these have the nature of possible solutions to the social abuses (the problems) at which the research is directed. In that case the testing method is a careful investigation of the extent to which the possible solutions can be implemented under the given conditions and have the desired effects. The conclusion of applied research comprises a policy recommendation and has the following logical form: $p$, $q$, and $r$ must be done to produce $Y$, so that $X$, the original situation, can be improved. What must be done is laid down in a development strategy. In the chapter devoted to that subject we shall look more closely at the methodology used in scientific studies of development process.

Applied research aimed at liberation is being carried out in Lusaka (Zambia), in the United Nations Institute for Namibia.

Here Namibians are trained to take over the government and the administration of their country as soon as it is liberated. In addition, research is being done on behalf of SWAPO. Special attention is paid to agrarian reform, the redistribution of land, the various forms of government institutions, political and economic structures, mining legislations, etc., so as to provide future government services with policy blueprints.

## Social criticism

Liberation science is critical of the poverty-and-wealth system and does not collaborate in making cosmetic changes to that system. It studies the mechanism by which the dominant groups operate the system, with the aim of bringing them down as a prerequisite of the emergence of better human relations. Some people are afraid that such studies may serve the interests of those who rule the system. That fear is not altogether unfounded, but the critical power of liberation science is so strong and so revealing and the information so useful for revolutionaries that, on balance, the research will be found to be of greater benefit to the resistance movement than to the enemies of resistance.

Liberation science is action-orientated and hence system-destructive. It is not interested in discussions with the rulers – discussion with the exploiters means closing an eye to oppression. Oppression must be combated, and that struggle brings one into head-on collission with oppression and oppressors.

The question arises whether liberation science can also be practised by people holding office in government, private institutions or in industry. To some extent it can, although plainly resistance work must then be camouflaged, and this calls for a great deal of courage, tact and patience.

## Change and continuity

The problems of the poor and exploited are examined as part of a process of development (or perhaps underdevelopment) or progress (or perhaps retrogression), as aspects of socio-structural changes, that is of changes in power relationships. This calls for an understanding of the history of the exploited groupings and – more generally – of the forces that determine the development of a given society. The relevant phenomena can then be viewed in historical perspective; at the same time an attempt should be made to discover how change can be encouraged.

Having stressed the importance of social dynamics, I would point out that the socio-economic problem should – initially – be viewed as being relatively static. The phenomena involved seem, alas, to change little if at all. This interpretation is in line with the way non-professional observers view social reality. They do not look at processes; they simply look (more or less clearly) at the society in which they have to live. Their attention is focused on phenomena that reveal themselves directly to the senses, for instance poverty and social inequality. That is why I give pride of place – in thought and in words – to these phenomena. I consider it of the utmost importance that my science should hasten the social awakening of people who have not enjoyed a good education. It matters little whether or not such people read, or indeed can read, my writings; by my way of formulating the problem, I simply hope to influence those of them who are in direct contact with my solidarity group.

Viewing phenomena initially just as they are is also of importance; contemporary phenomena must first of all be explained by the social context in which they occur today. Hence it is desirable from a methodological point of view to relate such phenomena as disrupted family life in the Caribbean first of all to the nature of contemporary capitalist society. Only then is attention directed at the historical events that affect the present. This approach is more correct methodologically than explanations that go back to Africa or to slavery, because the direct cause of a phenomenon is close to it in both space and time. From the standpoint of social change as well, explanations based on the contemporary situation are desirable: there is nothing we can change about conditions in seventeenth-century Africa or about the time in which workers were kept in slavery.

## Central concepts

Every view of social reality, by laymen no less than by social scientists, is based on a theory involving concepts and propositions partly moulded by these concepts and considered to be general truths. In other words, concepts are an integral part of every theory. That applies equally to the central concepts presented in this book. These were not derived from some sociology textbook but have had to be defined in accordance with the author's theoretical perspective. Liberation theory, which will not be discussed until Chapter 6, is thus embodied in the concepts presented to the reader here, in Chapter 2.

The author's system of concepts hinges on the concept of *social problems* because the author considers poverty in the Third World just such a problem and has made it the starting point of this book. Poverty is a consequence of *lack of power* and the poor are the victims of the power of their oppressors, which is based on a privileged position in the political system (*political power*) and connected with a favourable position in the economic system, expressed in the control of the means of production (*economic power*). These two forms of power will have to be wrested from the oppressors. A process of change will have to come about, namely *the liberation process*. That process is not possible without *leadership* and *organisation*. As soon as political power is seized by progressive forces, a process of *development* aimed at *progress* is ushered in. The italics indicate which concepts will be explained in succession below.

## Social problems

A great many books on social problems have been published, especially in the United States. The problems referred to in them form a varied collection: crime; prostitution; alcoholism; gambling; divorce; unhappy marriages; arguments about education; strife between religious denominations; illness (above all mental illness); unpleasant work; the class struggle; racial conflict; student unrest; war and many others.[6]

According to the North American sociologist, C. Wright Mills, this selection is based on a political philosophy.[7] He contends that social scientists who consider these problems fail completely or significantly to involve society as a whole in their discussions, let alone criticise it. They are more concerned with the contrast between town and country. Most of the problems they identify are considered so many consequences of a breakdown in values which, according to them, can only flourish in the countryside. Moreover, they blame problems on maladjustment but do not say to what the maladjusted fail to adjust themselves. Mills has few doubts about the answer. He realizes that what was meant is that they must adapt to North American middle-class ethics and manners.

From the writings of North American authors on social problems it becomes clear just how much people's view of social problems is determined by their class position. For the well-off, barely touched with social compassion, the poverty of others is no problem as long as the poor bear their lot quietly. Only when the well-off themselves begin to be inconvenienced, when the poor come out on strikes and demonstrations, does a social problem arise for the more prosperous. Hence it must always be made perfectly clear to whom, to what social groups, something is a social problem, and why.

Social problems are an important concept in liberation science, because social problems are its starting point. They are flaws in social life, seen from the position of the poor. This starting point is different from that used in more traditional social science. The latter starts out with a discussion of such neutral *subjects* as Indian marriages, Zambian youth, or the Colombian countryside. As far as this book is concerned, the central social problem is the poverty of the great majority and everything connected with it.

## Lack of power

Someone is said to lack power when his social position is such that he suffers want time and again. Whenever he enters into relations with the more powerful, they profit because they are able to impose their will upon him. If an orthodox sociologist considers this phenomenon, he views it from the position of those in power. Because I take the opposing view, I shall examine the concept of lack of power first.

It would be wrong, in discussions of lack of power, to dwell too long on pairs of relationships. Lack of power comprises more than a single relationship with powerful individuals who are your masters. Lack of power refers to a position in a system in which a constricting inluence is exerted from many sides. Those lacking power feel powerless in a host of spheres, and rightly so. The man lacking power is prevented from doing all sorts of things, and cannot satisfy his needs. The powerless poor are weighed down by a great mass of people who have much on their side, not just money – a great deal of money – but also knowledge, manners that are different and appear to be better, and fine houses set in secluded grounds. They seem to belong to a different species, to a mighty species with whom it is best to be on friendly terms: perhaps a crumb from their table will fall your way, perhaps you will be less harshly treated. Those who are part of the power bloc draw admiration and are met with respect.

The rulers' power is not always manifest. There is a great deal of potential or latent power, and the poor must take that into account. Peasants know how rich landowners and buyers would react if they combined to consolidate their position. They know that the power of the rulers would then become tangible indeed, that they would run the risk of being overwhelmed.

I have said that it is unsatisfactory to treat lack of power as a relation involving just two or only a few individuals. It is sociologically more correct to fit lack of power and power into the frame of the social system. A big landowner is able to exploit the dependent peasant because he is in a strong social position – he belongs to the class that controls the government apparatus. That is why it is true to say that the position of the powerless in an oppressive system is one that makes it very difficult for them to reach their objectives, since others make profits from them and place obstacles in their path. Between the prosperous and the poor there is an unequal exchange relationship, one that favours the party which owns the most.

It is the business of progressive political parties, assisted by liberation scientists, to help the oppressed gain some insight into the nature and defects of the power bloc that weighs them down. The powerless know perfectly well that they are powerless and what they can expect from those in power over them, but they are not always clear how the regional, national and international power systems hang together. They lack insight into the system of which they are an integral part.

*Power*

The concept of power has long been ignored by sociologists. Those sociologists who take a largely positive view of the society in which they live have had little inclination to study power relationships in that society because 'power' has a negative connotation. When they have finally turned to the subject nevertheless, they have arrived at definitions that painted power relationships in more or less rosy colours. They have tended to hide behind a smokescreen that part of social reality that was shaped by harsh power relationships. A definition found quite often in sociology textbooks is the following: 'Power is the ability to further the objectives of a person or group by limiting the behavioural choices of other persons or groups'. The results can be advantageous if those who do the limiting have altruistic motives, when they intervene for the benefit of others. Thus it is necessary to limit the behavioural choices of a small child during the winter lest it burn itself on the stove; at a later stage it must be prevented from falling into a river or lake. By and large, this limitation of behavioural choices is based on good intentions. Another sympathetic enough definition of power is that it is the ability to influence the decision-making process. There is little harm in that. Or that power is the ability to draw up rules for a group together with the necessary sanctions. A very necessary step, apparently. After all, there must be groups and they must be able to function properly. But the way they function is better for some than for others, and this aspect is what interests me most particularly.

Before I give my own definition of power, I should like to give the reader some idea of the kind of situation I have in mind. I read in a newspaper report of a South American military dictatorship in which three little girls, aged eight and nine, were found in a house, naked, bleeding and semiconscious. Neighbours said that the house was the scene of nightly visits by high government officials, army officers and even by the head of state. It normally accommodated ten such young girls. The witness who tried to bring these facts to the knowledge of the authorities was tortured for three days. If I look at these facts in a considered, 'scientific' manner, I find that this is indeed a question of limiting choices, but it is my considered opinion, too, that that is far from everything to be said on the subject. For the oppressed are being used for the advantage of others who do them harm and curtail their chances of progress. In that case, the oppressed enjoy no freedom whatsoever and are entirely in the power of the oppressors. The same was true of slaves, and to a somewhat lesser extent it is true of dependent peasants and of the servants who work in the houses of the middle classes. Generally, the exercise of power is less concerned with the ownership of the oppressed as with the ownership of their labour power. Power can also be used to appropriate goods.

I read in *Los Cachorros*, a novel by Mario Vargas Llosa, that the pupils of the elementary school in Miraflores, a fashionable suburb of Lima, would come out of school at four o'clock and by quarter-past four they would be on the football field. There they would play until just before five o'clock when the big boys from the secondary school would turn up and chase them away from the field. Here we have a scarce commodity (a football field) desired by the strong as well as by the weak. After five o'clock the desired object was beyond the reach of the weak, which was not to their advantage and impeded their development. The native population of North America, too, was driven away (and killed), as were the Algerian peasants who had to make way for the French colonists. Indeed, some of them had to work on French plantations. The powerful seized the productive forces of the weak and profited from their labour. In a village in Yunnan (S.W. China), Chinese sociologists came across peasants who had their land tilled by agricultural labourers while they themselves did nothing but enjoy pleasurable and comfortable lives.[8]

It will now be clear that the 'nice' definition given at the beginning of this section which reinforced the impression that power is a useful or at least not unpropitious factor in human society is unsatisfactory. In my definition of power as it applies to the Third World, I shall emphasise that it helps some to gain advantages at the expense of others. To me, power is an objectionable thing, not least because I side with those who are crushed by power.[9] What some people call 'positive power' I prefer to call leadership or positive influence.

It cannot be denied that people in power influence the behavioural choices of others, but this is not the crux of the matter. For me the most important thing is who profits as a result. That means that the usual definition of power contains too little information, is too abstract.[10] It is too wide, with the consequence that the distinction between harmful power and harmless 'power' is blurred. I shall try to explain my own approach with the help of definitions based on the limitation of possibilities, a rather vague concept which I shall attempt to define in my own way. To that end, I shall use a term that is sometimes used by my colleagues, namely the neutral term of *actor*. An *actor* may be healthy in body and spirit but he lacks capital and means of production. All he has is his own labour power, and in a capitalist system he has just two possibilities: to work with a company or government department that needs labour, or not to work and suffer hunger and want.

In West European welfare states there is yet another possibility for some, namely to feign sickness or pretend that no work can be found, and to draw unemployment benefits. The fact that there are only two (or at most three) possibilities is the result of the power of state and industry. It is they who have limited the choices. A person's possibilities can be schematised as follows:

(1) He can do things.
(2) He can limit possibilities.
(3) He can limit the possibilities of people.
(4) He can limit the possibilities of people who belong to his own social system.
(5) He can limit the possibilities of people who belong to his own social system for his own advantage.

or

(6) He can limit the possibilities of people who belong to his own social system for their advantage.

In this scheme, the term 'power' can be applied to all levels. Thus we can posit (Level 1) that someone who can do things has power. Someone who can bicycle has the power to move the handlebars; someone who can make a good speech has power over the use of words. Some may say that they wish to confine the concept of power to the limitation of free choice. Excellent: let them do so. See Level 2.

Most vague sociological definitions of power refer to Level 3. Someone in power is a person who limits the possibilities of human beings. I object to this not only on sociological but also on human grounds. The more abstract the definition we use, the more we treat people as manipulative subjects, as handlebars or machines. Abstract definitions are part of a dehumanised science.

A purely sociological objection is that the institutional character of power is not adequately brought out, the fact that power is associated with a system of complex relationships. My own definition is therefore close to Level 4, but it matters a great deal to me for whose advantage the possibilities are being limited. I confine power to Level 5 and refer to level 6 as leadership.

Someone has power who limits the possibilities of the powerless for his own benefit. In the case of leadership, by contrast, the possibilities of others are limited for their own benefit in order to help them improve their position. This is usually done with the agreement of the others. In the section on leadership I shall deal more fully with this subject.

It goes without saying that it is not always clear whether what is involved is power or leadership. When Nyerere forced part of the population of Tanzania to settle in communal villages he himself thought he was helping the development of his country, but some of the peasants no doubt regarded the measures as an exercise of power. In private companies and even in such democratic associations as cooperatives, leadership can easily degenerate into power.

My objection to abstract definitions (e.g. of power as the limitation of possibilities) is that they fail to make a distinction between, say, the power of Pinochet and the 'power' or rather (by my definition) the leadership of Castro. However, it must be remembered that neither is necessarily exclusive of the other. To some Chileans Pinochet is a leader and to others he is a man wielding power, a ruler. Moreover, a distinction must be made between his various leadership and power roles. Inasmuch as he is responsible for the smooth running of services that benefit (nearly) all Chileans, he plays a leadership role, whereas in other respects he is a ruler, at least as far as the great majority of the population is concerned. The same is true of Castro. To some Cubans he is a wielder of power, a ruler in some fields, but to many he is the recognised leader of the Cuban people in most fields.

Just like lack of power, so must power be seen in the framework of the social system. Power is bound up with certain positions from which power can be exercised. Positions of power are those (in organisations, industries, the state apparatus) from which the decisions are made. While those who make decisions wield power, those who persuade the men in power to take decisions in their interest wield influence.

## Political and economic power

Power relationships are usually expressed in terms of 'above' and 'below'. The powerful are set over the powerless, they are said to occupy the highest rung of the social ladder. The subjected are shown lying at the feet of the rulers who are seated on high thrones. In reality human relationships are played out on a horizontal plane, some drawing others into their sphere of power and being able to impose their will upon them. A judoka may end up on top of his opponent, but need not do so to have a hold on him. Both lie on the mat, more or less next to each other, on the same level. The main thing is not who is on top or underneath, but the hold.

To enrich oneself significantly one needs to have power over more than one person – the more the better, in fact. The struggle for power is a struggle to harness the work of others for one's own benefit. It is a very old story. The Inca princes, for instance, forced their subjects to do much of the work on the village lands for the priests and nobles (including the Inca himself). Admittedly their burden was eased with dancing and music and with offerings from the country's granaries, but this must have been scant consolation.

Regions in which everyone is able to look after himself and his family because there are adequate resources tend to throw up figures who succeed in forcing others to work for them. It was they who, according to the Dutch ethnologist, H.J. Nieboer, introduced the institution of slavery. Such processes took place in precapitalist times. Capitalism has its own forms of power: above all, dependent wage labour. A particular form of this phenomenon is debt slavery. Rubber tappers in Brazil, for instance, were encouraged by their employers to eat and drink their fill in company canteens. The greater their debt the more closely they were bound to their employers.

In the Inca empire, the labour of others was usurped by those wielding power in the state. That is political power. Those who, like capitalist entrepreneurs, use the labour power of others for their own benefit, wield economic power. They control the means of production. Now, those who own the means of production, or, more precisely, those who profit from the means of production, have a great deal of power. In other words, it is not ownership of the means of production that matters. This is what the poor experienced in Peru. Thanks to the agrarian reforms of 1969, a number of them became (often collective) owners of the means of production, something they considered an improvement. But it very quickly became evident that ownership does not necessarily ensure economic power. Their power was curtailed by the power of the state. The agricultural cooperatives saw much of their profit – sometimes all of it – flow into government coffers and the pockets of others. A better position than that of owner is that of controller, two positions that can coincide. The controller profits from a business, and can ensure his own advantage. He has control over the business. In modern capitalist society, control seldom rests with the owners. The actual power of control rests in a small circle of industrial managers.

It is important that the liberation scientist pays attention to the control of the means of production, to those persons and authorities who decide to what use the means of production are to be put. This is the crux of the productive relationship. Whosoever has control of the means of production determines how the means of production are to be used, what happens to the products, and how the profits are distributed. There are two main types of productive relationship:

– the joint decision by the workers as to the best use of the means of production, which are owned by the community at large;
– the domination of the workers by a minority of private owners or controllers of the means of production.

The means of production largely determine the social structure. Capitalist productive relations, characterised by the private ownership or control of the means of production and a pronounced division of labour, have led to the emergence of the bourgeoisie, a social class with a considerable say over the use of the means of production and a proletariat or class of workers dependent on the bourgeoisie.

## The liberation process

The liberation process leads from an oppressive situation to one in which the great majority enjoys freedom – above all freedom from want and fear. Liberation must pave the way for a change in power relationships if the position of the oppressed is to be improved.

## Leadership

Leaders play a crucial role in the liberation struggle. I have already said that some sociologists can see no difference between a leader and a ruler. In their theory, Somoza (the dictator of Nicaragua) and Ernesto Cardenal (the resistance leader and poet) must be placed on a par. Sociologists who are blind to the difference will accuse me of being biased in my attitude to power, of confining my examples to such repulsive incidents as the violation of young girls by army officers. They will, I suppose, admit that my examples do illustrate the wielding of power, but object to my omission of positive examples of the wielding of power. They might mention the case of an Akela leading a happy pack of Cub Scouts, with everyone chanting: 'Akela, we are prepared'. The children are deeply attached to her; she has them in her power. And she is unquestionably a fine leader. But in my view that very quality distinguishes her from someone wielding power, sets her apart from a ruler. Leadership is an essential condition of progress because a vanguard whom people can follow with confidence and enthusiasm can only further their advance.

## Organisation

Organisations are the means by which people can attain their (individual) objectives. There are organisations that help those whom they serve to exert pressure on economic and political rulers. In a cotton-growing region of Mexico, for instance, the peasants were able by an organised action campaign to force the President of the Republic to pass a long-promised land-reform law.[11]

It must be obvious that anyone studying the power structure of a country must pay particular attention to organisations and to their influence. To that end, he should begin by classifying the organisations he encounters. The character of the classification must reflect the aims of the investigation. Thus an analysis of a repressive system clearly calls for a different classification from the one we use to assess the development potential of a progressive regime. A so-called neutral classification that covers all contingencies is of very little serious use.

For the analysis of an oppressive system the following classification may be found useful: (1) organisations that mainly serve the interests of the oppressors; (2) organisations that mainly serve the interests of the oppressed; (3) organisations that serve the interests of all. The last category can be subdivided into (a) organisations that play an indispensable role for the oppressed, and (b) organisations that are not of essential importance to them.

In this type of analysis a clear distinction must be made between words and deeds. The investigators must not be taken in by what officials or rule books tell them about the objectives of an organisation or by what all sorts of factions expect from their organisation. What really matters is the so-called output: the effects the organisation has on the outside world.

A common complaint is that organisations in poor countries function badly. In my experience that is certainly the case with organisations in which some of the members profit at the expense of the majority. Once the gains of an organisation are shared out fairly, the prospects of genuine cooperation are greatly enhanced. This appeared from a study of cooperative irrigation schemes made by J.R. Siy of the Asian Institute of Management. According to Siy, organisations can best maintain the commitment of their members to the work of the organisation if every member's share in the organisation's total expenses corresponds to his or her share in the benefits.[12]

All organisations run the risk of degenerating into bureaucracies with a consequent widening of the gulf between leaders and ordinary members. The leaders become increasingly independent of the members and run the organisation as they like and often in their own interests as well. Such oligarchisation processes often beset the state machinery of Third World countries.

Organisations have all kinds of useful features. They can help people to gain skills that are important keys to future development: an organisation acts as a school of cooperation, as a training ground for organisational talent. In addition, it can increase political consciousness.

A friend of the South African resistance fighter Govan Mbeki has said that the first great trade-union federation for black South Africans, the I.C.U., helped to do just that. It was in the I.C.U. that Mbeki himself first engaged in political activities.[13]

The act of organising, too, is a prerequisite of development. Organising involves everything thought up and done to attain the objectives of an organisation. Unfortunately, organising skills in many poor countries leave much to be desired. Exceptions apart, the government sector no less than industrial life in these countries is run inefficiently, and political movements, too, are often badly organised. If these failures are teething toubles, if people learn from them, then this is not such a serious matter. Development is a series of ups and downs, of learning as one goes along. That is something Cuba experienced in rich measure. In the early 1970s, when everything seemed to be going wrong, posters went up with the slogan: we will turn set-backs into victory!

A country that tackles its development vigorously will provide training facilities to turn out capable organisers as quickly as possible.

*Development and progress*

Liberation is guided by values, and aims at the creation of a society in which the emergence of power blocs is virtually impossible, or, should it nevertheless occur, may quickly be corrected by democratic forces. The process culminating in a better society of this type is called progress. It is inspired by a view of the future in which the nation's spiritual and intellectual aspirations find their full expression. Islamic countries will strive for a different future from that sought in Buddhist or Christian countries.

Much less crucially moulded by spiritual and intellectual values is the general process of development, which is a more neutral concept than progress. Development raises the productive forces to a higher level and manifests itself in the greater productivity of human labour. This can be achieved by investments, by working more efficiently, or by raising the technical standard of the means of production. The Cuban government, which bought machinery to work the land more efficiently, to harvest, transport and refine the sugar cane more quickly and more easily, helped the development of native agriculture. This kind of process does not differ greatly from one country to the next, from one culture to another. In purely technical respects, improvements in production follow much the same pattern everywhere, but such improvements do not necessarily go hand in hand with the same productive relationships, which involve certain philosophical considerations.

Development is subsidiary to progress but is very important for all that; without increased production, without greater productivity, there can be no better society. That is why, after a victorious revolution, a great deal of energy must be spent on the development of the forces of production with the concomitant risk of attaching too much importance to economic growth. If circumstances permit and if the imperialist threat is not too great, the revolutionary process can simultaneously be aimed at progress and measures can be taken to create better human relationships.

## Macro/micro

Until the turn of the last century, European sociologists directed their attention mainly, if not exclusively, to society as a whole. This went hand in hand with a great deal of ideological criticism, considered to be an important branch of sociology. Subsequently, their attention shifted to smaller social units. Thus the German sociologist Leopold von Wiese concerned himself, among other things, with groups of two (*Das Paar*), three and more persons. As a result, he was able to shed much fresh light on human sociality, but very little on human society.

During and soon after the Second World War, interest revived in macro-sociological studies of the problems of society at large and their solution. The German sociologist Karl Mannheim, who fled from Hitler, linked the problems of European societies with a process of change of which he took a negative view. He followed his diagnosis with a cure: an alternative to the socialist or fascist form of society.

I hope that the fact of my having chosen sociologists from the rich countries as my examples will not give rise to misunderstandings. In fact, my own attempts to arrive at an adequate sociology for the oppressed in the Third World is not based on sociological trends in the rich countries. My starting point is the nature of the social problems of the poor countries and I endeavour to develop rigorous methods of arriving at solutions to these problems. That does not mean that there is harm in profiting from experiences gained elsewhere.

A general conclusion to be drawn from sociological investigations in the prosperous countries is that sociology becomes macro-sociology as soon as society as a whole is felt to be problematic. Now, in the contemporary Third World, social relationships, also on an international level, are indeed problematic. These relationships must therefore be examined in a wide, international context: the branch of learning devoted to the study of poverty must have a macro-sociological character. In macro-sociological studies, particularly of wide-ranging subjects, there is a great danger that the arguments may become too vague. That is why attention should also be paid to the fate of individuals. I accordingly plead for a macro/micro approach, a combination that provides valuable scientific and social insights.

## Decolonisation and the dismantling of elites

Many philosophers claim that man's thought is autonomous. Amidst all of life's transitory phenomena, human reason, for them, is a firm anchorage and its results proof against the ravages of time: thought is independent of social reality. This viewpoint can be refuted: the sociology of knowledge has shown that thought is largely determined by the thinker's social position. That is true of the thought of individuals no less than of knowledge as such. Our knowledge and understanding is largely shaped by ruling or privileged groups – both on the national and the international stage. That can be seen from the conclusions that investigators from the rich countries draw after visits to colonies or neocolonies. Thus various studies of conditions in Indonesia completely ignored the mechanism of class exploitation.[14] Instead, the investigators described Indonesian

society in terms of ethnic conflict and exaggerated the importance
of religious and nationalistic trends. By veiling class differences,
this kind of investigation supplies theories that serve those in
power as justifications of their system of oppression.[15]

The conservative nature of many sociological studies of the
(neo)colonies is also reflected in what I would call the
anthropological distortion of reality. Such distortion consists of
an undue emphasis on the specific character of local circumstances.
It is most commendable that social anthropologists should utter
warnings against the contamination of the culture of all who come
into contact with the 'Western' economy, but it is quite wrong of
them to ignore the fact that many local customs and traditions
blind people to what is happening all round them and hence
impede their emancipation. This phenomenon can only be seen in
perspective if the horizon is extended from the village to the
wider national and international framework in which the village is
set. If that is done, it often becomes clear that the preservation of
many local customs benefits no one so much as the ruling class.
Needless to say, this is no reason for rejecting all aspects of local
culture: I wish merely to warn against exaggerating the value of
the culture of people or groups to which the investigator does not
belong.

This anthropological distortion is an aspect of a wider practice:
placing a smokescreen round phenomena for the express purpose
of rejecting changes thought to be too radical. Any research that
contributes to that outcome, deliberately or otherwise, must be
called political propaganda. One common propaganda trick is to
concentrate on internal factors (conditions inside the poor
country) and to ignore or underestimate the external factors
responsible for underdevelopment. Thus in a fairly recent report
on Surinam, stagnation is blamed largely on internal factors: the
small scale of Surinamese society; a weak state with a
malfunctioning state machinery; the economic mentality of the
population; emigration, and – oddly enough – Surinam's
remoteness from the big trade routes when ship after ship goes up
the Surinam river to carry bauxite and other raw materials to the
rich north. Great stress is laid on mistaken policy decisions which
are largely blamed on the Surinamese government. Another
typical comment is that the Surinamese do not have what it takes
to modernise, such as ambition, a willingness to save and a

propensity for economic activities. I have no hesitation in calling this nonsense tropical madness. Surinamese have set up many kinds of industry large and small, and have done so with admirable application, but partly because of the power of foreign enterprises and also because of the country's colonial heritage, native entrepreneurs are lacking in expansion potential.

In any case, this type of sociological analysis is of no help to poor countries. Governments in 'developing countries' have an obvious reluctance, as I read in a report of a Dutch advisory commission,[16] to pay much attention to indigenous causal factors when discussing home affairs with representatives of the developed countries. 'That's understandable,' the right will say, 'they can't stand the truth'. But to the left it looks quite different: 'They are tired of all the lies, of all the deception'. I am becoming more and more inclined to dismiss all quasi-scientific statements that ignore the crux of the matter and argue around it as 'oppression science'.

An antithetic – indeed hostile – attitude to social science from the rich capitalist countries has a stimulating effect on one's own Third World studies, but one would be ill-advised to reject in a blind rage everything that originates from institutes and laboratories in hostile territory.

The rich countries have a need for hyperspecialists but the same need may not be felt in the poor countries. These would do better to study their own problems in their own way and not to feel obliged to copy the division of labour that besets the exercise of social science in the rich countries. In that case, they may well come up with their own subjects or their own faculties. Perhaps oppressed countries have a particular need for specialists engaged in interdisciplinary studies of the foremost problems of society. In this connection we need only think of (1) agricultural social scientists; (2) experts on non-agrarian trade and industry (including the trade-unions); (3) experts on public authorities (including development planning); and (4) liberation scientists.

However, social science in the Third World must not only be decolonised but must also be rendered less elitist. Social science often has the character of a hobby with little societal impact, a kind of luxury, a pleasant diversion for wealthy scholars. The research projects of these hobbyists are often self-centred; the student pursues his own personal interests. This does not agree with a Third World view in which the interests of the poor are paramount. In Surinam an old Amerindian woman, conscious of the elitist aspect of social science, said to a social anthropologist: 'If it were not for your studies you would never live among us miserable Indians'.

### Action research

In their attempt to make a useful contribution, liberation scientists have moved out of the ivory tower of 'pure' social science, in the conviction that social reality (and particularly the process of social emancipation) cannot be grasped properly unless its study is pursued in conjunction with the practical struggle for emancipation. Without broad knowledge in their academic field and the skills needed to do scientific research, they will not achieve a great deal. Moreover, they must also be able to put themselves in the position of the oppressed and of the activists, to view social problems from their standpoint.

Liberation scientists carry out their investigations in close contact with the leaders of political parties and similar action groups, and work with the active involvement of the oppressed. In so doing, they not only add to the knowledge of the oppressed, but, more important, encourage them to start gathering data by themselves and to interpret them. Research must be conducted everywhere and at all times, by adults no less than by young people, and must lead to an understanding of class relations and open up the prospect of liberation. The Brazilian educationalist Paulo Freire offers a prescription in his *Pedagogy of the Oppressed*. In particular, he wants people to make a critical analysis of their environment and social position in the hope that this will help them to work for their own emancipation.[17]

The research worker participates as much as possible in the struggle of the people who are the subjects of his studies. The object of the research is to plan actions that will help to change social relationships. Action research is a combination of investigation, education and struggle. This is called participatory investigation, and the Mexican sociologist Rodolfo Stavenhagen speaks of activist participation.[18] In Cuzco (Peru) an experiment based on this type of action research was recently planned by a university institute of social and economic research. The surveys were designed and executed in consultation with the organisations of those for whose benefit they have been devised. While doing their research, those responsible work in close collaboration with members of the solidarity group involved. They try to make themselves useful on the land, paint farmhouses, make calculations (for instance of crop yields) and give legal advice. The Danish investigator, Elsebeth Tarp, who believes that the study of women in the Third World calls for real participation, activism and commitment, pleads in favour of the use of leading questions – anathema to methodologists – provided that such questions help those interviewed to become more clearly aware of their situation and to express their views and feelings more adequately.[19] Action research demands a great deal of empathy: a feeling for others, the wish to get closer to them. Anyone unable or unwilling to provide that closeness had best not engage in action research. Of course one must also be able to be detached, keeping one's distance, but that does not gainsay identification.

Perhaps I should remove a possible misunderstanding. I certainly do not believe that action research should be done primarily by foreigners. On the contrary, academics from the country in which the struggle is being waged should be the main recruits, but it would be wrong to argue that foreigners should be excluded. At a Latin American university I met a European woman who was a fairly recent arrival but who was already helping to organise strikes. She was unreservedly accepted by all as a fellow fighter and was extremely well suited to doing action research in that country. Incidentally, it is possible to help the struggle with research at various levels, and at various distances from the scene of action. Not all of these contributions can be described as action research, but it strikes me as useful to dicuss the investigator's contribution in this connection.

In Surinam, a student told me that he thought it pointless to write the kind of progressive book on Surinam that I had produced. After all, the local peasants could not read it. I should instead have tried to make direct contact with the peasants and spread my ideas by word of mouth. This point of view must be strongly resisted, for it implies that all progressive writers, publishers and bookshops should cease their activities, and that response would bring great relief to reactionary forces throughout the world. Contributions to the liberation struggle can be made in all kinds of places in society, in the rich countries no less than in the poor, and all such contributions are welcome. We must not allow liberation science, or for that matter action research, to become the prerogative of an elite ('I am more progressive than thou'). In this section, I am chiefly concerned with action research conducted in close contact with the base, but whether this contact is protracted or relatively brief does not greatly matter. What I am concerned with is the result of the research and what can be done with it. A social scientist who lives a simple life in a slum for years can make a valuable contribution. But someone who stays among the slum dwellers for a much shorter time, but also studies the literature scrupulously, can do equally useful work.

To achieve the best possible results, action research should be conducted in the frame of an enduring organisation, one that will lead the struggle until victory is won. The link between the investigator and the militant organisation can differ, for tactical or other reasons, but a link there must be if the results are to prove useful. To what extent all these steps can be taken in practice depends largely on the nature of the oppressive regime. Clearly, the greatest possible caution is needed if the fighting forces of the resistance, including their scientific arm, are not to fall victim to those in power. It is of great importance that liberation scientists enlist the sympathy and protection of less progressive circles so that – if danger threatens – they can count on support from that quarter.

Liberation science will not have finished its job the moment a (progressive) change has taken place. The process of emancipation will still be under threat, and warnings must be sounded against those proposing to take the wrong course.

## Committed reports

Because liberation science aims to stimulate people with little education, it must be particularly careful about its use of language and presentation. All writing should be done in simple, everyday language, and if a scientific term cannot be avoided, its meaning must be carefully explained.

I am opposed not only to incomprehensible linguistic noises but also to the neutral presentation of research findings. A sociologist writing dispassionately will be able to give a calm exposition of how people are repressed, of how during protest demonstrations the police injure and kill them. He will be able to describe this as an inevitable phenomenon; after all you can't make an omelette without breaking eggs. It is just as happens in chemical reactions: some molecules are destroyed while others are formed and some solids are changed into gases and some gases into liquids. Whether the substances themselves like the idea or not, whether the chemist regrets or applauds it, is an extra-scientific question. Not so in liberation science. Liberation scientists do not ignore their feelings. Their publications bear witness to their negative attitude to oppression and their positive attitude to the struggle. Liberation scientists are human beings who react with passion to what is happening in the world; to massacres, wars, terror and to the victories that are being won. They give voice to that passion; they condemn outrages in cutting and harsh words, and they rejoice if there is cause to do so. They react 'irrationally', above all when a sober, rational report would convey the wrong picture, when a quiet, peaceful, euphemistic presentation would act as a soporific.

When describing labour conflicts in the West Indies, one would do violence to the realities if one did not report the feelings of the workers towards the sugar planters, preferably in the workers' own words, or if one failed to record what went on in their minds when, one night, they set fire to the fields and the hated canes went up in flames. Their subjective feelings are bound up with an objective fact, namely that burnt cane fields must be harvested as quickly as possible, which puts the managers under pressure to give in to the workers' demands.

Discussions with political opponents must sometimes be fierce and passionate. But though hostility may be justified, all exaggeration is damaging – if it goes beyond a certain point, an emotional account will prove counterproductive.

## The research worker's frustrations

In this chapter an attempt has been made to show how people emotionally involved with the oppressed do their research work. Their approach makes great demands on them and can easily become frustrating.

In order to keep a firm stand, a liberation scientist must have two sturdy legs: a scientific one and an emotional one. A scientific attitude it needed to arrive at useful and reliable results, and the emotional attitude supports that endeavour in three distinct ways: by lending direction to the research, by motivating the investigator and by helping him to bear disappointments.

The academic research worker who identifies himself with the oppressed is in a dialectical situation. On the one hand he benefits from a privileged academic position provided by the ruling class. As a result he is in constant danger of being alienated from the cause of the oppressed. Being in the vanguard of the struggle, too, causes difficulties: the research workers indicate how the struggle should be waged yet do not wish to play an elitist role. They would like best to join unreservedly in the activities of the solidarity group but are too often forced to draw attention to errors. To avoid, in these circumstances, any backsliding into the role of selfish academics in the service of the ruling class, the research workers must be members of an organisation that stands up for the cause of the oppressed and hence acts to some extent as a safeguard.

In their vanguard role, liberation scientists may risk trying to curtail the freedom of choice of the people in order to help them attain greater freedom in the long run. This irksome situation may turn the members of the solidarity group against them and the radical changes they advocate. The research workers may then feel deeply frustrated, the more so if they find it hard to accept that incisive changes can often take a long time to materialise. Most frustrating, too, is the realisation that the individual with his relatively short span of life can only contribute very little to the social progress he so desperately desires. The Third World expert Ankie M.M. Hoogvelt, who believes on theoretical grounds that our scope for influencing the course of history is very limited, nevertheless joins marches, stations herself and her posters in front of foreign embassies, and writes letters to generals, not in order to win great victories but to preserve her dignity. 'I do it to save my soul,' she confesses.[20] Working in groups of oppressed people and their sympathisers is another means of asserting one's principles and one's determination to persevere. People know that by banding together they become stronger; together they take cognizance of the work of writers and poets who long ago, rationally and emotionally, chose sides in a struggle that is still going on. The idea of handing on the torch to the next generation is a satisfying one.

## Summary

Since the social sciences of the privileged classes provide a distorted image of social reality, a separate form of social science is needed to defend the interests of the oppressed. That is what liberation science tries to be for the poor and oppressed in the Third World. It adopts an antithetic position to the official sciences of the rich countries, which in the main turn out knowledge that is geared to the needs of the rich countries. The poor have their own needs, and for that reason they must decolonise their education and research and also take it out of the hands of the elite. A Third World social science must be constructed to challenge the relevance of the social science of capitalist countries.

The liberation scientist's first task is to look into the causes of poverty and backwardness. The problems of the poor are studied in an interdisciplinary manner, with a view to change, development, progress and resistance. The poor themselves are not at first particularly interested in processes. What they need above all is an exposition of the way in which the social system of which they are a part works and how it stands in the way of their progress. The poor see few changes in their lives. That is why it is doubly important that liberation science should convince them that changes are possible and demonstrate to what extent.

Liberation science takes a dialectical view of social reality, which means that conflict and struggle are fully acknowledged. It is infused with the hope that the struggle to produce changes will lead to progress.

For educational reasons, but also to gather as much relevant information as possible, liberation scientists conduct their researches in close contact with a solidarity group and coordinate them with the practical side of the liberation struggle.

In his writings, the liberation scientist describes the social situation through the eyes of the victims, which in some cases necessitates the use of emotional language.

By adopting the scientific approach described above, the author is adopting a partisan way of undertaking research. Values form part of his scientific endeavour, and he makes sure that these values are stated explicitly. Because of this explicit formulation of politically or at least philosophically determined premises, the scientific work of the liberation scientist, other things being equal, is of a higher standard than that of his conservative colleagues who prefer to hide their value judgements behind a mask of objectivity.

In his gathering of data, the liberation scientist must be as objective as is humanly possible, constantly questioning the accuracy of the information he obtains, and his argumentation must be in keeping with the laws of logic.

This chapter has tried to sketch some aspects of a scientific research method that is a logical, or rather, a sociological, reaction to the type of oppression and domination that afflicts a large part of mankind. It is a science that helps the oppressed to diagnose their problems, that helps them to form and run organisations, as well as to elaborate strategies of effective social struggle and development. Liberation science deals with a phenomenon that is becoming more and more prominent: the liberation struggle of the poor of the Third World.

# 3 The Poverty-and-Wealth System

## Overview

Poverty is not one of the first impressions gained by a visitor to the city of Douala, in Cameroon, with its modern commercial centre, richly stocked main street stores and the many impressive buildings. But he does not have to look long before the darker side becomes evident: someone moves on stumps of legs between the little tables of the congenial pavement cafés along the Boulevard La Liberté. An obese, semi-paralysed man is being pushed along in a wheelchair, and a blind beggar woman is led around by a young girl. And all the time children hold out plastic cups for coins. Anything can be bought or hired at any time, including the bodies of women. Young men with nothing else to do sit or stand about along the streets. Fifty per cent of the working population is unemployed.

There is poverty, but also wealth in the Third World, reason enough to describe the social system in which this combination occurs as a poverty-and-wealth system. That term covers part of a division into four distinct phenomena based on two important characteristics: the total income of the system (including production for own use), and the distribution of that income. All in all, we distinguish between: (1) a system of uniform poverty; (2) a system of uniform wealth; (3) a developed poverty-and-wealth system, and (4) an underdeveloped poverty-and-wealth system. The last two categories are marked by considerable differences in income, but in the penultimate category the average income is high which, as a rule, means that the lowest-paid are not as badly off as they are in the last category. To avoid any misunderstanding I would just like to add that income is a broad concept covering everything by which human beings can satisfy their needs (without having to draw on capital). State provisions, too, are subsumed under this heading, and so are environmental benefits (pleasant homes), agreeable work, and so on.

In this book I shall be concerned exclusively with category 4, which for simplicity's sake I shall call the poverty-and-wealth system. It manifests itself on four levels: local, regional, national and international. The regional system is discussed in this chapter, the various aspects of the national systems are discussed in Chapter 4, and the international system is examined in Chapter 5.

If we place the poor, who are my central concern, in the centre of a circle, we find that they are surrounded by poverty-and-wealth systems which spread out round them in ever widening circles. The village is one such a system, as is the region, and the country; and the world as a whole is also a poverty-and-wealth system. The poor are involved in all these systems, and are the victims of every one of them.

Before we look at the various systems in detail, we must first consider some general socio-economic characteristics. The main characteristic concerns the mode of production. The poverty-and-wealth system is a system of private producers, that is, it is predominantly a capitalist system. Some of the private producers are poorly off; they are pauper producers, especially in small-scale agriculture but also in the retail trade. These poor producers have control over few means of production and the exchange relations are to their disadvantage, which is one aspect of the unequal distribution of economic power.

The non-producers among the poor are pinned down in low-wage jobs while social barriers prevent their social advance.

Characteristic of the capitalist poverty-and-wealth system is the contrast between, on the one hand, peasants and workers who are in a marginal position and, on the other hand, a very small group of entrepreneurs who control a fairly large share of the means of production. In every system and at every level can be found a dominant class that is able, not only because of its wealth but also because of its educational standard and political influence or power, to perpetuate the power gulf that divides that class from the poor majority, and even to widen it. The poor are exploited. Writing about the position of the poor rural woman in India, Miriam Sharma of the University of Hawaii points out that she has to contend with triple exploitation: first, as a woman oppressed by her husband and sexually abused by landlords and rich peasants; second, as a member of a general landless class, exploited by landlords and money-lenders; third, as a labourer exploited by the capitalist class.[1] The poor are powerless, badly organised and too divided to make sure that production is increased and that the profits of the increased production are shared out fairly.

Because the poor live and work primarily in a village or a quarter of a town, we shall begin with an outline of local and regional social life.

All descriptions in this and the two subsequent chapters of this book are highly schematised, i.e. reduced to the essentials. They do reflect social reality in the Third World, but for the sake of greater clarity certain aspects have been stressed, while others may not be present everywhere.

## The regional system

Among the thousands of officials who have tried to improve village life, also among the social scientists who encourage them, the naive idea that social equality can be found at the village level has long been rife. In fact, a village under capitalism is part of what, for capitalism, is a normal system, that is a system of oppressors and oppressed. In the village studied by the Pakistani sociologist Saghir Ahmad in the Punjab, the oppressors are managers in the service of absentee landlords. The cultivators of the land and the village artisans are subordinate to these managers, their position in many ways similar to that of workers in an industrial organisation.[2]

In rural areas the wholesale buyers of agricultural produce and owners of large shops are in a powerful position. Buyer and shopkeeper (and sometimes moneylender as well) are often one and the same person. Peasants who are short of cash while their crops are growing, and that is true of many of them, receive advances from the buyers or become indebted to the shopkeepers. Then, when the harvest comes in, they pay off their debt in produce at an unfavourable rate of exchange.

Another category of exploiters at the local level consists of healers and sorcerers, and often also of the lawyers who appear in the wake of quarrels between neighbours that are the direct result of envy due to poverty.

If the liberation scientist wishes to gain some insight into conflicts at the local level, he must divide people into groups according to the profits they gain from the production process. To that end, he must be able to see the social structure in historical perspective, the better to explain why one group receives more than another. In this connection, I would ask the reader to follow me to the Cuzco department in Peru, where there were 174 haciendas in the province of La Convención alone before the land reform of 1969.[3] The owners of these haciendas, the planters, let out part of their land in exchange for labour. The tenants were in many respects dependent on the planters, but their dependence was somewhat reduced when they found a way to sell part of their produce at good prices without the planters' intervention. As a result they were able to build up some capital, felt a little freer and stronger, and tried to reduce their obligation to the big landowners. They did this among other ways by subletting part of 'their' land to subtenants who took the tenants' places when the landowners summoned them for statutory labour. In their turn, the subtenants let out part of their parcels of land to sub-subtenants on the same conditions.

The land reform act dispossessed the planters, whereupon the tenants, subtenants, and sub-subtenants became owners of the land they worked, while the land formerly worked by the planters themselves – the best land – became the collective property of the former plantation landworkers and other employees. The landworkers had appeared on the scene after the tenants' disturbances had put an end to statutory work on the plantation.

Besides cooperatives holding land in common (communal cooperatives) there also appeared cooperatives of independent tenants (service cooperatives). This is not all that can be said about the Peruvian land reforms; the point to note is that not all the inequalities of the plantation period have been abolished. There remains the contrast between 'rich' peasants (the former tenants who were granted large pieces of land), middle-sized peasants (the former subtenants) and poor peasants (the former sub-subtenants and others). As in all rural areas, social contrasts to a large extent reflected differences in the size of farms and the associated ability to employ farmworkers and to purchase produce from other peasants and perhaps also to supply them with goods.

In the tea-growing valley of La Convención, the so-called rich peasants employ farmworkers and in addition act as traders or operate haulage businesses (using lorries). The former tenants have to some extent stepped into the shoes of the old planters. They are the leaders of the newly-formed service cooperatives and have considerable influence on government officials. There is a conflict of interests between them and the members of the communal cooperatives. They, the ex-tenants, had waged a bitter and dangerous campaign against the planters, while the members of the communal cooperatives (the *socios*) had profited from the agrarian reforms for the simple reason that they were farmworkers. The ex-tenants felt that they had had the worst of the bargain, but that was not the only cause of their resentment: the 'rich' peasants and the *socios* were also competitors in the labour market. Both groups needed labourers and the supply of farmhands was particularly short in this district. The cooperatives had an advantage here because they could offer higher wages and also because they observed all social regulations.

The history of the small tea-growing valley in the militant province of La Convención shows that the Peruvian land reforms did not abolish the most fundamental social contrast in the countryside, that between small and large farmers. After the land reform, the large estates became the communal property of groups of peasants, but the contrast between these large-scale cooperatives (the former haciendas) and the small farms of the remaining peasants remained, and with it the conflict. In various parts of Peru, land not worked by the cooperatives has been occupied by small peasants, a situation that often gives rise to fighting.

It must be remembered that the tea-growing valley is part of a wider productive system. An agrarian region is, as a rule, run from a regional centre, a medium-sized town in which produce is normally processed in factories. It is here that most of the money is earned, and the peasants, the primary producers, resent that fact. 'The town is the centre of our oppression,' said a peasant in imperial Ethiopia.[4]

Because of the economic role of the town, the availability of cheap food is important to it, so that workers' wages may be kept in check. Cheap food is supplied by the oppressed rural areas. Since that means poverty for those in the countryside, the population migrates in large numbers to the towns. The regional poverty-and-wealth system flows from the national poverty-and-wealth system, which will be dealt with in detail in the next chapter.

# 4 The National Poverty-and-Wealth System

## Production

### Overview

The national poverty-and-wealth system will be examined through the various subsystems we can distinguish in it. It goes without saying that we should start with the production subsystem because the contrast between poverty and wealth is an integral aspect of the prevailing mode of production. Moreover, the remaining subsystems are partly determined by the productive system. We shall look at each subsystem from the position of the poor, and in so doing we shall discover time and again that the contrast between the poor and the rich is a central feature of every one of these subsystems.

We shall examine small producers, middle-sized entrepreneurs and big businessmen in that order. These three groups are linked by means of exchange and power relationships. The middle-sized entrepreneurs profit from the small producers and the big businessmen profit from both the small producers and from the middle-sized entrepreneurs.

After describing the production system, we shall successively discuss the social structure, the political system, the cultural system, the system of mass persuasion and the maintenance of these systems.

### The small producers

The category of small producers is largely made up of peasants. In this section, I shall confine myself to them alone. They cannot

73

be described as entrepreneurs (for instance, they employ no workers), but as producers they do have relationships with the rest of the economy. If they are largely self-sufficient, they will sell part of their produce (what is left after home consumption) on the market, which is a part of the regional, national and international capitalist system. In addition, many peasants all over the capitalist world devote a large part of their land – compelled or otherwise – to growing cash crops for the international market.[1] Total self-sufficiency is the exception rather than the rule. Thus Adolfo Figueroa, Professor of Economics at the Catholic University of Peru, tells us that a typical peasant family in the southern sierra of Peru has to rely for approximately 40 per cent of its income on wage labour.

The peasant is beset with a host of problems, and many writers devote themselves to drawing up long lists of these. The lists bear witness to their scholarship but add little to our understanding. They place a smoke-screen round the true problems if – as generally happens – their authors look at peasant enterprises from a mainly technical point of view: the peasant's fields are too scattered, the soil is poor, the location is unsatisfactory, the barns, wells and seed are of poor quality; the peasant uses no artificial fertiliser and works with primitive tools. In my view, this is a mistaken approach. The reason why the peasant works with poor material is entirely due to the fact that he is poor. That is his real problem and it is a political one: the peasant is the victim of a political system, he is being exploited. His main problem is not that his barn or house are inferior, but that he receives too little payment for his labour. That is a direct result of his lack of power. Liberation science accordingly defines the peasant as an exploited producer of agricultural products.[2] He is exploited because others profit more from his products than he does himself; his hourly earnings are less than those of any connected with his production: landlords, wholesalers or carriers. Indeed, even consumers may be said to exploit the peasants whenever they buy produce that gives the peasant a much lower hourly income than the consumers themselves earn. Here the same thing happens as occurs in unequal exchanges in international commerce (see the section *Unequal exchanges* in Chapter 5).

Exploitation can assume such virulent forms that the peasant decides to produce nothing for the market any more. He withdraws into self-sufficiency. This is what I found in Peru, and the Iranian revolutionary, Bizhan Jazani, reported the same reaction in Iran during the pre-Sha era.[3]

A great many exploited peasants are, in fact, wage-labourers who would supplement their meagre income with outside work, if they were able to find any. I call them agricultural proletarians; they are (partly) unemployed workers.

'Peasant' is a political concept, as I have just said, but in many countries it is also an historical concept. The peasant is not only exploited, he is also being driven into a corner. Thus when the Inca peasants in Peru lost their land to the Spanish conquerors, they were forced back to the highest and at the same time the worst parts of the Andes, where they tried to keep themselves under extremely difficult circumstances. Those who could not hold out any more tried their luck elsewhere in Peru. They came down from the mountains in their hundreds of thousands and made for the coastal plain where trade and industry flourished.

## The middle-sized entrepreneurs

On the regional level we come across a group of middle-sized entrepreneurs who appropriate a good part of the profit to be made from agricultural products: traders who exploit the peasants, small industrialists and other entrepreneurs who enrich themselves through their workers. The better-off peasants, too, are enemies of the small peasants. The difference between the two groups is that the former (together with the big landowners) live predominantly from the rent on their land and from the proceeds of the work of agricultural labourers. The small peasants, by contrast, live on their own labour. Because of their need for supplementary work, they have an interest in high wages; the better-off peasants, on the other hand, have an interest in keeping wages low.

Medium-sized and small industrialists treat their workers badly. In India, for instance, legal protection of workers' rights in small-scale industry is almost non-existent, while physical working conditions (especially hygiene and safety) are poor. The workers draw very low wages and have to accept a subordinate position.

Without a small piece of land on which to grow food and without
the additional income of household members, they are unable to
maintain their families.[4]

## The big businessmen

Many of the middle-sized entrepreneurs are dominated by big
business: local buyers by wholesalers in the city, small industrialists
by big industrialists.

One complaint about big industrial enterprises is the very low
wages paid to the workers together with the shedding of labour.
Those involved may include industrialists from Western Europe
who have moved their factories to low-wage paying countries: an
example would be the Dutch garment companies in Tunisia. The
main reason why big industry in Indonesia can pay very low
wages is the political impotence of the workers, a direct
consequence of the liquidation of the labour movement in 1965
and 1966.

There are, admittedly, some industries that pay their workers
relatively good wages. This is particularly true of foreign
companies in which the wage factor is of subsidiary importance,
for instance in mining and oil refining. These companies,
moreover, are interested in creating a favourable impression, in
having public opinion on their side. For the same reason, they
will also subsidise cultural institutions.

Another complaint against large industrial enterprises is that
they introduce increasingly more advanced machinery, these new
machines producing more goods with a smaller workforce. Thus
in the Netherlands Antilles workers in the old industries were
dismissed in large number. At the same time, mechanisation and
automation helped to increase the demand for highly qualified
staff from Europe and the United States. In 1952, the oil industry
gave work to 21 000, but by 1976 there were only 4100 workers
left in the industry.

In Indonesia, the scale of the textile industry was greatly
enlarged, which meant an increase in production, but that went
hand in hand with a decrease in the number of jobs. In the period
from 1966 to 1971, textile production rose from 250 million
metres of material to 600 million metres, but more than half the
jobs were lost. Small, labour-intensive industries were no match

for the large labour-exclusive industries. And under the Indonesian system no work means no income.

It is not only big industry but large-scale farming that gives work to too few people. In addition, the yield per cultivated hectare is low and much land is left to lie idle. In pre-revolutionary Cuba a single family ran 80000 cattle on 200000 hectares – 2½ hectares per animal, something that may be permissible in thinly-populated Texas but that was completely irresponsible in Cuba.

## Social structure

### Social classes

There is a prevailing difference of opinion in the literature on the Third World concerning the extent to which classes exist in underdeveloped countries. Africa, in particular, is said not to be ready for genuine class distinctions. One writer has claimed that in the rural areas of Africa there are only classes-in-the-making. This is not entirely incorrect, but it must be borne in mind that the creation of classes in Africa has been proceeding for some considerable time and that it is currently taking place at an accelerated tempo. A class system appeared in Africa, as elsewhere in the Third World, following the introduction of capitalism by the colonial powers. In Nigeria, for instance, there emerged a native petty bourgeoisie dominated by a foreign ruling class drawn from the British middle class. The lowest social class in the colonial situation was made up of the great masses of peasants and workers. In some towns one could occasionally come across a class of workers who, according to Bade Onimode, an economist from the University of Ibadan (Nigeria), had lost any independent means of livelihood.[5] Once national independence had been gained, a class of industrial labourers emerged, people who had to sell their labour in order to survive, but according to the Tanzanian political scientist, A.M. Babu, this class is still numerically small.[6] I might add that even in rural parts of Africa, capitalist productive relationships have appeared: in many places a top stratum of prosperous agricultural entrepreneurs faces a large group of pauperised agricultural workers and poor peasants. The creation of large state-owned farms, too, for instance in

Zaire, has led to the appearance of class distinctions between the workers and privileged government officials.[7]

It has to be said that classes and social strata in Africa are rather complex because a capitalist mode of production (in state industries and in the private sector) still goes hand in hand with a feudal mode of production (for the benefit of princes and nobles) and also with a communal mode of production (by and for individual families). In Ghana I was told that these three modes of production can sometimes be found in one and the same region and involving the same people. Tribal chiefs force peasants, who are largely self-sufficient, to hand over part of their surplus to them, which they then sell on the national and international markets. It is well known that Latin America has marked class distinctions, but Asia, too, is class-ridden. Thus David Selbourne met a number of classes in India who 'rode on the backs' of hundreds of millions of peasants, landless, unemployed, semi-employed and homeless people. In Indonesia, Sritua Arief and Adi Sasono have distinguished nine interacting components of the national economic system, including landlords, an industrial bourgeoisie, a petty bourgeoisie, and the rural and urban poor.[8] In rural Thailand there are widening inequalities between farmers, medium-sized peasants, marginal peasants and landless labourers due to the absorption of the local economies into the national and international exchange economies.[9]

I agree with Ankie Hoogvelt that, though the social structures differ in the three continents, their dominant features are similar, deriving as they do from their similar positions in a global power system.[10] I shall be discussing the nature of the global system in the section devoted to the capitalist world economy in Chapter 5. Here I shall confine myself to classes.

The distinction between entrepreneurs based on size, and hence on their respective power and influence, provides the main criterion of class distinction. The relationships between the various types of entrepreneur are in fact class differences, with some exploiting others. My conservative colleagues often forget to mention this fact and affect to believe that classes are independent of one another. They also use an approach which I prefer not to follow. They begin their catalogue of classes with what they call the highest; with the 'better circles' or the elite. With my social commitment, I begin with the 'lowest', though I shall try to avoid the terms 'low' and 'high' as much as possible, because they suggest a qualitative difference: the 'better' circles may occupy the top rung of the social ladder, but they are not better people. This impression must be studiously avoided. Similarly I eschew the term 'elite' when referring to the rich and powerful, for that term implies that we are dealing with a select and superior group.

The definition of classes based on exploitation is a simple but very illuminating one. To take an example: when you hear people advocating small-scale technologies for small businessmen you will realize at once – thanks to my clear definition of 'petty bourgeoisie' (see p. 82) – that this policy entails exploitation of the poor.

The enrichment of businessmen sometimes takes illegal paths. In Peru and Jamaica, for instance, fortunes are made in the narcotics trade. But much more far-reaching than enrichment by unlawful means is the appropriation of a surplus value in accordance with the rules of the system.[11] That is obviously done at the expense of the workers or the producers. If the appropriation of surplus value were a reasonable reward for the entrepreneurs' trouble, there would not be so many objections to it. But that is impossible in a capitalist system which hinges on the accumulation of the greatest possible fortunes for use in further investments. As a consequence, we have a situation in which just a few people determine economic developments.

The social group whose nucleus decides on the use of the chief means of production is the bourgeoisie. It is a class that is in a position to exploit the rest of the population. Because class divisions determine the lives of all who are subject to them, I consider them the most important structural aspect of a capitalist system.

In some countries it seems as if the population is mainly divided into power blocs based on ethnic, cultural and religious differences. After discussion of social classes, I shall go on to say a few words about these differences, from which it will appear that there is often a close connection between class conflict and other conflicts.

The main criterion of membership in a social class is not ownership of the means of production but control over them. On that basis, we can distinguish between those with no powers of control, those with moderate powers of control and those with considerable powers of control. The group that does not own any means of production and has no economic control is the proletariat, and the group with a great deal of control is the bourgeoisie, with the petty bourgeoisie holding a place somewhere between the two.

Below we shall be considering the following classes: the sub-proletariat; the agricultural proletariat (consisting of farm labourers and part of the peasantry); the factory workers; the petty bourgeoisie and the bourgeoisie.

I do not, of course, suggest that all these classes are to be found in every country, but like all the phenomena described in this book, they can be encountered in many parts of the Third World (and sometimes in the First and Second Worlds as well) and – if they occur – they are of crucial importance. This book is also a methodological work; it contains a survey of the phenomena to which we must pay attention and which we must look for if we want to get to know a society in the Third world. The liberation scientist will also try to discover the social concerns of all those who are victims of the bourgeoisie. As for the class enemies of the proletariat, he will draw attention to those facts which, as they become known, undermine the position of the enemy or bring him into discredit. For the liberation struggle to succeed it is also of great importance to make a study of any (potential) opposition between the enemies of the oppressed.

*The subproletariat*

Proletarians depend on paid work. Their problem is that there are so many wage dependents and so few jobs that the pickings are very thin. A great many have-nots have no regular jobs and take on casual work as unskilled labourers, garden boys, domestic servants and the like. Some, without money, start up a small business: hawking anything they can lay their hands on, cleaning shoes, offering themselves as prostitutes, touting for customers for hotels and brothels, etc. They are called subproletarians. Their number includes beggars, some of whom make use of maimed children, and people like Carolina Maria de Jesus, whom we met in Chapter 1 and who searches dustbins for food and things to sell. Subproletarians are found mainly in the big cities.

They live on the fringes of the capitalist system, but their activities constitute a part of that system. The economy of the slums and workers' districts is usually named the informal sector, labour conditions in it being almost completely unorganised and difficult to register. However, I can see no sense in separating this type of fringe economy from the rest. The subproletarian, too, makes a contribution to a system of production that is dominated by other classes. Petty-bourgeoisie contractors find him work and charge commission and the middle-classes can find bargains at flea-markets. The established order benefits from the cheap labour of people with no fixed occupation.

According to the Dutch anthropologist, Paul van Gelder, it is a characteristic of the informal sector that economic activities in it are not governed by legal provisions.[12] This applies equally, I believe, to many economic activities of medium-sized and large enterprises with a corporate status but which practise tax avoidance and enrich themselves through all sorts of questionable activities not sanctioned by the law. It is typical of bourgeois sociologists, among whom I do not wish to include Van Gelder, that they close their eyes to the informal sector or black economy run by their own class.

## The agricultural proletariat

Agricultural proletarians play a modest role in the capitalist system of their country, profit little from it, but do make a contribution to the enrichment of others.

Among the agricultural proletariat I include those peasants (with or without plots of land of their own) who work as labourers on the land of foreign or local entrepreneurs, and also those who eke out a living on the land but are, in fact, wage-dependents without work.

Peasants know perfectly well that they are being exploited. According to an old Javanese proverb, the peasant's property belongs to the prince during the day and the thief at night. And a Jamaican peasant said to me: 'The rich man rob you money, the poor man t[h]ief you crop.'

Those peasants who are forced to move to the city constitute an urban proletariat with strong roots in the countryside in which they grew up.

*The factory workers*

In my opinion, those workers who are more or less permanently employed in (more or less) modern factories, and are relatively advanced and organised in trade unions, constitute a separate class. They are better off than other workers and many of them claim middle-class status. During an enquiry conducted by my institute among the staff of a gas and electricity company in Surinam, two-thirds of the employees declared that they counted themselves among the middle classes.[13] Similar attitudes have been recorded in other countries too, such as India,[14] which is why Breman speaks of a labour elite.

*The petty bourgeoisie*

The core of the petty bourgeoisie is made up of exploiters of the proletarian class. Especially at the local level, middle-men wield a great deal of power over poor peasants and workers and profit from their cheap labour. The various petty-bourgeois groups do not necessarily hold the same political views, but on the whole they are interested in maintaining the capitalist system, albeit they would like to hold a more favourable position in it. By and large, the petty bourgeoisie acts as a prop of the big bourgeoisie. A large section of the clergy, too, is part of the petty bourgeoisie and acts above all to preserve the system.

A formidable threat to the proletariat comes from the armed forces, whose officers enjoy middle-class status thanks to their antecedents and income.[15] It would be an oversimplification to claim that the military in the Third World invariably look after the interests of the upper class. Primarily, they look after their own cause, particularly that of the top brass usually referred to as the 'national interest'. And this, according to the Syrian political scientist, Bassam Tibi, does not coincide with the interests of the proletariat.[16]

Officers tend to adopt a conservative attitude, both because the right has a great deal of power and because the rich are able to be of service to them – as a group they are willing to lend the army financial support, though sometimes they may have to be forced to do so. Moreover, essential social changes introduce too many uncertain elements, and the fierce anti-communism that is rife in many armies springs, according to S.E. Finer, from the fear held by the military that their group interests would be threatened if the left came to power.[17]

African writers see their continent, at least as far as the black population is concerned, as a petty-bourgeois continent. The African petty bourgeoisie derives its power, not from the ownership of the means of production, but from ownership of the means of distribution and from domination of the state apparatus and of state-owned enterprises.[18] Thus various African countries have government agencies which buy products from the peasants, possibly process them, and often export them as well. The difference between what the peasants receive and what these government concerns collect is considerable, and it seems likely that a large part of the difference finishes up in the bank accounts of senior officials.

A part of the African middle class works hand in glove with metropolitan economic interests; it is in the service of the international bourgeoisie. Since I myself attach less importance to the ownership of the means of production than to their *control*, I place these people in the international bourgeoisie. But no matter what we call him, the African bourgeois is a 'ruthless type, less refined than his metropolitan master; he is crudely ostentatious in his tastes, sometimes wears diamond rings on each finger big enough to be noticed even from a fast-moving car', writes A.M. Babu.[19] In other countries, too, we find similar types, people who, unlike their European counterparts, have not, or not yet, learned to hide their greed and ambition under a cloak of hypocritical modesty – which, in Europe, is of Christian origin.

### The bourgeoisie

The bourgeoisie in the Third World often has a different composition from that in the prosperous countries. The industrial element is less strongly represented because it is almost impossible for local businessmen to compete with foreign competitors on the industrial plane. The local bourgeoisie has accordingly settled for trade and the state machinery. The position of those who control the latter in particular is very strong: they constitute a *bureaucratic bourgeoisie*. In Iran this class was made up of officials in the Shah's court, army officers and managers of state enterprises.

Bizhan Jazani, who finished up in one of the Shah's prisons, where he was murdered, wrote that many of them grew rich on corruption.[20] Closely allied to the bureaucratic bourgeoisie in many Third World countries is what the Sudanese social scientists El-Wathig Kameir and Ibrahim Kursany have described as a *parasitic bourgeoisie*. It is a class that acquires wealth by the embezzlement of public funds, the appropriation of agricultural land as a result of the privatisation of state farms, and the acquisition of shares in commercial companies supported by the government. It is a parasitic class because its income is derived chiefly from non-productive activities.

It is useful to classify the bourgeoisie in yet another way, by distinguishing between a *national bourgeoisie* and a *dependent bourgeoisie*. The last subclass maintains close relationships with foreign economic powers on whom it is strongly dependent. The national bourgeoisie consists of businessmen who feel hampered by the foreigners and therefore turn against them. They want to develop as freely as possible and favour protection against foreign competitors.

Because the dependent bourgeoisie is a tool of foreign commercial and industrial companies (confining itself, for instance, to the production and export of raw materials), this class, which contributes little to national development, has been called 'lumpen-bourgeoisie' by A.G. Frank, an expert on the economy of developing countries.[21] In my book on Surinam I myself used the term 'footooboi bourgeoisie' (errand-boy bourgeoisie) to stress the fact that this class serves the interests of the foreign groups that are in control.

It should also be noted that the four parts of the bourgeoisie we have distinguished often overlap and there can also be conflicting interests between them. According to Mahmood Mamdani, an economist connected with Makerere University in Kampala, Uganda, capitalism in many neocolonial countries has a dual character because the state plays a major role in the production process.[22] This explains the powerful position of the bureaucratic bourgeoisie.

Reverting to the military, I might add that in various countries power has come to lie with a military bourgeoisie that looks after the interests not only of their own caste, but also of the rich entrepreneurs. In Indonesia, the ruling military bureaucracy is responsible for a parasitic diversion of national resources to people in power.[23]

The bourgeoisie strengthens its own position by giving the impression that it is superior to the great majority of the people, not only in wealth but in cultural respects as well. Thus the rulers of pre-revolutionary Cuba contended that there were just two classes: 'leaders shouldering responsibility' who were also 'men of culture', and 'the simpler people', those who belonged to the 'lower classes' and who had therefore to do manual labour.[24] Quite often the upper-class culture, which is considered to be so superior, is of foreign origin, derived from the dominant rich countries.

*Other structural elements*

Apart from class conflict, ethnic, religious and regional conflicts are often at work as well. It must, however, be stressed that these conflicts are often the result of actions by governments that look after the interests of the ruling class at the expense of other population groups. These groups react, *inter alia*, along ethnic, religious and regional lines, with a consequent danger that the class conflicts may become hidden behind a smokescreen of ethnic, religious and regional ideas and sentiments. Govan Mbeki, the recipient of an honorary doctorate from the University of Amsterdam, learned how to see through that smokescreen; with greater awareness, his outlook began to change. At first, he looked upon the differences in the standard of living and in the privileges of black and white South Africans respectively as a racial problem, as the result of the domination of his people by the white colonists. But later, when he examined his country's situation more deeply, he came to see these differences in the light of class distinctions. And there are many more such Africans as Mbeki. In Nigeria, for instance, Bade Ominode has observed that during the nationwide strikes ethnic and class affiliation often coincided.[25]

I mentioned the conflict between the sexes earlier, when discussing the pattern of poverty in Chapter 1. We saw that women are suppressed in the home and at work, that is, in the production process as well as in the reproductive process. Many men behave as if their women were their servants, in a subordinate position.

Maria Mies has described the oppression of women in Narsapur, India. There women undertake outwork on commission from traders, labour that is badly paid and often prolonged. They work in their huts from sunrise to late at night, by the light of oil lamps, turning out lace, textiles and pottery, much of which ends up in the rich countries where, thanks to the low wages of these women, it can be bought at bargain prices. In Narsapur the exploitation of women is facilitated by an ideology that keeps women in their homes, barring them from work outside the house.[26]

It may be apposite to point out at this stage that I do not for a moment suggest that women in the Third World and the poor in general would have been better off if the conquerors from the rich countries had left them in peace. They would then, I assume, have been oppressed by different means, in which case a different theory, and a different liberation struggle would have been needed.

## The political system

The poor have no, or very little, political power, not even in a poverty-and-wealth system based on parliamentary democracy, because the latter, too, is a capitalist system in which the economically strong make their presence felt more forcefully than the economically weak. Sometimes this is partly due to divisions among the progressive forces resulting from differences of opinion about the nature of the struggle to be waged and the system to be introduced after victory. That sort of argument is conducted in the main by academics and other theorists, with the proletariat as impotent listeners. They would undoubtedly like to put a stop to what is often no more than idle speculation but they are unable to do so owing to a lack of knowledge, weariness and dejection.

In many poor countries, broad social groups are kept in the political cold; the various ministries take decisions without consulting them or even taking their interests into account. Intellectuals imagined things differently before independence;

none of it fits into the theories they propounded. They advocated a one-party system, run by a strong party that would be able to weld the nation together, eliminating tribal and local self-seeking. The one-party state would encourage mass participation and defend the interests of the entire population. And this is what has ostensibly happened in such countries as Zambia and Tanzania. Here the people choose those political leaders they believe will best look after the interests of their region. Those elected choose the leaders of the party councils at the regional and national level, people drawn from all strata and all regions. But even from newspaper reports published in these two countries it appears that the system does not work. Thus a senior official felt it necessary to point out to prospective candidates that they must not stand for office for the financial rewards alone. And a Zambian political commentator wrote: 'Most of our political leaders fail to understand the humanism our party advocates'. Zambia has degenerated into a state capitalist system in which the bureaucratic bourgeoisie manipulates and exploits the nation, and things are not very different in Tanzania. For that matter, we find that in most of Africa the one-party state represents privileged urban groups and especially the bureaucratic bourgeoisie. Those who control the state do so mainly in their own interest.[27]

The poor section of the population, which is excluded from political influence, has no alternative but to try to enter into personal relationships with those who are better situated, with those who have the economic or political power and are therefore in a position to do their friends small, and sometimes big favours. This sort of system is known as clientism. It is a system of businessmen in politics in which the big political entrepreneurs have subcontractors or agents to look after their interests in all kinds of places in society. The top entrepreneurs in politics, the people who are eligible for ministerial posts or parliamentary seats, get the money they need for advancing their political careers from businessmen in the productive system who are anxious to obtain (legal or illegal) facilities from the authorities, or who – in a more general sense – are interested in the maintenance of the status quo.

A system of parliamentary democracy in which a class of businessmen in politics holds a powerful position can be described as a manipulative democracy. During the elections, the voters are misled by intensive campaigns that only well-funded political parties can afford. The ruling class does business in the political system by doling out functions – in the party and in the government machinery; its propaganda is based on appeals to personal egoism with promises of presents or other material advantages. What benefits the politically weak manage to obtain are generally short-term or insignificant: temporary work, minor local improvements and so on. In the long run, their encapsulation in corrupt political cliques is anything but in the interests of the oppressed, because it cannot possibly lead to a structural improvement of their position. Clientism weakens the tendency to effect structural changes in the society.

In a social system in which clientism flourishes, the state machinery, too, is corrupt, and very little is done for the weaker groups in society. Whenever conservative experts try to explain this phenomenon, they use the phrase 'political will'. There is a lack, they say, of political will to do anything for the poor. This is another typical smokescreen phrase which hides the real power relationship. 'What a pity the rulers do not want to play the game; what a pity that they are so self-indulgent. If only they had more willpower, everything would be fine,' goes the implicit argument. The conception is false. The rulers do indeed want to play a game, and the name of that game is preserving the status quo.

## The cultural system

The culture of the poor and oppressed often differs from that of their rulers and offers them poor chances for growth and advancement in a society dominated by the rulers. One result is that the culture of the poor contains elements of dissent. In the primitive little churches of Jamaica which are called 'God's poor people's churches', the people give vent to their dislike of the values and manners of the rich and of the churches attended by solid middle-class worshippers. Their own religion is a mixture of Christian and African rites.

Resistance can also take the form of poking fun at their rulers in private while showing respect for them in public. And things become ominous for the rulers when popular sects and organisations arise to demand equal rights for all.[28] One of the reggae numbers of the Jamaican Rastafarians is called 'Equal Rights'. It is, however, important to bear in mind that many of the oppressed have a strong desire to appropriate the culture of their rulers.

## Mass persuasion

### Introduction

The dominant culture in a society is propagated in many different ways by interested parties. At the same time, however, one can feel the pressure of contrary cultural currents: every idea that is propagated implies the rejection of that idea, for the simple reason that its converse must occur to the minds of all those interested in the opposite idea.

An idea propagated by defenders of the established order is that this order has been ordained by God. Rebellious people, by contrast, feel that God must have intended something quite different, for instance equality. This idea invariably occurs to them and they will express it freely just as soon as the existing order shows signs of strain. When that happens, we have the emergence of a counterculture,[29] and that can be the beginning of the end of the existing order.

Mass persuasion includes the kind of education provided in schools, but also by the media – the press, radio and TV – and by all sorts of institutions, for instance the church. And we must not ignore the fact that society itself is a kind of school. The prevalent ideas (usually those of the ruling class) are stamped upon the daily round of the production process: as they work, people are taught such ideas as the value of competition, the struggle for existence, efficiency, and then they make them their own.

### The mass media

Mass media is a short way of saying the means of mass communication, and that is a misnomer, inasmuch as these means do nothing to foster real communication. Rather do they obstruct communication, because what they are primarily concerned to do

is to mould public opinion. A mutual exchange of views is not in
the interest of the rulers because it would threaten their cultural
monopoly. In most poor countries, the media are used for
repressive ends. Their main objective is depolitisation, or
deflecting public attention to subjects that pose no threat to the
rulers.

It must be remembered, however, that people may not always
be taken in. They belong to various groups (family, neighbourhood,
work, etc.) in which certain attitudes prevail to which the
members prefer to adhere. It is not easy to make them change
their minds.

In some Third World countries, it is still possible to sound a
note of opposition, particularly in the press, and sometimes an
illegal pamphlet may be distributed, but this cannot be considered
a serious counterbalance to the influence of the mass media.

## The church

The church propagates views that are intended to keep the poor
and oppressed in their place. It cannot be denied, of course, that
religion also inspires people to social resistance, but in many
Third World countries the social effect of religion has for centuries
been a mainly conservative one. It goes without saying that
religion does not have this social function alone. Its appeal lies, in
the first place, on the personal plane, but that particular aspect of
religion falls outside the scope of this book.

In many religions, attention to worldly problems is deflected by
the promise of a better life in the hereafter. Muslims are enjoined
to rest in Allah, and Buddhists to empty the mind, to suppress all
desires, to seek Nirvana. They are then far removed from this
earthly vale of tears which has so few good things to offer to the
poor.

Officials of the church tell us of poor people who are addressed
by mysterious forces, hear inner voices, and are proclaimed
saints, from which it appears that the poor, too, can be superior
human beings, with the help of divine intervention. A most
comforting thought.

Religion enjoins people to respect the powerful, the unknown,
and the many things they cannot grasp with their modest intellect.
In sermons and so-called sacred texts, they are confronted by

elevated thoughts and beings to whom they fell inferior and who make them fell that they are lowly creatures. In this way, religion inculcates people with the very intellectual attitudes that help to keep them oppressed: during their melancholy earthly existence, they had best keep on the right side of the rulers. Religion is a good exercise in this art: they learn to insinuate themselves into God's good books by addressing Him with folded hands, by kneeling down before Him. These methods may easily be adapted to dealing with earthly rulers.

However, other sounds too can be heard in clerical circles, especially among the lower ranks, some of whom have taken up the cudgels for the oppressed out of a sense of human solidarity. In Latin America, Catholics have been infected with a new mode of theologising: liberation theology, which Gustavo Gutiérrez from Peru has called a gospel-inspired reflection by people who oppose injustice and who stand for a just and fraternal society.[30] At the end of the 1960s, even some of the Catholic hierarchy in South American were forced to speak up, though they quickly recanted. And at present the highest clergy of all, those in the Vatican, are trying to cast suspicion on liberation theology by reproving it for using Marxist concepts to account for poverty and oppression.

*Education*

The poor are eager for their children to go to school and are prepared to make sacrifices to achieve this. But the children do not find it easy. Many are weak and sickly, which does little to encourage learning, and their school environment, too, is far from good. The classes are too large, there is a lack of teaching material and in addition the children are taught in a language they do not fully understand: the language (or the usage) of a different social class or population group. The result is that many poor children leave school early or are repeatedly kept down.

The children of the poor are given the sort of education that meets the needs and requirements of the middle class and that reflects the life style of the petty bourgeoisie. If the parents want their children to prosper in the existing social system, then they must provide extra coaching in the practices of a culture that has left so deep a mark on education. But this they cannot afford, with the result that the children of the poor are 'selected out'. Moreover a great many children do not even get as far as the first class of primary school.

At the universities, students often form groups opposed to the existing order and in some countries the effect of bourgeois education may well be tempered by teachers with progressive ideas. This is particularly true of Peru.

## Maintaining the system

### Introduction

When I wrote the Dutch version of this book, the town of Estelí in Nicaragua was being bombarded. There were repeated sounds of explosions and clouds of smoke hung above the town. Estelí was one of the towns that had rebelled against the regime of President Somoza. Somoza, for his part, tried to maintain the system – a system that favoured himself and his friends – by a military force made up of Nicaraguans, Cuba counter-revolutionaries and the like trained in the United States. But a system need not necessarily be defended by military force alone. We shall see below that there are other means of maintaining a status quo that benefits the few at the expense of the many.

Though I am dealing with the maintenance of systems as a separate issue, the reader must remember that it is inseparable from all the subsystems discussed in this chapter. The separate treatment is, however, justified because those who want to change a poverty-and-wealth system cannot ignore by what means the system manages to remain as it is. However, the reader must also remember that every system is subject to change. Because various people and groups seek power in it, a social system has an internal dynamism of its own. Individuals and groups who can expect few advantages from the system try to improve their position and in so doing set up tensions between the privileged and the dissatisfied. Such tensions may well lead to changes.

I shall show below that there are 'safety valves', such as a parliament, in which the opposition can let off steam. These institutions have a system-maintaining function but may also give rise to change. The safety valves can become a clarion call to struggle. The liberation scientist must study how this comes about and how it can be encouraged.

There is a good chance that this section will cause despondency, that the conclusion will be drawn from my remarks that it is very difficult, if not impossible, to change an oppressive system. That conclusion would be over-hasty. In a later chapter devoted to the liberation struggle, I shall show that changes can indeed be made. Like all my observations, these too are partly of a methodological kind. I shall show to what aspects the investigator must pay special attention when studying the social factors that prop up an exploitative structure. These are the maintenance of unequal control of the economy; the geographical and social isolation of the proletariat; the strengthening of the position of the bourgeoisie; and oppressive culture; various safety valves to reduce social tensions; physical violence.

## System maintenance

In colonisation schemes in Surinam, it has been the custom for many years now to allow peasants only a very small piece of land, too small, in fact, for them to live on, so that they are forced to seek work elsewhere. This is, of course, in the interest of entrepreneurs since there is a shortage of cheap labour. In poor countries, where labour is not scarce, by contrast, peasants are exploited with high rentals. Either way, the result is the *maintenance of unequal control of the economy*.

Inequalities in economic power are also maintained or encouraged whenever government departments do little or nothing for the poor while performing various services for the rich. Thus the Surinamese government did very little to assist the work of poor peasants but provided substantial sums for investment in large-scale agricultural projects.

A large section of the proletariat suffers *geographical and social isolation*. This phenomenon was particularly marked in colonial Rhodesia, and is still reflected in the 'urban-landscapes' of Lusaka (Zambia) and Harare (Zimbabwe). Harare in particular, it must be said, appears at first a splendid city, conspicuously clean and well-kept, and with no trace of poverty. On closer inspection, however, it becomes evident that all this magnificence covers a small area. Take a car and drive a few miles out into open country and you will then come across the localities of those who are less well-off, the townships of the Africans. And the further afield you go, the worse the poverty.

When the Europeans trekked up from the south (the Cape Colony) and founded Rhodesia, the African population was driven towards the periphery of the conquered territory, where the soil is poorest, and left to their fate. Many of them, it is true, were forced to work on the farms of the European conquerors, but they were among the poorest in the land.

There are also social barriers between the classes, reinforced by physical and geographical distance, to make crossing the divide between the classes more difficult. Thus social life takes place mainly within one's own circle, in one's own club, one's own swimming pool, and so on. In education, too, there is a gulf between the classes. The children of the rich and of the poor go to different schools and they receive a different education. 'Apartheid' also exists in industry, where blue-collar and white-collar workers have separate canteens. The workers have a trade union and the staff have a professional association. If you think that sort of thing is normal, you must realize that it is only normal in a certain social context; in a society riddled with class conflict and powered by competition between individuals and groups.

One way of separating proletarians from the rest of society is to belittle and intimidate them by what might be called psychological oppression. In Jamaica, I observed that a 'garden boy' was repeatedly told, when being handed his weekly wages, that he had done next to nothing to earn it once again. This was a humiliation at the very moment when the oppressed is most aware of his dependence on his employer.

It is also possible to divide the proletariat from the middle classes by the creation of a buffer layer. This happened in Peru, where the military government used land reforms to bestow privileges on one section of the peasantry by making them collective owners of cooperative farms.

As long as methods of oppression manage to maintain fear, they help to maintain the system. But they also arouse hatred and that is something the oppressors fear. Both sides are afraid of each other.

As soon as the middle class feels threatened it tends to close ranks and to reduce conflict within its own class. Once it does that, its position is consolidated. And there are other ways as well of strengthening the position of the bourgeoisie. One of these is a legal system that protects its interests, and forces the oppressed to observe the rules.

Another method used by the middle class to protect its interests is to enter into personal relationships with selected members of the other classes, a system we mentioned earlier. It also helps to maintain the status quo if occasional handouts (charity) are given to the poor. Then even those who come away empty-handed may hope that it will be their turn next, and remain fearful of spoiling their chances by adopting a rebellious attitude.

The bourgeoisie tries to blunt class conflicts further by making small improvements and also by passing sham progressive measures and creating sham progressive organisations, especially in the so-called social work sphere.

By granting various subsidies, the ruling class tries to win over potential opposition groups, to ensnare trade union leaders and to curry favour with a section of the peasantry (a small subsidy here, a little credit there).

Sociologists have been pointing out for quite some time now that the role of many organisations devoted to change, and even of some progressive organisations, is to maintain the status quo.[31] Conservatives also establish organisations for the specific purpose of preventing the radicalisation of the masses. Thus the military rulers of Peru founded a trade-union to take the wind out of the sails of the communist trade union, and with the same aim also organised Peruvian peasants in a national organisation with local branches.

The oppression of a population or group is not only a structural phenomenon; it also involves the *cultural* sphere. This happens in various ways, but firstly it involves silencing the culture of the oppressed. Thus slaves in Surinam were forbidden to play African music. In the second place it means indoctrinating people with an ideology useful to the ruling class. Thus in capitalist countries, the prevailing ideology shores up the system of private enterprise, i.e. the interests of those who are best equipped to operate successfully in a capitalist economy.

Even culture in its scientific and artistic forms is often turned to the greater glory of the ruling class. In Cuzco (Peru), local artists were encouraged to produce splendid paintings glorifying the religion of the ruling class. All the persons depicted on those canvasses were of Spanish descent. Again, in the nineteenth century, Latin American painters turned out a large number of portraits through which the bourgeoisie could vaunt its power. Only at the turn of the last century, when the working class and the oppressed peasantry began to make their presence more strongly felt, did painting in that part of the world become more socially committed. Even so, many artists continue to be the servants of the bourgeoisie.

We have seen that the ruling classes like to present themselves as culturally superior and that they like to depict the victims of their exploitation as inferior human beings. This whole attitude serves above all to perpetuate the status quo, especially if those discriminated against can be made to believe in their own inferiority. The result is a culture of resignation, the more so if the oppressed feel that they have little chance of ascending the social scale or if they believe that class distinctions are divinely ordained. However, we must always remember that such attitudes invariably go hand in hand with resentment and that they can easily turn into their very opposites.

If there is resistance, if tensions appear, then the bourgeoisie can open some of the *safety valves* we have mentioned. One of these is social advancement: some of the more intelligent members of the working class get a chance to raise themselves up a rung or two on the social ladder. Another method is to focus attention on events in rich foreign countries, or on heaven, where the poor can enjoy a plentiful life.

Sport, too, makes people forget their everyday cares and temporarily reverses the social hierarchy. Those workers who watch football matches on the field or on television (in Peru I saw lorryloads of peasants from the mountains being driven down to Cuzco to follow the feats of the national football team on a public screen) hero-worship men of their own class. Moreover when the conversation turns to sport, they feel like experts, people whose opinions must be taken seriously.

The boosting of national sentiments with the achievements of national teams, but also with the threat of war, is another important safety valve.

Parliament and elections also have that function. At election time, people can vent their resentment against real or assumed enemies, and parliament offers people a chance to let off steam vicariously between elections or when following its debates. The possibilities of voicing objections on a limited scale and of fighting minor political skirmishes also helps to preserve the status quo.

I have examined the various system-preserving methods used by the bourgeoisie, each in turn. How could it be otherwise? But the reader must realize that they are all interrelated, that they are part of one and the same system of oppression. This is also true of the physical violence used to cow the opposition, invariably in combination with other techniques. It will only be used as the ultimate threat, when all else has failed, for instance when economic pressure is no longer effective. The weaker the position of the oppressors the more they are forced to resort to physical violence.

In many poor countries, the struggle against the so-called 'internal enemy' is the main justification for having any army. Some people are astonished that soldiers are willing to kill their own compatriots, but it must be remembered that most suffered misery and want before they joined up, that life itself has made them hard. For them there was little choice and the army seemed attractive. For many, moreover, violence is a welcome way of releasing their pent-up frustrations on fellow human beings, who are in fact fellow victims.

Those who speak up for the oppressed are boycotted, persecuted or killed. Class justice decrees severe punishment for any disturbance of the public order. The power of the state is sufficient to maintain the status quo in the absence of a vigorous opposition. Should the power of the opposition grow, then the ruling class may have to enlist the support of foreign countries. Anti-guerrilla groups and police officers are trained on foreign soil to put down all who resist the hegemony of the ruling class.

# 5 The International Poverty-and-Wealth System

## Introduction

In the preceding pages we have examined regional and national social structures and in both cases we encountered the same sad fact: great differences in wealth and great inequalities. To explain these inequalities, we turn to the situation on the international plane, only to find that 75 per cent of the world population lives in the Third World, but the rest, or one quarter, can lay claim to 83 per cent of the gross national product of the world; uses 75 per cent of all energy and 70 per cent of all cereals; owns 92 per cent of all industry and controls 95 per cent of all technological innovations; and accounts for 89 per cent of all the money spent on education throughout the world.[1] (The gross national product is the total value of all goods and services produced annually.)

International relationships do not do the poor in the world much good. Thus the Chinese textile industry was destroyed by the import of cloth from Great Britain. Only occasionally do poor peasants profit from international trade. In the 1870s for instance, Jamaican peasants were able to improve their position when the bananas they cultivated for export rose in price, so much so that many of them were able to purchase the land they had previously worked as tenants. A class of small tenants thus became a class of small property owners. But this was an exception, and their prosperity was, moreover, short-lived.

Production in the poor countries by small, medium-sized and large producers is usually linked to production by companies in the rich countries, and generally in a way that is disadvantageous to the producers. Organisations in the rich countries usually have the upper hand and can dictate terms (financially, technically, and also militarily). People in the Third World are weighed down by a multifarious power bloc. They are oppressed.

Domination on an international scale is just one aspect of the capitalist world economy which comprises the rich and the poor countries and which is characterised by a division of labour and by exchange relations from which the economically powerful profit and the poor suffer. The exercise of power by capitalist enterprises established in the rich countries and supported by their governments is usually referred to as imperialism.[2] Imperialism is based on the old principle that the (neo)colonies are there to be exploited for the benefit of the mother country.

It is therefore understandable that the wealthy capitalist countries should wish to maintain their hold on the Third World and that they should be opposed to those countries disposed to align themselves with the Soviet Union. Below, we shall be examining the draining of capital from the poor countries through commerce with the rich countries and the exodus of skilled workers (the brain drain). Since all these developments favour the rich countries, those countries have little interest in incisive change.

In this chapter we shall confine our attention to the capitalist world economy and to the social forces that help the economically strong to preserve their privileged position.

## The drain of capital

From the poor countries large amounts of money flow to the rich countries in the form of profits, technology payments and interest. In Indonesia, for instance, 2.71 US dollars are siphoned off for every US dollar's worth of direct foreign capital investment made during the period 1970–77.[3] And in 1979, North American companies alone made 12.7 thousand million dollars profit in the Third World and shifted it to the United States.[4] In addition, many of the local rich transfer their money to banks in the prosperous countries.

If an underdeveloped country grants favourable terms to foreign countries, it can count on a generous slice of development aid, mostly in the form of credits. Now, it is partly as result of such credits that the poor countries are so badly in debt, and these debts are growing. Between 1970 and 1984, the outstanding medium and long-term debt expanded almost tenfold to 686000 million US dollars.[5] Ten years earlier the debt was still a mere 119000 million. Such an increase is not necessarily a bad thing. If the economy is growing quickly, then the foreign debt may safely be allowed to grow as well, but this is not what has been happening: compared with the growth of the gross national product and of exports, there has been a clear increase in the burden of debt.

There has been a marked increase in indebtedness to such private creditors as foreign banks, which has meant a higher interest rate and shorter loans. It does not have to be stressed that banks only lend money to those regimes they consider creditworthy, such as Chile, where the government spends little on the welfare of the masses. Governments that try to help their poor and become financially embarrassed as a result are too great a risk for the banks. These governments can then appeal to the International Monetary Fund, a bank in which all countries of the world are represented but in which the rich capitalist countries have the final say.[6] And these make high demands. To obtain help from the IMF, a government must first arrange its finances in such a way as to make sure that it can pay off its debts and is able to contract new loans and to order goods from the rich countries, all of which greatly benefits foreign banks and foreign business. The great majority of the population is made to suffer in the wake of these arrangements inasmuch as their wages are frozen, there is less money for social services and food subsidies are reduced or abolished. Everisto Arns, the bishop of São Paulo, must have been thinking of this when he declared at a conference in Havana that what was at stake was the life of millions of people, against which the claims of international debtors weighed not very heavily in the balance, the less so as it was not the people but their rulers who had contracted the debts in their own interest. The Havana conference on the problem of South American debts was called in August 1985 on the initiative of Fidel Castro and was attended by 1200 delegates of political and other organisations from thirty-three South American countries.

## Unequal exchanges

Poor countries hold an unfavourable position in international trade. One handicap they suffer is that the rich countries have no wish to buy finished or even semi-finished goods from them. Their system of import regulations is governed by an 'anti-finishing policy', by a kind of value added tax. That means that levies on imported goods are the higher the more finished are the goods: for example, 0 per cent on skins, 4.8 per cent on leather, 11.9 per cent on shoes. The rich countries give preference to unfinished products lest their own industries suffer, and as a result the development of industries in the Third World is gravely impeded. Moreover, the industrial countries are increasingly adding further impediments,[7] quite apart from non-official protectionism. In the European Community, for instance, whole industries or industrial sectors enjoy large-scale state subsidies. In return, it is usually understood that a state-supported industry will not order materials or goods abroad that can be obtained at home, say cheaper steel from a poor country. One good turn deserves another.[8]

Even so, some poor countries have been able to step up their industrial exports. Industrialisation in the Third World has made great headway during the last two decades; indeed in the period from 1960 to 1968 the increase was more rapid than in highly developed capitalist countries. But this increase is insignificant if it is related to per capita income. A number of industrial products flow out from the poor countries; the proportion of manufactured goods in the total exports rose from about 15 per cent in the early 1960s to nearly 50 per cent in the early 1980s.[9] The countries with the lowest incomes, by contrast, produced much less favourable figures. More than half the exports from Third World countries come from just five countries.[10] The newcomers among the countries exporting manufactured goods specialise in less sophisticated, labour-intensive products.[11]

It is clear that the export of finished goods has risen in a small number of poor countries, but the figures do not tell us who profits. It may well be that the chief beneficiaries are foreign companies.

Among the relatively unfinished products that leave the poor countries, minerals rank first. They come from the so-called extractive sector of the economy, syphoning off raw materials and energy mainly intended for the processing industries of the rich countries.[12]

As for imports, many poor countries are forced to buy expensive machinery, tools and the like, abroad. In addition, several are dependent upon oil imports. Remarkably enough, large amounts of foodstuffs that could easily be produced at home are also imported. Cereals, soya beans, cotton, sugar and similar products travel from the rich countries to the poor. Of the total amount of agricultural produce exported by 'Western' countries, about 20 per cent goes to the poor countries. The peasants in these countries are unwilling to grow these products because a horde of profiteers has seen to it that they are grossly underpaid; and in some cases the peasants find it more attractive to concentrate on cash crops for export.

A remarkable phenomenon is the import of luxury articles for the privileged social classes. The Dutch journalist Jan van der Putten gives the example of French wines to be seen freely on sale in Santiago de Chile (while Chile itself produces excellent wines). Caviar, too, and other luxuries are available for the refined taste of a small but well-funded upper stratum. No one needs to be told that the foreign currency required for the import of these delicacies is earned by the work of those for whom French wine and caviar will always belong to a remote and unattainable world.

In addition to food, the means of death, too, travel in the direction of the Third World. We know what happens to them. It was with North American arms that the Nicaraguan National Guard inflicted massacres in defence of a social system that favoured those in power.

The poor countries are an attractive market for the rich countries. They absorb some of the rich countries' overproduction, and shoddy or faulty goods may be disposed of in them. This applies, for instance, to medicines prohibited in North America and Western Europe, and to insecticides that the rich countries do not allow on their fields.

For every country without its own supply, oil is an essential import. An increase in its price is unwelcome to every consumer, but for the poor countries it is a disaster. Towards the end of 1973, they were delivered a staggering blow when the price of oil almost quadrupled; oil imports in the poor countries rose from 8000 million US dollars in 1973 to 24000 million in 1974. In addition, the cost of their other imports also rose, since the industrial countries were having to pay more for their energy. At the end of 1978 there was another energy crisis and the price of oil in the poor countries doubled again, almost overnight. To make things still worse, their chances of exporting goods to the rich countries were severely curtailed by economic stagnation in the latter.

In exports no less than in imports, the rich countries make more money than the poor countries. According to some authors this is the most important cause of the growing poverty gap between rich and poor countries. There is a constant siphoning of labour value from the poor countries to the rich. Samir Amin, an Egyptian specialist on economic development, has calculated that in the middle of the sixties the loss to the poor countries from unequal exchanges amounted to about 22000 million US dollars a year. That was twice as much as the 'aid' and private capital received by the Third World.[13]

Unequal exchange: the name says it all, indicating that during commercial transactions one party gains more advantage than the other. There are two types of unequal exchange: one is due to differences in labour productivity, and the other to differences in wage level.

As a simplified example of the first type, we shall compare a North American rice grower who eats a plate of Thai rice in the evening and a Thai peasant who is served a bowl of North American rice.[14] Both consume the same amount of rice, but the North American 'eats' more work than the Thai. The Thai peasant produces no more than two kilograms of rice per hour of labour while his North American competitor produces 200 kilograms. Yet a kilogram of rice fetches the same price on the world market, no matter where it is grown. The American farmer has higher production costs because, among other things, he makes use of complicated machinery, but his profit per hour of labour is much higher all the same. That means that the poor peasant working hard for a hundred days a year with his primitive tools earns enough to buy just a small portion of the goods imported from the rich countries. His entire annual income is required to buy an article on which a North American worker need spend just one day's work. And we must also bear in mind that a North American does not work a hundred days a year like the Thai peasant, but three hundred. The difference is due to differences in the respective ways in which the capitalist system functions in the Third and First Worlds: in the Third World, there are considerably fewer possibilities of making a living. This difference will be discussed in the section devoted to the capitalist world economy.

The second form of unequal exchange is linked to differences in wages. Here, too, we shall use an example: the manufacture of identical radios by a multinational concern in both rich and poor countries, using exactly the same technical equipment. Though the labour productivity is identical, the wages of the workers in the poor countries are approximately one sixth of the wages of the workers in the rich countries. If the radios are exported to a rich country, the latter acquires products that – if they had had to be manufactured at home – would have been considerably more expensive, while the poor countries must import products that they could produce much more cheaply at home if only they had the means. The workers employed by export companies in the poor country are paid low wages and the consumers (some of whom are these very workers) must pay relatively high prices for imported goods. The situation is a disadvantageous one for the people in the poor country, quite apart from the fact that the radio factory is in the hands of foreigners and a large part of the profit goes to the rich countries.

When the question of low wages in the Third World is raised, people in Western Europe will often tell you that a Thai, a Peruvian or a Nigerian can buy much more for his money in his local market than a European can in his supermarket. But that is by no means always the case, and is, moreover, a false conception of the actual state of affairs. If we calculate how much a worker, for instance in Belgium, pays for everything he buys during the year, we shall find that someone in the Third World would have to pay a great deal more for the same consumer's package. And to do it, he would certainly have to have a much better job than the Belgian worker.

### The brain drain

One ghastly consequence of imperialism is the literal sucking out of human beings. This happened, among other places, in Haiti where companies from the United States collected blood for use in luxury hospitals in North America. On a much larger scale, the Third World suffers a brain drain, although that term does not, of course, have to be taken literally.

Between 1961 and 1972, some 300 000 highly skilled workers left the underdeveloped for the developed countries. Most of them went to the United States (90 000), Great Britain (84 000) and Canada (56 000). The largest number of immigrants came from Asia (more than 50 per cent), above all from the Philippines and India. Most of these were engineers (25 per cent), followed by doctors and surgeons (20 per cent) and scientists (10 per cent). It has been computed that the educational value of the qualified labour force that left the Third World for the United States, Great Britain and Canada between 1960 and 1972 was 50 900 million dollars, vastly more than all development aid put together.

Had the West had to pay for this brain drain there would, according to an UNCTAD report, have been a 50 per cent reduction in the foreign debt of the Third World in 1972.[15]

### The capitalist world economy

We saw in the last section that a great deal of wealth is pumped from the poor countries into the rich. Why does this happen and who is responsible for it? To find the answers we must examine the origins of the domination of the poor countries by the rich.

Capitalism emerged in Western Europe when the bourgeoisie acquired possession of the means of production created by the work of others.

The members of this social class seized the surplus value of the work performed by people who did not own the means of production. With the capital acquired as a result, the entrepreneurs were either able to step up production very considerably in Europe, or else – if higher profits could be made that way – they tried their luck in the colonies.

In the sixteenth century, ships sailed to what is now called the

Third World ostensibly to trade, but what went by that term was often little better than robbery. At a later stage, Europeans founded colonies for the express purpose of encouraging the cultivation of crops whose export to Europe promised large profits. By contrast, simple industrial products, for instance textiles, were exported to the colonies. This was the beginning of a division of labour on a world scale introduced for the benefit of the ruling class in Western Europe. Later, from the end of the nineteenth century, an increasing amount of ore and oil was removed from the Third World, having been extracted with capital supplied by the rich countries.

European penetration did a great deal of damage to autochthonous production in the poor countries. In his book *How Europe Underdeveloped Africa*, the Guyanese historian, Walter R. Rodney, has shown to just what extent colonisation by the European powers has had a negative effect on the development of Africa. That continent was in the process of developing its own productive resources when the Europeans arrived and brought such development to an end. Africa, thus doomed to impotence, fell further and further behind Europe.

Other continents experienced other developments, but none brought improvements for the native population. Asia, Africa and Latin America, before being introduced to the capitalist division of labour on an international scale, were quite unfamiliar with such phenomena as landless peasants, slums and massive unemployment or underemployment, as Samir Amin has observed.[16] The European bourgeoisie must bear full responsibility for these.

During the colonial period, the exploitation of the colonies served European interests above all. However, after the Second World War, the balance shifted in favour of North American business.

While the Europeans were at one another's throats, the North Americans were able to seize their chance. Thus a study by the Council of Foreign Relations came to the conclusion that the North American economy needed the largest possible sphere of influence. The report, which was approved by the North American government, went on to suggest that the British colonial empire as well as the territories occupied by Germany and Japan would have to make way for a Western sphere of influence in which the

North Americans would have an 'open door' for their trade and capital.[17] In 1947, this wish was granted when the General Agreement on Tariffs and Trade (GATT) was signed, creating a free-trade zone in which North American businesses and banks could operate both in Europe and also in the (former) European colonies.

This ambition of the rich countries was not ignored in the poor countries. Many people realized that their newly-found independence, which the North Americans welcomed, had brought them no real social or economic changes. The colonies had simply become neocolonies. The term neocolonialism, which was coined in Africa,[18] applies to the continuation of imperialist exploitation of economically backward countries, according to U.O. Umozurike, of the University of Nigeria in Enugu.[19] The essence of neocolonial relationship is that powerful and wealthy countries enrich themselves at the expense of various groups in poor countries.

To this day, the economies, and especially the commerce, of the poor countries are strongly tied to those of the rich countries. A report published by UNCTAD tells us how this came about: many trading companies in the poor countries are subsidiaries of firms established during the pre-independence period, and the international transport and communication network of many underdeveloped countries is geared to markets in the rich countries. Moreover, the so-called aid of the rich countries is often bound up with the sale of supplies to the poor countries, while transnational enterprises in the rich countries tilt the balance of trade further in favour of the North.[20]

As they did in the colonial period, so the poor countries must still supply the rich countries with raw materials and other goods at low prices, while they themselves must pay a high price for those goods they buy from the rich countries. Even oil earned the poor countries little profit for many years, a trend that, as everyone knows, was dramatically reversed not so long ago. Metals, by contrast, have become cheaper.

Surinam is an example of the extent to which a poor country can be economically dependent on the economy of the rich countries. Surinamese industries exist largely by the grace of foreign companies with factories in Surinam, and these are governed by decisions made in Pittsburgh (USA) or The Hague

(The Netherlands). If there were no foreign industries in Surinam, very little indeed would be produced in that country.

The economy of a country such as Surinam is rightly called a dependent economy, but that term does not cover the whole reality. The rich countries, too, are dependent on the outside world. Thus the industrialised countries import large amounts of food (such as fats, sugar, coffee and cocoa), together with rubber, mineral oil and various types of ore, for instance Surinamese bauxite. However, the dependence of the rich on the poor is quite a different matter. If the United States believes it has a grievance it can do something about it by threatening retaliation or by actually using force.

When the term 'dependent' is applied to the economies of the Third World, a qualification must be added: we must speak of subordinate dependence.

To appreciate fully to what extent a rich country can profit from a poor country we require just a few crucial pieces of information. We need to know how much profit it makes from investment in the poor country and how much the poor country earns from money it has invested in the rich country. The second sum will be found to be very small indeed. Apart from investments, we must also consider loans. Money lenders in the rich country make profits when they grant loans – they charge interest, though some governments also make low-interest loans (so-called soft loans). The interest saved through these may then be considered a windfall for the poor country. Another important piece of information we need is how much people earn in the underdeveloped country from the export of goods and how much others in the rich country profit from the same goods. Similar data are needed for the imports of the poor countries: how much do the native producers earn from the same goods? To that end, we can do no better than complete the following list:

| *Receipts of rich country* | *Receipts of poor country* |
|---|---|
| Profit from investments in the poor country* | Financial advantage from investments by the rich country in the poor country |
| Financial advantage from investments by the poor country in the rich country | Profit from investments in the rich country* |

| Receipts of rich country | Receipts of poor country |
|---|---|
| Interest on loans | Financial advantage from loans granted by the rich country |
| Financial advantage from loans made by (inhabitants of) the poor country to the rich country | Interest on loans to rich country |
| Interest saved through soft loans | Interest saved through soft loans |
| Value added to goods imported from the poor country | Value added to goods exported to the rich country |
| Value added to goods exported to the poor country | Value added to goods imported from the rich country |
| Financial advantage of immigration from the poor country | Financial advantage of immigration from the rich country |
| Transfer of earnings home by foreign subjects working in poor countries | Transfer of earnings home by foreign subjects working in rich countries |
| Gifts from poor country | Gifts from rich country |
| Total | Total |

\* Including profit from the export of knowledge (patents, licences, etc.). It is obvious that some figures in the first column will be very low or even nil.

This list should be considered an invitation to establish the relative advantage of imperialist relationships. My experience is that conservative economists tend to decline such invitations, with the excuse that the work is much too complicated, which is not true. It takes very little trouble to work out how much the Surinamese make from the cultivation of bananas and how much foreigners profit from it. I did just that and found that foreigners earn at least thirty-five times as much from Surinamese fruit as the Surinamese do themselves.

The favourable position of the rich countries is not exclusively due to such spontaneous processes as unequal exchanges – the protectionist policy of rich countries must also be taken into consideration. Thus 32 per cent of all animal products, 31 per cent of all textiles, 29 per cent of all vegetable products, and 28 per cent of all prepared food and tobacco products are subject to import restrictions in the wealthy countries. In addition, the governments of the rich countries assist ailing exporters with elaborate schemes.[21] European agriculture, in particular, is so heavily subsidised that imports of food (*inter alia* from poor countries) is only possible in those areas where European production falls short. Moreover, if subsidised farmers produce more than the inhabitants of the European Community can consume, the surpluses are reduced with the help of export subsidies and dumped on to what is often an oversaturated world market, so that prices drop further and it becomes increasingly difficult for anyone in the poor countries to make money from crops.

If we reflect on the structure of the capitalist world economy, we shall find that it is largely in the hands of three great power groups: the big international corporations, the big international banks and the dependent bourgeoisie of the poor countries. The latter, who are hand in glove with those who run the political machine in their countries, render considerable services to the other two power groups. In her *Third World in Global Development*, Ankie Hoogvelt speaks of a tripartite collaboration between international finance capital, the multinationals and Third World governments in the exploitation of the Third World. The resulting power structure bears a great deal of similarity to that of the colonial period. Then, too, the governments in the poor countries saw to it that foreign capital could exploit resources and labour under the most favourable conditions.

The big multinational corporations are the leading actors on the international stage. One cannot help admiring them. To set them up and to keep them going requires a great deal of energy and intelligence. They are among capitalism's greatest achievements: in 1978, the four largest multinationals between them had an annual turnover greater than the total GNP of the whole continent of Africa.[22]

The importance of the multinationals is reflected in the scope of their commercial activities, mainly conducted by affiliated companies.[23] Statistical tables give the impression that world trade takes place between countries, but this is far from being the case. There are divisions of multinationals that supply goods to other divisions of the same corporations. Moreover, many of these goods are also manufactured by the multinationals to whom international production is more important than international trade. In one of her books, Hoogvelt points out that as early as 1971 the combined production of all multinational corporations outside their countries of origin was greater than the total value of goods and services that make up the trade between countries (outside the Socialist bloc).[24]

It is partly because of investments by the multinationals that the Third World, too, has experienced a considerable degree of industrialisation. The multinationals do this because production costs in the poor countries (including wages) are low. Their power is great enough to stop developments that might lead to wage increases, and they can count on the support of the local economic ruling class whose interests in this area are the same as those of the multinationals. As a result the unequal exchange mentioned on page 103 can be maintained.

There is no question but that the activities of multinational corporations are disadvantageous to the great majority in the Third World. True, a small number of privileged people in the poor countries profit from their presence, albeit in a very limited way. Local employees are assigned the less highly paid jobs, the senior staff being recruited in the rich countries. Nor is local production boosted to any great extent. Thus Philips-Chile imported 81.7 per cent of the raw materials it needed in 1968, 87.2 per cent of its spare parts and 94 per cent of its machinery. The multinationals, moreover, do very little to hand on advanced knowledge and skills, and they are masters at avoiding taxation. If they do well, the subsidiaries of the multinationals in the poor countries minimise their declared profits with various kinds of bookkeeping tricks (by increasing the ostensible costs of products and other materials obtained from the mother company). The biggest local beneficiaries of foreign industries are found among local businessmen and government officials who supply different services and labour to the foreigners. In addition, when it suits them, members of the bourgeoisie are only too happy to dispose of their businesses to foreign interests. Thus statistics show that a large part of the investment of foreign companies is devoted to buying up viable local businesses. By the end of the 1960s, 65 per cent of 2904 subsidiaries of 396 North American and other multinationals in underdeveloped countries had been bought in that way.[25]

Capitalism is of little benefit to the great majority in the Third World. Indeed, it is no exaggeration to say that it causes a great deal of suffering. But perhaps that is not the whole story, since after a period of social misery in Europe and North America it brought prosperity to a good many people. That, at least, is how it looks to my solidarity groups; in the rich countries themselves there are many who complain about the results of the capitalist system. Still, the poor in the Third World would gladly change places with them, a fact that has persuaded quite a few writers that capitalism has not exploited the Third World as much as it might have done. If the capitalists were only allowed to have their way, these writers continue, they would bring prosperity to the Third World as well. This way of thinking is quite absurd, as I shall try to show in the section of Chapter 8 devoted to capitalist strategy. Here I shall simply confine myself to quoting Samir Amin,[26] who argues that capitalist production in the underdeveloped countries is based on cheap labour and does not greatly stimulate internal demand, with the result that few industries geared to the national market can develop. The economy of the poor country has been distorted by an export bias, which may suit a small minority. For this group, luxury goods are imported freely, as anyone can see in, say, large cities in many parts of Africa. However poor that continent may be, the stores are full of consumer goods for the better-off.

The economy of the rich capitalist countries is much healthier than that. Here, high wages and salaries have helped to boost purchasing power and hence mass production of consumer goods. Despite the high labour cost, industry has been able to make good profits and to acquire what capital equipment was needed to step up output dramatically. The combination of the mass production of consumer goods with the large-scale production of capital goods is the true explanation of the favourable economic position of the rich capitalist countries. That position was largely created by trade unions who managed to keep wage rises roughly in tune with increases in productivity. The workers were able, as Amin puts it, to wring a social contract from the employers in which it is laid down that consumers must be paid enough to spend freely, and employers must be able to retain enough to make sizeable investments. The social contract reflects a balance of power between organised workers and organised employers, with the state acting as a kind of referee: it makes sure that both parties keep the 'contract'.

Amin calls development in the North Atlantic countries autocentric: it generates its own expansion, at least in general, for without some profits in the Third World, Western Europe and North America would not fare nearly so well.

Some Third World countries, too, seem to show signs of autocentric development, for instance South Korea and Brazil, but such signs are misleading. From about 1966, the Republic of Korea has been the scene of labour-intensive developments focused on the export of industrial goods. The consequent increase in the gross national product did not, however, lead to a significant increase in internal buying power. True, social provisions were made for large groups of the population and there were also – especially in the seventies – some wage increases, but real wages rose less than GNP and productivity. A low wage level is and remains the basis of South Korean industrial development. It helps to make South Korean products considerably cheaper than similar products from other countries. Foreign enterprises, too, profit from the low wages for, as the South Korean expert Sun-Hwan Jo explains, they are able to swamp their home markets with highly competitive imports.[27] The peasants in South Korea are forced to make a contribution to this process by growing cheap food for the factory workers. That spells poverty for the rural areas and explains why millions of people have moved to the slums of the cities, where they swell the labour supply and thus help to keep the wages of the factory workers low.[28]

The low wages of the workers and the low incomes of the peasants mean that the buying power of South Koreans is low, but this is not considered a serious complaint by the rulers, writes Phyllis Kim, because the production is mainly geared at foreign markets.[29] And here we come up against the central flaw of the South Korean development model: the economy is *not* being guided towards an autocentric system. Because the country has no trade unions with enough influence to impose a different policy, improvements in the lot of the masses can only come about if a scarcity of labour forces the employers to pay decent wages. The resulting increase in purchasing power would lead to increased production for the internal market, which would bring further wages increases, and so on. This, at least, is the view of Dieter Senghaas,[30] though I doubt whether spontaneous economic processes will ever bring the desired result; without a powerful labour movement no substantial wage increases can be expected.

According to Senghaas, there is no sign that the labour factor in South Korea will ever grow scarce and hence expensive. This is prevented by demographic factors, by a surplus of labour in agriculture and by the acquisition of labour-saving machinery. Nor should the political influence of the employers be overlooked. They know how to make sure that further mechanisation does not go hand in hand with a shorter working week, something that did happen in Western Europe. In South Korea the workers still put in long hours. In 1982, for instance, women still worked an average of 52.9 hours per week.

In Brazil, the future of the poor looks no rosier. Here, too, production is strongly geared to exports. There is a great deal of development by foreigners in the interest of foreign countries, which leads to great social contrasts. *Time* magazine has called it a social scandal: while the Brazilian economy is growing spectacularly, more than two million children have been deserted by their desperate parents to roam about the streets. Another fourteen million children live in such poor circumstances that they would probably be better off if their parents deserted them as well. Altogether one Brazilian child in three is destitute.[31]

The relationships between countries and between regions can be presented in schematic form, roughly in correspondence with Johan Galtung's 'structural theory of imperialism'. If we take two capitalist countries, one poor and one rich, we must distinguish four elements. In the rich country situated at the centre of a world economy $C$, we distinguish between the centre $cC$ and the periphery $pC$; in the poor country, which lies at the periphery of the world economy $P$, we distinguish similarly between a centre $cP$ and a periphery $pP$. $C$ and $P$ have opposite interests, but some groups in $cC$ and $cP$ have common interests; while there is a conflict of interests between $pC$ and $pP$ in some respects. Figure 5.1 represents the relationship between the elements; the arrows show which way the gains flow on balance.

Without doubt, persons in the centre of the central country $cC$ profit from their favourable economic situation, but it is more correct to say that it is the companies which profit, and the

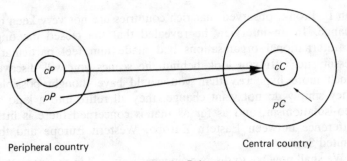

Peripheral country                    Central country

**Figure 5.1**

companies include employees, many of whom are found in *pC*. Experience shows that employees and their organisations in the central country are primarily concerned to further their self-interest.

Because of common interests, the social class in the centre of the peripheral country consists to a considerable extent of members who do menial services for economic forces in the central countries. Inasmuch as the centre of the periphery serves the interests of the centre of the central country and hence serves as a kind of bridgehead of the rich economies, the governments of the rich countries will support the subservient class. Hence the resistance to the Sandanistas in Nicaragua who have curtailed the power of the bourgeoisie. The rich countries fear that revolutionary governments may ensure that the interests of the periphery prevail in the oppressed country.

According to Johan Galtung, the capitalist world is made up of elements that rob one another of wealth. This is also true of every individual country. The capital city drains wealth from the provincial towns, the provincial towns from the villages, the villages (the merchants) from the peasants, the peasants from the farm labourers, and the men from the women. The main losers are the poverty-stricken women and children in rural areas of the Third World.

## Maintaining the system

The former Dutch Minister of Development Cooperation,

Jan P. Pronk, observed that rich countries are not very keen on
change. In an interview he revealed that the closed meetings
of international organisations had made him feel particularly
pessimistic.[32] 'If you look behind the scenes you will discover
much more hypocrisy than you would have thought possible.
They simply do not want change, they all retire into a kind of
neo-isolationism, and as far as that is concerned there is little
difference between Eastern Europe, Western Europe and the
United States.'

We shall now try to discover in what way, and in the interest of
which economic forces, the international power structure is being
maintained, and in so doing we shall find that similar factors are
at work on the international level as we have encountered on the
national stage.

## The consolidation of inequality in economic power

The creaming off of wealth, discussed in the previous paragraph,
is the main system-maintaining factor. The crux of the inequalities
between various countries or between urban and rural groups is
that the rulers syphon off wealth from the ruled, from the
oppressed. If the system works 'well', the poor countries keep
growing poorer and so do the poorer regions of a country. And
the system works quite well. It is based on a division of labour
and an unequal exchange that is disadvantageous to those who
are badly placed in the system.

Development aid is often based on the maintenance of the
status quo. It is a kind of umbilical cord, writes A.M. Babu, that
ties the underdeveloped countries to the economies of the rich.[33]
A major part of the so-called aid is used by Third World
governments to service loans from banks in the rich countries.
Another part is given by the donor countries to help their own
exports and to enable their own businesses to invest in the Third
World. Thus the development aid given to Surinam was largely
directed at the improvement of the infrastructure for the benefit
of international capital, for what is so euphemistically called the
improvement of the investment climate.

*Isolation of the poor countries*

It has taken the poor countries a long time to close ranks. In 1964, the United Nations Conference for Trade and Development (UNCTAD) was founded for the express purpose of furthering international trade in a way that would help the development of the poor countries. The staff at UNCTAD has calculated that the growth rate of the poor countries could increase from 3.7 to 6.4 per cent in the period 1982–90 if only they imported more consumer and capital goods from one another and became more self-reliant in the field of such industrial inputs for the agricultural sector as fertilizers and agricultural machinery.[34] Economic cooperation among the poor countries has been a major concern of UNCTAD from its inception.

The creation of UNCTAD was a reply by the Third World to such 'rich nations' clubs' as ECOSOC (Economic and Social Council of the United Nations) and GATT (General Agreement on Tariffs and Trade). A 'Group of 77' made up of countries in the Third World succeeded in 1964 in turning UNCTAD into a permanent body of the United Nations with a secretariat and various commissions. The 'Group of 77' meets from time to time in order to prepare for possible confrontations with the rich countries. Special mention must also be made of the organisation of non-aligned countries in which the poor countries are in a majority. Unfortunately these organisations are too divided to exert tangible pressure on the rich countries, with the possible exception of the oil-producing countries. One of the reasons is that many of the poor countries are represented at international conferences by rich people or members who represent the interests of the rich, and that these interests often coincide with the interests of the rich countries. The viewpoints of these representatives are bound to clash with those from Cuba, Tanzania, Algeria and other countries that champion the poor at home and abroad. Similar conflicts can also be found within Africa, as a result of which the Organization of African Unity (OAU), founded in 1963, has been doomed to impotence.[35] In short, there is little collaboration between the economically weak countries, while the rich countries have banded together into powerful economic blocs with few internal trade barriers and a united front towards the rest of the world.

*Strengthening the position of the rich countries*

Just after the Second World War, the United Nations was a kind of power bloc for the rich countries, but when the situation changed and the rich lost their grip on that organisation, they shifted their allegiance to NATO and such economic and financial organisations as the OECD, EMS, IMF, the World Bank,[36] and, last but not least, the Big Four or the Big Six. Another important group is the European Economic Community. Faced with these concentrated power blocs, the underdeveloped countries are helpless: so many beggars asking for alms now and then in order to import a few items.

As on the national level, clientism is also rife on an international level. The rich countries support certain poor countries (bilateral development aid) or grant them minor trading privileges (the Lomé Agreement between the EEC and poor countries in Africa, the Caribbean region and the Pacific) in the certain knowledge that they will receive a multiple return.

Poor countries in the capitalist world which border on socialist countries and in which there are strong socialist movements have a particularly good chance of receiving aid. One such country singled out for aid by the United States is South Korea, a buffer between the capitalist and the socialist modes of production.

There are social as well as geographic buffer zones. A great many well-paid international experts and officials are hired, and many of these come from the poor countries. They are interested in the maintenance of the status quo, and the same is true of the officials in the Third World who are paid out of the development kitties of the rich countries.

There is also charity, albeit on a small scale, for instance in the form of food supplies to starving people. The EEC is able to offer this kind of help because it is flooded with surpluses built up in the wake of the lavish subsidies enjoyed by European farmers.

*Pseudo-progressive organisations*

Since the Second World War, many people throughout the world have paid lip-service to the idea that poor and rich alike are interested in building a world based on collaboration and cooperation for the good of all. A large number of organisations claim that they are working towards this noble objective. One of these is the World Bank which, in granting aid, ostensibly gives preference to projects intended to help the poorest in the Third World: aid to peasants (in order to improve agricultural output), for slum-clearance, education, etc.

## Holding out bait

Time and again new promises are made. The representatives of the poor countries are invited to talks, but very little happens. One of the tricks used by the rich countries is to protest vigorously against this or that (for instance, at the stabilisation of raw material prices), only to proclaim themselves champions of the idea at some conference. The next steps is to recant and to assert that while everyone agrees that the idea itself is excellent, it has to be examined in much greater detail.

A.H. Boerma, the former Director General of the Food and Agricultural Organization, is not very optimistic. 'I have attended enough conferences to have little hope left.' Self-interest is too strong, he believes. In an interview he described the high-flown resolutions adopted by the United Nations as twaddle.

## Cultural domination

Invariably, economic power goes hand in hand with a flourishing of art and science. It happened in the past and it still happens today: art and science thrive in those prosperous capitalist countries where – and this is just an example – visitors from all parts of the world can crowd into the museums.

The influence of the powerful countries is not confined to science and the fine arts. The rich countries are also powerful generators of ideas that shore up the international poverty-and-wealth system and emphasise the contrast between the West and the so-called Eastern bloc. Among the ideas that prop up the international poverty-and-wealth system, the principles of free enterprise, of free wage negotiations and free trade hold pride of place.[37] When people in the underdeveloped countries adopt these principles they adopt ideas that are not in the interest of the great majority in their country because these ideas help to preserve inequality in the world. Theories about communism and capitalism, too, are – with ostensible objectivity – poured into the Third World, as so many justifications for sanctions against countries that dare to harm the interests of rich power groups. Such countries are labelled as communist without further ado.

Organisations in the rich capitalist countries send a large number of missionaries with well-filled purses to the poor in the Third World in order to proclaim a doctrine that undermines the will of its followers to engage in social struggle and reform, and results in submissive resignation pending the return of Christ and the changes He will bring about.[38]

## Social safety valves

The main international safety valves are the meetings of the United Nations, UNCTAD conferences, and so on. Here delegates from the poor countries can voice their displeasure and also let off steam. If they want to, they can even shout their protests; that has a most calming effect, but achieves very little. Now and then they are allowed – within reason, of course – to give more tangible expression to their dislike of the policies of a rich country, for instance in the diplomatic sphere. Thus the United States allowed Jamaica, Guyana and Barbados to express their sympathy for Cuba by setting up links with this rebel against the international system. But if they should go too far, the North Americans are bound to hold threatening manoeuvres off their shores.

## Violent oppression

When the imperialist world system functions smoothly in the economic, cultural and political sphere, the big capitalist powers do not have to use violence to defend their interests. But if other mechanisms prove inadequate, the use of arms is first threatened, and if that does not have the required effect, weapons are then brought out. Notorious is the enormous devastation wrought in Vietnam for the sole purpose of maintaining a regime favourable to the North Americans in Saigon.

# 6 Liberation Theory

## Theories for rich and poor

After the Second World War, a great deal of thought was given to the causes of poverty and underdevelopment. The theories then put forward fell into two categories: modernisation and dependency. The first contends that the poor countries are not yet adequately modernised, that they are backward. The second emphasises the subordinate, dependent position of the poor and of the poor countries; their dependence on groups at home or abroad.

Modernisation theory originated in the rich capitalist countries. It held up the development of the rich capitalist countries as an example to the Third World and scorned the approach of the socialist countries. Modernisation, it claimed, is encouraged by elite groups made up mainly of politicians and businessmen who know how to make the best use of modern technology and of highly trained non-manual workers. Most 'modernisers' believe that people in the underdeveloped countries have a great deal to learn and that foreign companies are their best training grounds. They portray businessmen from Western Europe and North America as rational people who, moreover, can also bring other intellectual faculties to bear on development. Thus at least went the, usually unexpressed, premise of the psychologists among the modernisers. They argued that people in the Third World lacked ambition and empathy (the ability to place oneself in the situation of those who are 'different' or who occupy other positions), that they were not creative enough and that they had narrow horizons.

One objection to this kind of psychological approach is that it takes too little account of the socio-structural factors, of the circumstances that allow certain psychological characteristics to come into their own. The psychologists concerned failed to realize that one's social position determines what one can do with one's psychological characteristics, 'the need for achievement' among them.

A typical 'moderniser' is the North American economist W.W. Rostow,[1] a man who, far from hiding his anticommunist views, has enshrined them in the subtitle of one of his books: he called his study of the stages of economic growth a non-communist manifesto. The message he has for the military in underdeveloped countries is that they must protect their country's modernisation from those progressive politicians who would hamper it.

In what Rostow calls the 'pre-take-off' stage of development, natural resources are exploited efficiently with the help of foreign businesses and a class of home-grown businessmen emerges. If this process runs its full course it is followed by the take-off stage and finally by the mass-consumption phase characteristic of the rich North.

Modernisation theory awakens hopes: that the welfare-spreading capitalist mode of production will penetrate to the furthermost parts of the earth. It is a false hope, argue the opponents of the theory. An early critic of this optimistic approach was the Peruvian journalist and founder of the Peruvian Communist Party, José Mariátegui.[2] In the twenties, he pointed out that a great many explanations of the plight of the native population were imperialist excuses. According to Mariátegui, the misery of the native population was caused by the rulers. They had been robbed of their land by the Spanish conquerors.

Had he been granted a longer life, Mariátegui would surely have been a supporter of dependence theory. That theory was developed in the Third World itself, and treats underdevelopment from the point of view of the oppressed countries or of oppressed groups in them. It stresses the nefarious influence of economic forces in the rich countries which keep the Third World in a position of subordinate dependence. This ensures that the system of production in the poor countries is largely determined by economic developments in the rich countries. While the latter develop along more or less independent lines, the dependent economies must follow the line drawn by the dominant economic powers.

Dependence theorists contend that the North Atlantic countries have developed partly at the expense of the rest of the world, and that the development of the rich West went hand in hand with the underdevelopment of what is now called the Third World. Underdevelopment does not precede development, as Rostow would have us believe, but occurs simultaneously. Development and underdevelopment constitute the obverse and the reverse of the coin of international capitalist expansion.

Some dependency theories are of Marxist origin and stress the transfer of surplus value to the ruling class at home and abroad. Release from dependence, according to the Marxists, lies in the liberation struggle waged by peasants and workers. All dependence theories that ignore class conflicts must be considered so many bourgeois ideologies, so many justifications of the status quo. They blame foreign powers for what must be blamed in part on the ruling class of their own country: the fact that the great majority of the population is poor.

More recently dependence and modernisation theories have drawn closer to each other, but they continue to remain theories of the poor and of the rich respectively. Both nowadays refer to the international economic system as a whole and to the development possibilities of the Third World within that system.

According to Hoogvelt, nowadays there are just two theoretical frameworks: (a) the liberal theory of growth, and (b) the Marxist theory of imperialism.

The liberal or bourgeois theory no longer advocates the copying of the example of the West. Instead, it argues that the solution of international problems calls for an international political approach. This is because all parts of the world have become interdependent. There must be a global administration of resources, increased international cooperation and a rejection of narrow nationalisms. A profound transformation of the capitalist world will, according to bourgeois theorists, help to preserve the capitalist system. Here, the Third World will be able to play a complementary role to the First.

The bourgeois theory supports an international economic system based on competition and production for profit rather than on human needs. The progressive thinkers among the bourgeois believe that poverty can be eradicated by a spirit of global political cooperation.

Marxist theorists, by contrast, believe that capitalism cannot help generating poverty and wealth, underdevelopment and development. They accordingly advise the Third World to pursue a policy of national liberation and collective self-reliance.[3]

## Towards a liberation theory

The theory adopted by liberation science must be a theory deeply anchored in the experiences of the people on whose behalf it is put forward. And those concerned, of course, the poor, must be able to understand it. No complicated, academic theory, therefore. In my view progressive social science is too often far too abstract. Masters of Arts in social science no doubt love to hear that the feudal mode of production is a 'borderline' case of the tributary mode, and that a new, capitalist, mode of production articulates with an already existing (pre-capitalist) mode of production, which explains why foreign businessmen can acquire products at very low prices by extra-economic means. The peasants and labourers for whom I do my work know only too well that they receive too little money for their labour, but they have no idea what to make of such learned observations as the above. Indeed, a number of academics, too, have arrived at the conclusion that they cannot get anywhere with such abstract reflections. This became clear to me during my lecture tour of Latin America in 1983.

A liberation theory may be expected to offer as concrete as possible an explanation of why so many people are unemployed or semi-employed and earn too little money. For the poor it is most important to know what sort of people are responsible for their plight. First and foremost, these are the buyers of their products and the bosses for whom they work. But there are also the people who work in the dark and whom you do not see, as Bertolt Brecht would put it. Some of these live in distant lands where the goods produced by the poor are freely on sale: tape recorders from Hong Kong and coffee from Colombia. In addition to pointing out this sort of thing, the theory must also be able to offer the poor an escape from their plight.

The first part of the exposition that now follows must be considered a summary of the propositions implicit in what went before. I shall then show what solutions can be derived from these propositions. The solutions will be examined in greater detail in the chapters that follow.

Just one more comment: it is impossible to list all the relevant aspects of my starting point (the position of the poor in the Third World), of all possible solutions and of all my own assumptions in this section. I shall therefore confine my remarks to the most important points. These are of four types: facts and problems; (part) causes of facts and problems; solutions of problems; and ethical and theoretical assumptions. The last have been placed in brackets. From what I have said it appears:

– that the great majority in the Third World is poor and that the lot of the poor does not improve; even where there is economic growth, poverty increases;
– that the incomes of the poor are so low that they have great difficulty in participating in the life of society at large, of the local community or even of their family;
– (that the conditions of the poor in the Third World are inhuman and in urgent need of improvement);
– that the poor live in a society that also includes prosperous people: the local community to which the poor belong is a (poor) poverty-and-wealth system, and so is the region, the country and the world of which that country is a part;
– that their poverty is a consequence of the unfavourable position of the poor in all sub-systems to which they belong. This is particularly true of the economic and political sub-systems;
– that the small producers (mainly peasants) are poor because they are exploited by entrepreneurs who wield more power. As a result, the small producers are paid low prices for the goods they produce;
– that the big producers provide work for a few, whom they pay low wages;
– (that economic power is wielded by those who are able to get others to work for them in the framework of an unequal exchange relationship. An exchange relationship is unequal if one of the parties involved in it receives more for his labour than the other. In that case we speak of exploitation. As a rule, those who do the exploiting profit from the labour of numerous persons and have resources that they can turn to their own advantage. The direct exploiters of the poor are exploited in

turn by persons with even greater economic power. As a result we distinguish between several social classes);
- that there are three main classes, namely the proletariat, the petty bourgeoisie and the bourgeoisie. In the Third World, the proletariat consists largely of agricultural labourers, but also includes independent peasants with little land. The latter must be considered as wage-dependants unable to find work. The proletariat is exploited by the other classes;
- that factory workers constitute a numerically small group better off than the great majority of the agricultural proletariat;
- that the bourgeoisie is the most powerful class, due to its wealth, knowledge and political control. The core of the bourgeoisie is made up of persons and groups in control of the most important means of production of their country;
- (that exploitation and domination involves various sub-systems: the productive, the political, the cultural and mass persuasion. In other words, the exploiter's advantages are not merely material; he also accumulates knowledge and information. The more knowledge a person can absorb, the stronger he is. Generally, though not invariably, one and the same person or group will hold the same position in all or most sub-systems. This is a hallmark of all exploitative structures);
- that the proletariat is the victim of unequal exchange relations because it lacks economic power, is culturally weak and can exert no influence on political decisions that affect its life. The state is controlled by the bourgeoisie or by the army, which largely defends the interests of the bourgeoisie;
- that the poor are in situations where they are unable to attain even a small measure of what society as a whole considers desirable;
- that the poor generally look upon poor neighbours as competitors, and feel that they must look to their own salvation (individualism);
- that they are by and large politically passive – the poor are driven by fear of growing hunger and misery and of the power of the rich;
- that life on the edge of survival offers the poor little opportunity for joining forces, the less so as the oppressors are bound to take reprisals the moment they feel theatened. This explains

why the poor have no political power, exert very little influence
and have no money;
- that of all the poor, women are the worst off: fear, individualism
  and lack of organisation affect them to a particularly marked
  degree;
- that the poor would like to rise into the ranks of the petty
  bourgeoisie, which means that they are not really interested in
  radical social transformations;
- that the disadvantaged position of the poor can also be
  explained by international factors, inasmuch as every national
  poverty-and-wealth system is a part of a global poverty-and-
  wealth system, in which it holds a subordinate and dependent
  position. There is a syphoning of wealth (surplus labour value)
  from the poor to the rich countries, based on foreign
  investments, unequal exchange relations and the flow of highly
  skilled personnel to the rich countries. The governments of the
  rich countries support Third World investments by their own
  nationals with tax concessions and political pressure, and
  protect their home markets by impeding or preventing the
  import of Third World products;
- that capitalism in the rich countries works much more to the
  advantage of the population at large than does capitalism in the
  poor countries. The difference is largely explained by the
  power and influence of the organised workers;
- (that attempts to improve social conditions, to change the power
  of control over men and resources, in short to usher in socio-
  structural change, lead to the exacerbation of social tensions. We
  speak of social tensions when a large number of people,
  especially in organised groups, try to improve their lot along
  paths not approved by the ruling class).

So much for the survey of the main facts, problems and causes
discussed in earlier sections and amplified with some ethical and
sociological assumptions. From the causes it is possible to derive
solutions. These will now be outlined in brief, to be discussed in
greater detail in the following chapters:
- to effect progressive socio-structural changes, the poor must
  wage a liberation struggle with the ultimate goal of seizing
  political power;

- a resistance organisation (political party or political front) brings together the most politically conscious and active of the oppressed and leads them in unarmed, and if necessary in armed, struggle;
- (the society of the future must be based on fraternity, equality (justice) and the experience of freedom, and be anchored in structures that make the search for excessive material advantage look unattractive. Control of production will be vested in the working class whose actions will be largely guided by the interests of the community as a whole);
- the main goals of a development policy geared to the emancipation of the oppressed are improvements in economic relations with foreign countries and changes in the national power structure;
- an improvement in economic relations with foreign countries can only be achieved by sharply reducing dependence on the capitalist world economy and by entering instead into close relations with the socialist countries. To that end, the Third World countries can do no better than join together in regional economic communities for the express purpose of stimulating industrialisation and strengthening the bargaining power of all members;
- society at home is changed by the removal of those elements which impede development and progress and by strengthening those elements which help development and progress;
- the bourgeoisie is stripped of political power and the social position of those who were previously oppresed greatly improved;
- society will have to be organised as a mobilisation system to ward off internal and external enemies. Resources must be mobilised and there must be a concentrated effort by the population, under the leadership of the state, to achieve great economic growth and to introduce trenchant social changes;
- during the period of mobilisation, a political party and organisations connected with that party and defending the interests of the oppressed will play an important role. Women's organisations will further the emancipation of women;
- as soon as circumstances permit, political control must be transferred to the population;
- the aims of economic policy are: an increase in the quality of

life of the whole population, economic growth, an equitable distribution of incomes and productive labour by the native population for their own benefit, with their own means of production;
- because the great majority of the oppressed are peasants and because land is generally the most important natural resource, the development of agriculture must have high priority;
- a satisfactory standard of living can only be attained through industrialisation; moreover, the development of agriculture involves a large number of industrial concerns. The development of agriculture must be geared to that of industry and be able to rely on the best available technical resources;
- foreign companies (including those from capitalist countries) may be allowed to play their part in these developments, but only under stringent conditions aimed at preserving the national interest;
- the mass media must be used to strengthen the confidence of the people. Education has the same effect, while also increasing the level of technical skills.

As I mentioned before, this theory, inasmuch as it affects the solutions, will be discussed in greater detail in the following chapters.

# 7 The Liberation Struggle

## Introduction

In the summer of 1980, after twelve years of military rule, the Peruvians were allowed back to the generals' polling booths. A great number of parties, three on the right and some ten on the left, competed with each other for the presidency and for parliamentary seats.

The parties of the left made a militant impression. Their followers marched through the streets of Lima with flags and banners shouting revolutionary slogans. The red columns were preceded by stewards with helmets and truncheons: the shock troops of the movement. And while the demonstrators converged on the Plaza San Martín from various directions, the loudspeakers broadcast the songs of the oppressed from the sierra, interspersed with such slogans as '*Patria o muerto, venceremos*' (Our country or death, we shall be victorious).

The election symbol of one of the parties was a burning torch – the torch that lights up the consciousness of the people and points the way to revolution. Almost the entire left in Peru is revolutionary; it does not expect to come to power through elections organised by the bourgeoisie and manipulated by the right. Many workers to whom I spoke were agreed on that; they believed only in armed struggle, a slogan they chalked up on numerous walls during the elections together with the word *revolución*. The Peruvian Communist Party (PCP), popularly known as 'Sendero Luminoso' (The Shining Path) did not take part in the elections: it had started to add actions to words and was engaged in a guerrilla campaign near Ayacucho, in the Andes.

Elsewhere, too, there is active resistance. And if we look at the Caribbean we find that this resistance is not of recent vintage but that the slaves rose up as early as the seventeenth century. One

130

of those resistance groups in Jamaica was led by a woman: Nanny. Not much is known about her, but the village of Nanny Town was named after her, and after the declaration of the independence of Jamaica, three centuries after she took up arms, she was proclaimed a National Hero.[1]

Part of the resistance of the poor takes the form of escapism. Thus the Jamaican Rastafarians dream of an African country where life is good for blacks, a country they call Ethiopia and which they would love to exchange for Jamaica. They reject both Jamaican citizenship and Christianity. Their god is the god of Ethiopia.[2] Like so many similar resistance movements in the Third World, Rastas have turned against the appalling society in which they are forced to live and have placed their trust in a millenial kingdom on earth where life is pleasant under the rule of their divinity, their messiah.

For modern freedom fighters it is of great strategic importance to know which enemy the revolutionary movement must tackle first: the internal enemy (the bourgeoisie) or foreign governments. Experience has shown that the answer differs from one part of the world to the next. In Africa the struggle was mainly about liberation from colonial oppression, which, as the resistance leader Amilcar Cabral has explained,[3] held back the development of the African peoples. André Gunder Frank, whose thought is strongly influenced by developments in Latin America, argues in his later writings that the struggle must be aimed primarily at the internal enemy, since foreign economic powers are harder to hit than the national and regional bourgeoisie and their governments.[4] That is true of most of the Third World today. Writing about Africa, Elenga M'buyinga wrote: 'the African working class and poor peasantry should take hold of the leadership of the revolutionary movement in each country'.[5]

In many cases, resistance to the ruling class has taken the form of war. Of the 120 armed conflicts that the world has known between 1945 and 1977, 115 were fought in the Third World,[6] and two-thirds of these were civil wars directed against the regime: sections of the population fought their government in an attempt to create a fairer society.[7] Their object was to make sure that their labour and their country's natural resources are used for national development, not for the profit of rich enterprises from abroad and privileged families at home.

In this chapter we shall be discussing the following aspects of the liberation struggle: the conditions which make the struggle possible (when is the time ripe?), organisation and leadership, the driving forces, possible allies, the role of women, political consciousness, cultural resistance, armed struggle, diplomacy and reaction (by the enemy).

It is important to consider these aspects and to look for general resistance patterns from which resistance fighters in various countries might benefit. It should not be overlooked, of course, that the situation will differ from country to country, since the distribution of power, the economic situation, the geographic circumstances, the culture, the character of the population and relations with foreign countries are also different.

The penultimate section of this chapter, entitled 'The Third World War for control of the Third World', will deal with the conflict between the two superpowers that seems largely to be concerned with the Third World. The chapter ends with a reflection on the links between the liberation struggle and the nature of the development strategy deployed after liberation.

### When is the time ripe?

The basic cause or necessary condition of social unrest is dissatisfaction with one's social position, but such grievances are not a sufficient condition. Another important element is a weakening of the ruling class, a fact to which James Scott has drawn particular attention.[8]

The absence of resistance even when conditions appear rife for it is sometimes attributed to a kind of fatalism shored up with religious dogma and other ideas that support the status quo. Examples of the latter are the belief in the caste system and in reincarnation: the poor are persuaded that if only they live a resigned life in the present their position will improve in the next life. But Scott does not attach great importance to that aspect. He believes, and I agree with him, that the power of the oppressors is the most important factor in preserving the status quo. It is only when that power begins to waver and the people feel reasonably confident that they will entertain the idea of an uprising. This is what happened in West Bengal, after the left-

wing United Front had won the 1969 elections and the peasants
believed that the police and the authorities were on their side.
They then spontaneously seized the land.[9]

A temporary weakening in the power of the authorities may
facilitate an uprising or civil disobedience, but does not usher in a
revolution. For that more is needed. A revolution also depends
on a weakening of the authorities, but such weakness has to
assume very serious proportions. That is what happened in Russia
in 1917, when the Tsar's army had been beaten by the Germans
and there was a state of national emergency. Peasants, among
others, then seized their chance. Their leaders called for 'land to
the peasants', and the peasants heeded their revolutionary call.

The above remarks show that three important factors go into
the makings of a revolution: a serious disruption of the political
system, most often by economic circumstances, a marked increase
in the class consciousness of the oppressed, and the presence of a
determined revolutionary leadership which, as a rule, takes the
form of a political party.[10]

## Organisation and leadership

An important prerequisite for the success of a liberation struggle
is the intensification of contacts between the poor which can be
facilitated by organisation. The resistance of the poor and the
oppressed will prove abortive without proper organisation. An
organised movement, i.e. a party or possibly an armed force, is
needed to lead the resistance and to consolidate it.

One of the first tasks of the party is to adapt the experiences of
resistance movements in other parts of the world to the specific
situation of their country; to frame a revolutionary theory of their
own. The leader of the resistance movement in Guinea-Bissau,
Amilcar Cabral, has repeatedly emphasised the need for careful
studies of the national situation because the national liberation
and also social revolution are mainly the results of national
circumstances. Only if there is a correct evaluation of the social
structure of national urban and rural conditions can the resistance
struggle be organised in an appropriate way.[11]

Soon after the Second World War, nearly all African politicians
contended that a single political party was what their country

needed. They believed strongly that only through unity could colonialism be conquered. Every African, irrespective of class, was entitled to join the single party in his country. Now, while that view may have been correct at the time, liberation from oppression in the Third World today demands parties exclusively made up of peasants, workers and their leaders.

The leadership of the organisations that look after the interests of the poor must include academics and others who do not belong to the proletariat. That does have its dangers, but these are generally unavoidable. The oppressed are seldom able to initiate the revolutionary process by themselves; they need the assistance of educated people during the struggle and even after the seizure of power when the course of reconstruction has to be decided. However the intellectual leaders must all be known champions of the cause of the poor, and must wage the struggle against the oppressors with and amidst the masses. Even so, differences remain and hence the danger that the vanguard will degenerate into an elite, into a power group that manipulates the masses, with the result that the masses may lose all say over the tactics and strategy of the organisation.

Another objection to organisations is that they incline towards inflexibility if too much attention is paid to maintaining their structure. In order to avoid confrontation, the leaders tend to make substantial concessions to the authorities. Unfortunately not much can be done about that and the risk that things may go wrong will simply have to be run. It is irresponsible to argue against the creation of powerful organisations, because such organisations happen to be indispensable for effective action and struggle.

## The driving forces

In the European Marxist tradition, factory workers are considered to be the motor of the revolution – because they hold a key position in the productive process, the entire capitalist works grind to a halt if their mighty arm so decrees. The factory proletariat is a class that can be organised more readily than all other oppressed people, and its class consciousness is boosted time and again by its active struggle for improved living and working conditions.

Most European Marxists see the peasants as allies in a proletarian revolution but cannot see them as the spearhead. The peasants, according to them, are part of the petty bourgeoisie because they own their means of production and only rise up when their middle-class position is threatened. Lenin thought differently. He viewed the peasantry as a potential revolutionary force, just like the industrial workers. And Mao Tse-tung, whose ideas, like Lenin's, were moulded by revolutionary practice, discovered that the Chinese revolution must be a peasant revolution first and foremost. The guerrilla armies created by the Chinese Communist Party had the support of the peasants because these armies fought the peasants' greatest enemies, the big property owners.[12] In a large part of the Third World, the peasants are filled with revolutionary longing for more land or better returns for their produce. In China, Vietnam, Algeria and also in Cuba the impoverished peasant population either joined actively in the struggle or gave it their support. In Guinea-Bissau, too, the armed struggle against the Portuguese was fought mainly in the countryside.[13]

Various experts have tried to discover what type of oppressed peasant is most likely to engage in revolutionary actions if the circumstances are favourable. Theda Skocpol of the University of Chicago has made a special study of the ideas of some of the experts, namely of Wolf, Migdal, Paige and Scott, and has come to the conclusion that a rebellion cannot be started by powerless peasants. The rebels must have room to move, that is, must not be under too much pressure from the rulers. This is true, according to Wolf, of smallholders and tenants who live in communal villages outside direct landlord control, no less than of peasants who live in geographically marginal areas, relatively inaccessible to government authority. These people have some material and organisational advantages in putting up collective resistance against the oppressors.[14]

Among the peasants who live in circumstances that encourage revolutionary action we can distinguish several categories. There are peasants who are the victims of an apparently irreparably depressed market situation; peasants who feel threatened as an ethnic group; peasants who are exploited by their traditional leaders; and peasants who are the victims of capitalist estate owners.

It is of great importance to realize that peasants have seldom fought for the triumph of a revolutionary theory, but rather for the vital and tangible stuff of subsistence: bread, land, tax relief.[15] The radical intelligentsia, by contrast, is motivated by theories and ideals by which they distance themselves from capitalism and imperialism.

However, the peasants are not the only revolutionary group. In Peru, Dutch investigators discovered a strong potential for revolution among mineworkers, whose trade-union activities went hand in hand with the radicalisation of the rank and file.[16] At meetings and in pamphlets, the mineworkers declared their solidarity with other groups such as peasants and teachers, and called for a restructuring of Peruvian society, partly by the nationalisation of industries. The miners looked and continue to look upon themselves as a vanguard which stands up for the interests of the entire working population.

As far as the revolutionary potential of the industrial working class is concerned, investigations suggest that it is strongest among those workers and unemployed who realize that their plight is a consequence of their class position. This was detected by Maurice Zeitlin among the unemployed in Cuba.[17] He also discovered that low wages alone do not lead to radical actions; here, too, it is true that the understanding of the social causes of poverty fosters radicalism. This understanding is greatest among groups who are slightly better off financially than the majority, but who see no way in which they or their children can ever enter middle-class occupations. Many skilled workers in Cuba resented the fact that they were being paid less than fellow workers with the same skills and experience who were employed by foreign companies. Among these resentful men the percentage of communists was high.[18] Zeitlin argues that most of these workers blame their relatively unfavourable position on the capitalist system and its many injustices.

## Allies

The organised poor cannot achieve very much without internal and foreign allies. Peasants need the support of workers, workers need the support of peasants, and both groups need the support of academics and students and of other petty-bourgeois, and sometimes even of bourgeois, groups in favour of waging a national struggle against imperialism. It is part of the task of liberation science to determine precisely which groups can make what contribution to the liberation struggle.

The oppressed have no confidence in the army, but whenever sergeants do manage to overthrow their officers and proclaim a progressive course hopes nevertheless rise high. This is what happened at the end of the thirties when the Cuban sergeant Batista seized power, and it happened again in 1980 when Sergeant Bouterse seized power in Surinam. It is my clear impression that even after such changes in power, the military looks mainly after the interests of its own caste and quickly finishes up steering a course to the right, but if the radical groups have allies in the army this alliance can stand the revolution in good stead. In 1917, for instance, before the October revolution, groups of soldiers crowded into lorries, and drove through Petrograd, their guns at the ready and red flags flying. Shouting 'All power to the Soviets', the 1st Machine-Gun Regiment marched through the streets, other regiments joining them until thousands and thousands of armed soldiers were on the move. Their actions made a considerable contribution to the success of the revolution.

The Iranian revolution led by Khomeini also profited from divisions in the army. From Paris, the Imam had warned army commanders not to ignore the wishes of the people and had called on young officers in particular 'not to be a party to abominable crimes'. Later it appeared that some of the conscripts had heeded Khomeini's appeal to desert from the Shah's army.

An observer of the Russian revolution has stressed the class-consciousness of the Russian soldiers. They felt that they belonged to the masses and refused to shoot their own people.[19] But this must not be generalised. There are countless cases in which the sons of workers and peasants, in uniform, have shot working-class and peasant demonstrators, trampling the struggle for freedom underfoot.

As I said earlier, the people must be on their guard against the military and treat all military *coups d'état* with suspicion. Often what the military do soon after they seize power seems worthy of applause. In many African countries, leaders of military coups roundly declared their intention 'to redress the gross imbalance between the disinherited majority and the educated few who have betrayed the poor,' when, in fact, they did no more in most cases than bring about the embourgeoisement of the army. Isaac Mowoe of the Department of Black Studies at Ohio University, who reached this conclusion, has also observed that there are exceptions: in Benin, Ethiopia and some other countries.[20]

As a rule, liberation movements gladly accept support from foreign allies, from other Third World countries, from the highly-developed socialist countries and also from progressive groups in rich countries. The idea that the proletarian revolution must be made by the proletariat alone is an antiquated one. The military machine, the economy and the political power of the imperialists, and of the North American imperialists in particular, is so strong that no anti-imperialist revolution in the Third World is possible unless the proletariat can count on the help of strong and reliable allies. Thus, North Korean needed the help of a million Chinese soldiers to drive the North Americans back.

The Algerians who fought against France were helped by Arab and socialist countries. The French soldiers armed with NATO weapons were shelled with Chinese mortars and Chinese batteries, and the Algerian *guerrilleros* ate Bulgarian jam on their bread.[21] Hundreds of Algerian students were trained at universities in socialist countries.

Cuba gives very considerable support to the liberation struggle. Immediately after his seizure of power, Castro demanded the right to intervene in the struggle of the oppressed Latin American people. He claimed the authority of José Martí, poet and liberation hero, who had died in 1895 fighting the Spaniards and had clearly perceived the danger of American imperialism. Martí contended that America consists of only two countries, but countries with completely different souls. And he believed that Cuba was a province of one of these countries, the Latin American. Given this definition, Cuba has the right to help the oppressed in El Salvador, Guatemala, Chile, etc., which are so many political divisions of a single fatherland. Nor is that Cuban approach confined to Latin America. In January 1966, the Three Continents Conference in Havana decided to found an organisation for the solidarity of the peoples of Africa, Asia and Latin America (OSPAAAL) and Castro declared that every revolutionary movement, no matter where in the world, could count on Cuba's support.[22] South American guerrilla fighters are being trained in Cuba side by side with Africans.

The development aid that Cuba renders to African countries and liberation movements with the help of both its soldiers and citizens, is most impressive for so small a country. Cuba lent support to the resistance movements in former Southern Rhodesia, in Mozambique and in Guinea-Bissau, and is helping the liberation struggle in Namibia and South Africa. Cuban instructors trained the militia in Equatorial Guinea, and in Tanzania. Cuban technicians and advisers are helping to build roads and secondary schools, just as is done in rural Cuba itself. In Mozambique, Cuban technicians, engineers, doctors and nurses perform a host of predominantly non-military tasks. Cuba has also given a great deal of support, including military aid, to Ethiopia. The neocolonial powers are anxious to spread or consolidate their influence in Africa, and in this struggle the position of Ethiopia and the surrounding territories is of crucial importance.

Cuba also gives massive aid to Nicaragua. If the Dutch decide to help in the education of a poor country they usually send a few young teachers and perhaps add a modest package of educational aids. But Cuba does such things on a much grander scale – it sent over two thousand teachers to Nicaragua. The Cuban government can be believed when it claims that it wants to improve the position of the poor, for that is exactly what appears to be the case from its actions.

The Cuban contribution to the liberation of Angola aroused strong emotions in the Caribbean. Those Caribbean citizens whose ancestors were brought across under humiliating circumstances and put to work under white, capitalist masters, were oppressed for centuries and for centuries also practised resistance, were overjoyed in 1975 when armed black men in Cuban uniforms helped Mother Africa to repel the white intruders from South Africa.[23]

It goes without saying that little Cuba cannot fulfil its important international role without the support of the Soviet Union, but it is quite wrong to assume that the initiative comes from the Soviets.[24] Cuba has often stood up for the oppressed in the face of opposition from its Soviet ally. It needs no stressing that the Cuban government runs great risks, that the country could be overrun or destroyed by the United States at any time.

The oppressed also have allies among the rich countries. Norway and Sweden are renowned for their official aid, and in the Netherlands private organisations make a considerable contribution. It is remarkable how many Dutch committees have for years and with unflagging devotion given support to liberation movements: the Angolan fight against the Portuguese oppressors and the resistance in Mozambique both received help from private quarters in the Netherlands. Dutch action groups, the Vietnam Medical Committee not least among them, stood firmly by the Vietnamese people in their struggle against the North American intruders. With much patience and persistence many people busy themselves with small things which, when added together, have an appreciable effect. The struggle for the liberation of the oppressed in the Third World is thus being fought on many fronts and in many different ways.

## The role of women

In 1974, twenty-seven women in a village in Uttar Pradesh (India) prevented nearly sixty men from going to the forest to fell trees; they acted in order to protect their source of firewood, the forest round the village.[25]

In Africa, too, women will rebel if their interests are threatened. The widespread riots of women in southern Nigeria in 1929 will long stand as evidence of the unity, determination and strength African women can display.[26] The women who had acted as intermediaries in the sale of palm oil and kernels to foreign companies were hard hit by a drop in prices, while the imported goods they purchased and resold to villagers had risen in price. By 1929 these women had come to fear that a government tax programme would be extended to them, and the accordingly organised mass meetings and demonstrations under the slogan of *ogu umunwanye* (women's war). Their actions were also directed against the extortion and corruption of native courts. The buildings of these courts were attacked and ten of them were destroyed. The colonial government moved in and shot thirty-two of the women. The riots were put down but some of the women's grievances were nevertheless met. The Nigerian historian Nina Mba, who made a study of the campaign, came to the conclusion that it was very much a feminist movement in the sense that the women were deeply conscious of the importance of women to society and of their rights as women *vis-à-vis* men.[27] This feminist aspect was also evident in Trinidad and Tobago. In her study of the women's struggle in this former British colony, Rhoda Reddock dispels the sociological myths that these women have always kept to their homes, which precluded their participation in social and political movements and struggles, and that women constituted a politically conservative force. Reddock produces a great deal of evidence to show that women participated in underground resistance during slavery, and that after the abolition of slavery they took part in many strikes and disturbances and were active members of trade unions. In addition, women of both African and Indian descent bravely resisted the attempts of their men, supported by the colonial state and church, to domesticate them.[28]

In various other countries, too, women have participated in the liberation struggle. In Algeria, their activities were originally supportive – they carried messages or fed the fighting men – but at a later stage women, having themselves urged that they be allowed to do so, also participated in the armed struggle.[29] In the Portuguese colonies women were involved in the liberation struggle from the outset. In Guinea-Bissau a large number of women took part in the running of local affairs, the staffing of clinics and elementary schools, and some of them also fought in militia groups.[30]

From the beginning of the resistance struggle in Namibia, women have been involved in its work. Thus there are detachments of the SWAPO Women's League that transport arms and other supplies, which they camouflage with children's clothes. Because Namibian women can acquire travelling documents more easily than their men they also do service as couriers and spies.

According to Maria Navas, a Salvadorian teacher and

representative of the women's organisation AMES, women played a very important role during the beginning of the national resistance struggle in that country. The conduct of two national teachers' strikes (1968 and 1971) fell largely on the shoulders of women. Their intervention led to a breach in traditional relationships. Originally women had played a helping role, looking after the infrastructure while the men did the fighting, but later women acted more independently and sometimes even took command of groups of men.

In the Third World women from different classes have never joined forces against men – the contrasts between the classes are too great for that. That is why Janet Bujra believes that only a revolutionary movement which stands for the abolition of classes will be able to bridge the gulf between women.[31] Women must be on their guard because even among progressive men there are many who are opposed to women's emancipation. They must therefore stand together within the liberation movement, in order – particularly when the class struggle has been won – to ensure the equality of women. The emancipation of women, as Ho Chi Minh repeatedly pointed out, must go hand in hand with the eradication of feudal and bourgeois ways of thinking. He also enjoined women not to wait for government or party measures, but to rely on themselves, to wage the liberation struggle themselves. That is precisely what women in Africa have done, forming ancillary associations within national movements and political parties to protect their own interests.[32]

## Political consciousness

To be immune from the temptations of their rulers, the oppressed need a heightened political consciousness. In his *The Wretched of the Earth*, Frantz Fanon, a resistance fighter born in Martinique, has stressed the importance of historical knowledge and of a grasp of power relationships. Resistance fighters must know who the profiteers are, and who the reliable allies, and accept that everything depends on the masses. And finally, they must know what the better society for which they are fighting will look like.[33] Political conciousness is rooted in the daily experiences of the oppressed. Better educated and more conscious comrades and party members help them to grasp the nature of social relationships. The resulting (class) consciousness is a prerequisite of a successful struggle against relations that impede the development of the oppressed.

It is a mistake to suppose that revolutionary consciousness is forged automatically, that social circumstances impose it upon those concerned. Consciousness must be awakened by a revolutionary vanguard (drawn from various classes), one of whose tasks it is to inform the peasants' and workers' vanguard about the revolutionary significance of their actions.

Political consciousness, a prerequisite of successful struggle, spreads very slowly. Fears and doubts about the desirability of eliminating the 'superior' ruling class cause the oppressed to hamper the attempts of their own leaders. Paulo Freire, who sides strongly with the oppressed, has observed that many of the oppressed are afraid of their liberation and that they tend to identify with the oppressors to some extent. Quite a few, indeed, would prefer to join the ranks of the oppressors themselves.[34]

## Cultural resistance

Freire's educational work in Brazil must be considered a form of cultural resistance. He experimented with a form of education geared to the needs of peasants and urban slumdwellers but also aimed at increasing their consciousness of the causes of their unfavourable position. In accordance with his views, the Peruvian education law of 1972 laid down consciousness of one's own environment as a principle of education. This law speaks of *concientización*: taking cognizance of the need for liberation and participation in a process aimed at abolishing dependence and domination.[35]

Art, too, can make a contribution to the awakening and deepening of the consciousness of the oppressed; it can be of great assistance in the struggle. The work of the Mexican painters Diego Rivera, José Clemente Orozco and David Alfaro Siqueiros, and that of their Brazilian colleague Cándido Portinari, had political overtones. Portinari made striking paintings of the suffering of the oppressed people, while the Mexicans depicted the oppressed in their pride and struggle.

Siqueiros wrote that he and his supporters objected to the cultural domination of his people by a bourgeois culture imported from Europe. They condemned formal paintings and all other academic art which they rejected as aristocratic. 'We extol monumental art because it is the property of all.' 'We declare that at this moment of transition from a mouldering to a new social order, the creators of beauty must exert themselves to the utmost to ensure that their work is of ideological significance to the people.'[36]

Rivera, Orozco and Siqueiros were commissioned to paint the walls of public buildings, and in Allende's Chile artists bore witness to their revolutionary vision on large murals in the streets. Into these, they incorporated political texts, as well as verses by Pablo Neruda, popular motifs and symbols. They were avant-garde and traditional at one and the same time; aesthetic and popular. They helped the development of new ideals for a new society.

The priest and poet Ernesto Cardenal used his writings to protest against the Somoza regime in Nicaragua. In one of his poems, *Somoza unveils the statute of Somoza in the Somoza stadium*, he has the dictator explain why he had erected a monument to himself: he knew that his subjects would hate it. Ernesto Cardenal wrote for the people. That meant writing his poems in simple and clear language. He considered it his duty to use plain terms to awaken the nation to its situation. He himself did not participate in armed struggle; his weapons, he declared, were words, poetry and his interpretation of the gospel to which he attributed a radicalising effect.

Religious leaders also played a crucial role in the Islamic revolution in Iran which, according to Asaf Hussain, has a pronounced anti-imperialist character, and is based on the needy and oppressed.[37]

In Kenya, it was the writer Ngugi wa Thiong'o who joined in the struggle. In 1973, he made a passionate plea for the languages, oral traditions, dances and sculpture of his people in an attempt to breathe new life into what the bulldozer of white civilisation had attempted to flatten. In his *Petals of Freedom* (1977) Ngugi expressed his disappointment at conditions in his country: African culture was shamelessly being disposed of in the seasonal sale that kept the tourist industry going, and the traditional dances were being commercialised into easily digestible, custom-built slices of 'wild life'.

Uneducated people, too, can make a contribution to the culture of protest. Many stories and songs that originated among the people carry a political message, formulate problems, express suffering and voice hope.

## Armed struggle

A distinction must be made between unarmed and armed struggle, though these two forms of resistance are not entirely unrelated. Armed struggle is a continuation – by other means – of unarmed struggle. The two must be geared to each other and reinforce each other. Those who, often for many years, generation after generation, have led the unarmed struggle know that they have been doing the spadework for a struggle that must be brought to an end with arms. And once arms have been introduced, there must be close collaboration between those organisations that fight with arms and those that fight without them. When the *guerrilleros* moved down from the mountains near Estelí in Nicaragua they found that the town boasted a flourishing secret branch of the Sandanista National Liberation Front which had prepared the people for the struggle.

It is the task of the political branch of the resistance movement to lead the armed struggle as well. It would be wrong to assign a dominant political role to the guerrilla army as demanded by the so-called *foco* theory, in vogue in Latin America after the success of Fidel Castro and his *guerrilleros*. According to that theory guerrilla forces, not the party, must take the political lead and prepare the way for the popular party of the future. Guerrilla experience, Régis Debray contended, must precede political leadership. However, the Vietnamese general Giap rejected this view: in his opinion the army must be subordinate to the leaders of the political party. The party educates the fighters, and it is through the party that the army can fulfil its revolutionary task.

Armed revolutionary struggle involves three phases. The first takes the form of sporadic attacks to frighten the ruling class, to undermine the morale of the army and to stiffen popular resistance. Sometimes the aim is also to exacerbate class conflicts and to tempt the ruling class into taking steps that increasingly unmask them as enemies of the people. The second phase brings the consolidation of areas completely under the control of the freedom fighters, from which attacks can be launched, and to which the *guerrilleros* can withdraw after battle. In these areas, a standing army is established which, if the balance of power permits, will engage the armed forces of the state. This is the last, decisive phase of the popular war: the guerrilla campaign has been transformed into full-scale war. The word 'guerrilla' does not mean 'small war' as some people think: it is a form of struggle characterised by surprise attacks of short duration, followed by a swift withdrawal into safe areas, a struggle that can be waged against a large army by small fighting units.

The military operations of guerrilla groups are only possible if they can rely on the support of the majority of the population. And such support will only be given if the population appreciates the justice and necessity of the struggle, and if the peasants and workers are aware that the *guerrilleros* are peasants and workers just like themselves, people who fight for a better future for the class to which they belong. In regions freed of counter-revolutionary state repression, the revolutionary leaders will offer the peasants such collective benefits as education, medical services and a voice in the administration. Sometimes it will even be possible to distribute the property of large estate owners among the poor. In Vietnam, popular support had an organised character. In every village, in every town, people's organisations provided food and shelter for forward army units. Children were taught to spy on the enemy and to lead the revolutionary fighters to their objectives. Workers assisted in moving supplies, while student organisations provided political instruction and tried to show enemy soldiers the error of their ways. Women's organisations attended to the wounded.

The struggle in Guinea-Bissau followed much the same lines. In the more or less liberated regions political village committees of five members were formed, always including two women. In addition, mobile political action brigades helped to organise and to train the people. This activity went hand in hand with generally beneficial measures, for instance the introduction of school medical services.

In Peru, by contrast, the politico-military infrastructure was small during the guerrilla struggle in the 1960s. There were no leaders – not even among the middle cadres drawn from the peasant population.[38] Throughout Latin America, the main weakness of the guerrilla movement is that it has not emerged from political organisations and does not collaborate with a party that defends the same interests as the *guerrilleros*.

As a soldier, the resistance fighter will behave impeccably. He will certainly not do what the Dutch army did in Indonesia: kill citizens not involved in the struggle or torture prisoners. He does not operate in a foreign country among foreign people but among his own people, and will do his utmost to win over government soldiers, who are also his compatriots. As a human being, the *guerrillero* must be several cuts above soldiers in the oppressors' army. That does not mean he must be soft. Thus Indonesian freedom fighters attacked village administrators who collaborated with the Dutch occupiers, and Colombian revolutionary forces were forced to execute peasants who acted as government informers.

The *guerrilleros'* class enemy considers guerrilla warfare to be unlawful and treats *guerrilleros* as criminals. Needless to say, they are nothing of the kind in the eyes of progressive observers and of humane members of the liberal groups. They see the *guerrilleros'* struggle as justified resistance to injustice which means that the *guerrilleros* have the right to the same status as regular army soldiers.

African lawyers examining the legal aspects of the independence struggle of colonial people concluded that the law of nations recognises the right of self-determination of all people and also recognises the legality of armed struggle against foreign domination.[39] E.C. Udechuka, and expert on international law who agrees with this conclusion, does not say what he thinks of armed struggle by the majority of a population against the tyranny of the national bourgeoisie. The Geneva Convention for the Protection of War Victims of 12 August 1949 does have something to say on the subject, however. Article 3, which deals with armed internal conflict, stipulates that non-combatants, those who have laid down their arms, and the wounded, must be treated humanely. Unfortunately, resistance fighters are generally considered to be traitors and criminals, and quite a few countries have entered reservations to Article 3. K. Skubiszewski of the

University of Poznan (Poland) points out that every government is nevertheless bound by the UN Charter to act in accordance with its international duty to observe human rights. As soon as an established authority deploys police or military force on a massive scale to deal with internal conflicts, the application of international law is called for.[40] In my own view, these resistance fighters, too, must be covered by The Hague and Geneva Conventions which, *inter alia*, govern the treatment of the wounded, of prisoners of war and of civilians.

In his *La Guerra de Guerrilla*, Che Guevara dwells at length on the problem of arming the *guerrilleros*. Most must manufacture their own weapons and for the rest depend on the arms they capture from enemy troops. (Photographs of the struggle in Nicaragua showed just how primitive the weapons of the resistance fighters were.) According to Che Guevara, tanks are best immobilised with Molotov cocktails fired from a gun. As far as I can tell, however, such methods no longer work. Since the Cuban guerrilla war, the arming and also the training of reactionary forces had been considerably improved, and it seems almost impossible that government troops in other parts of the world can be beaten as easily as by Castro and his courageous band. The people must have arms capable of bringing down aeroplanes and destroying heavily armour-plated tanks. If they have, then they can inflict heavy damage on the enemy and in so doing deal him a severe psychological blow. That means that the guerrilla struggle must be well prepared and that at least some of the fighters need to have technical skills, in which many resistance movements are still lacking. In Nicaragua, for instance, when a tank was captured by the Sandinisats, it turned out that there was no one who could drive it.

Since the rich capitalist countries are unlikely to supply the weapons needed for guerrilla warfare, the movement must make contacts with the socialist countries and smuggle in what weapons it can.

The reader may have gained the impression that I am naturally inclined to answer violence with violence. But that is a misunderstanding. I admit that generally there is no alternative, but it took me a great deal of heart-searching to arrive at that conclusion. Many of my students have looked for alternatives to violence, and they deserve great credit for that, but they have

failed to come up with an acceptable answer. Hard necessity
forced many of them to come to the same conclusion as I did,
namely that, as a rule, the class enemy can only be beaten by
force of arms.

I would now like to draw attention to a form of armed struggle
known as terror. Can freedom fighters resort to terror and yet
maintain the irreproachable standards of behaviour expected of
them? Che Guevara's answer was that they cannot. He wrote that
terror is a negative weapon which opens up a gulf between the
revolutionary movement and the people and, moreover, inflicts
suffering on the people that bears no relationship to the results
that can be achieved. Terror may only be used when it is essential
to eliminate an important and vicious leader of the oppressive
camp. But never, Guevara insisted, must ordinary persons be
killed: that can only lead to further oppression.

Now, it is an open question whether the removal of a vicious
enemy of the people should be described as terrorism. That
depends on the definition of that concept. Let me emphasise that
I do not reject violence when it is used as a last resort. I agree
with Edward Hyams that there is a causal connection between
violence by the people and a country's laws. If the main purpose
of these laws is the protection of the position and privileges of the
ruling class, violence will persist until there is social justice. In the
meantime, the right of minorities to use violence as a last resort
must not be challenged, not even in democratic countries, says
Hyams.[41]

Nineteenth-century Russian anarchists, Indian independence
fighters, Tupamaros in Uruguay, the Baader-Meinhof group in
West Germany, the Palestinian resistance, the Jewish underground
in Palestine (the Stern Group and the Irgun Zvai Leumi), all
perpetrated acts of violence, attacks and abductions and took
hostages. Were these people soldiers (*guerrilleros*) or terrorists?
According to Walter Laqueur, the author of a book on terrorism,
they were certainly terrorists, but that is because his definition is
rather wide. Terrorism, he contends, is covert violence by a
group for political ends.[42] Terrorists, he goes on to say, seek to
cause political, social and economic disruption and to that end
frequently engage in planned or indiscriminate murder. This last
phrase – planned or indiscriminate murder – contains what I
believe is a useful distinction, namely that between (a) killing or

trying to kill specific persons who have shown that they are enemies, and (b) killing persons in the enemy camp of whom it is not known on what side they are or if they participate actively in the struggle. In the last case, their assassination is rightly called the killing of innocent people. They belong to the enemy camp, of course, for no resistance fighter would take it into his head to take the life of his own people.

I confine the concept of terror to attacks on unknown people believed to belong to the enemy camp and on their property. Attacks on known oppressors and their henchmen, the blowing up of buildings important to the enemy, etc., must, by contrast, be considered as acts of armed resistance in a civil war context.

Terror as a form of regular warfare is often adopted by the standing armies of capitalist powers. The Germans conquered Poland after terrorist bombing raids on Warsaw, and the United States forced the North Vietnamese back to the negotiating table by ravaging their country. Hiroshima and Nagasaki were acts of terror, and so was the British destruction of Dresden at the end of the Second World War. The Dutch criminologist, W.H. Nagel, believes that such actions are on a par with other military tactics. According to him, therefore, terror is an integral part of comprehensive military strategy.

I am unable to judge all terror bombings and comparable actions by their military and political impact, but it is my firm impression that terrorism has often been effective. This claim is difficult to prove because in politics a number of factors are at work simultaneously. It seems likely, however, that various violent episodes have brought the cause of the Palestinian freedom fighters home to the world at large. Many people have started to think again as a result, and have come to the conclusion that these acts were the desperate deeds of people fighting for a just cause, and now look upon the armed Palestinian struggle as a fight against the main force obstructing freedom, namely imperialism. Edward Hyams, too, believes that terrorism has had many successes, but also thinks that terrorist organisations rarely or never manage to reach their, generally radical, objectives. As a result, the position of the more temperate, often of those who reject violence, is strengthened.[43]

I believe it is wrong to claim, however, that violence does not pay. Consistent violence, given certain conditions (a responsive public; responsible political leaders) has often made an appreciable contribution to the political struggle.

My conclusion can be summarised as follows: if the socio-economic and political violence of the ruling class leads to intolerable exploitation and restrictions, it has to be opposed and, if that cannot be done in peaceful ways then it must be done by violent means.

There are spontaneous acts of resistance by courageous people acting on their own initiative, but in order to overthrow entrenched regimes an organisation is needed and armed resistance must be put up under the leadership of a responsible political party or political front. Now, it is that political leadership which must decide during which phase of the struggle violence, and exceptionally terror, may be used. That decision must not be left to those groups which are prepared to carry out the acts of violence.[44]

Europeans living in comfortable circumstances tend to reject violence in all circumstances, but if they are honest with themselves, they have to admit that violence is sometimes the only way of putting an end to the violence and domination of the opposing side. But even if they do, they generally hope that after the revolution the masses must be told that there is no need for further violence. Here I must disappoint them. After the revolution, it will become clear that the struggle must be continued, especially on the international front. Imperialism will continue to threaten the revolution, and, moreover, the pressure must be kept up until imperialism has been defeated throughout the world.

## Diplomacy

A number of successful revolutions in the Third World have been associated with large-scale diplomatic activities, as a result of which the colonial and neocolonial rulers have suffered severe political setbacks. What is often forgotten is that the military might of the people was often quite considerable. Spurred on by hatred of the exploiters and by ideals, the *guerrilleros* fought with great courage, only to discover that the fire power of the enemy was greater. The Somoza army supported by the United States was materially much stronger than that of the Sandanistas, but the position of the latter was greatly strengthened by political support throughout the world. Many South American countries sided with freedom in Nicaragua, as a result of which direct military intervention by the United States became a political impossibility.

In order to speed the liberation of Guinea-Bissau, Amilcar Cabral launched a successful diplomatic offensive. He called on the Pope at the head of a delegation from the national liberation movement, and he also succeeded in obtaining humanitarian help from the Scandinavian countries. Partly as a consequence of these diplomatic successes, a special commission of the United Nations visited the liberated regions of Guinea-Bissau, whereupon the Decolonization Committee of the United Nations recognised the resistance movement. The General Assembly quickly followed suit and the Security Council condemned Portuguese colonialism.

## Reaction

The conservative forces oppose the insurgency of the masses with counter-insurgence.[45] The United States, in particular, has made huge investments in this struggle. They have done so in the interests of what they call national security, which to them means much more than protecting their own borders: it means safeguarding North American interests in as much of the world as possible. Hence the talk of global security. Every movement in the Third World that, according to Washington, threatens the capitalist system must be fought and is pilloried as an excrescence of religious fanaticism and above all as a communist threat. The North–South conflict is interpreted as much as possible in East–West terms and presented as a struggle against international communism and the menace to the 'free world' it poses.[46] Anticommunist feeling has to be constantly stoked up by the mass media, because North American attacks on liberation movements dubbed as communists can only be launched if large numbers of the North American public – that is of the voters – are behind such attacks.

The methods by which the North Americans try to defend their interests have changed a few times. Until the end of the fifties, their military exertions were directed in the main against the Soviet Union, but a series of conflicts in the Third World have persuaded senior North American officials that the 'communist threat' comes more from rebellious peasants in Africa, Asia and Latin America than from the Soviet Union. For that reason, a rapid deployment force was set up in 1961 that could reach any part of the world within 72 hours. The high costs of military intervention (the war against the Vietnamese people proved very expensive) and growing opposition at home paved the way for the Nixon doctrine: friendly governments must try to repress rebellions with their own troops, for which purpose they will receive generous economic and military aid from the United States. A strong police force in friendly Third World countries would discover 'subversion' as quickly as possible and nip it in the bud. Since then, a great deal of money has been invested in the internal security of many poor countries plagued by 'instability'. The number of army personnel trained by the United States for service in the Third World has greatly increased since 1966, and under Nixon the sums voted for military help in the form of equipment, etc., doubled. In addition, the United States has considerably stepped up aid to police forces in the Third World. Between 1950 and 1976, a total of 483 019 foreign soldiers were trained by the United States, including 6883 from Chile; 1925 from El Salvador; 11 025 from Iran; 16 008 from the Philippines; 4998 from Indonesia; 33 844 from South Korea and 19 150 from Turkey.[47]

According to the North American political scientist, M.D. Wolpin, the training of army officers includes the study of economic development models, based on such *laissez-faire* ideas as free trade, free enterprise and the role of private investment in the development process.[48] Moreover, officers are encouraged to play a leading role in the solution of the socioeconomic problems of their country.

Distatorships are often able to further the interests of the United States. Now it is a fact that while the United States government protests in public against military seizures of power (especially in Carter's day), the resulting military regimes are far from hostile to economic interest in the United States. In Latin

America, most military coups involved soldiers trained in the United States.[49] Once the army is in power, it almost invariably takes measures that encourage the inflow of foreign capital.

The armed struggle waged by the rulers of capitalist Third World countries, mostly with foreign support, against the rebellious masses assumes various forms. One of the tactics is to oppose *guerrilleros* with guerrilla tactics. Thus the government forces use decentralised military units to seek out the freedom fighters, quickly following up with helicopters and airborne troops. In the Philippines, the army is trained in jungle warfare: units of eight men, armed with machine pistols and a light machine gun, learn to steal up on the resistance fighters before opening fire and finishing them off with knives. These small units are covered by a mortar detachment that secures their withdrawal.[50]

Like the *guerrilleros*, so the government troops, too, try to win over the population. To that end, they have strict orders not to loot and to pay for everything they need. The strategy of counter-guerrilla warfare is based on the assumption that at least half the population is neutral and that this indifferent mass may be made to yield the recruits needed to fight the resistance troops. In order to woo the population further, modest reforms are introduced and the masses are seduced with tales about the long-term advantages of so-called modernisation.

W.W. Rostow, in his study of economic modernisation, participates actively in counter-insurgency education. He believes that the best way of fighting guerrilla groups is to prevent their emergence, and he is therefore a champion of village development and indoctrination.[51] At a lecture to the Counter Guerrilla Force of the US Army's Special Warfare Center, which specialises in training foreigners, Rostow declared that communism was best explained as an illness during the transition to modernisation; the communists simply exploit difficulties during that transition. They are the scavengers of modernisation.[52]

If it is impossible to gain the support of the people in the struggle against the liberators, the army will try to prevent the masses from aiding the guerrilla groups. This is done by destroying crops, slaughtering cattle, and confiscating or burning produce. Another strategy was used in Indonesia: to bring in brutal measures first (in Indonesia half a million 'communists' were eliminated) and then to appease the masses with kind words. Expert manipulators of public opinion appealed to them with the help of shrewd sociological methods in an attempt to reassure them and then to organise them into 'anti-communist' groups.

## The Third World War for control of the Third World

We saw that the United States intervenes in the struggle waged by the oppressed in the poor countries, and the same is true of the Soviet Union. The focus of confrontation between the superpowers has shifted from Europe to the Third World, where they have been locked in constant battle for a good thirty-five years now. It is a war that affects practically every continent and which will decide who has the final say over the Third World – reason enough to speak of a Third World War for control of the Third World. This fact is not fully understood in Western Europe, but it is by no means ignored by the US media. In an issue entirely devoted to the Soviet Union, *Time* magazine of 23 June 1980 blamed the end of the *détente* between the Soviet Union and the United States to the role the Soviet Union had begun to play in the Third World. The magazine went on to explain plaintively that the Soviets were penetrating mineral-rich Africa, the oil-rich Middle East and the Pacific routes. Former Secretary of State Henry Kissinger expressed much the same views in *Newsweek* of 29 November 1982, and his most recent successor, George Shultz, agrees with him: early in 1984 he delivered an address, reprinted in the April issue of the *Department of State Bulletin*, in which he argued that the danger of Soviet expansionism lay mainly in the Third World. He went on to explain what US interests were threatened as a result.

More than half the growth of US exports since 1975 can be attributed to the Third World, and in 1980 the poor countries took forty per cent of all US exports. One in every twenty US industrial workers and one in every five acres under cultivation supplies markets in the Third World. In return, the poor countries produce forty to forty-five per cent of all US imports. According to Shultz, the Third World supplies more than half the bauxite, tin and cobalt processed by North American industry, and accounts for more than half the imports into the United States of some eleven other strategic minerals.

Unlike the United States, the Soviet Union has a small economic stake in the Third World. It barely needs imports from the Third World, because it exports energy vectors and is practically self-sufficient in raw materials. But Moscow would, of course, very much like to see the capitalist interests in the Third World reduced. While the United States still enjoyed nuclear supremacy, Soviet activities in the poor countries were limited in extent. Moscow feared for its own safety. But since 1970, when nuclear balance was established, Moscow seems to have grown bolder. It now openly supports, with threats of military intervention, deliveries of arms and military training, those countries in the Third World that have taken the socialist path, together with countries that, though they have a capitalist system of production, do not wish to be dependent on the 'West' alone. Since the beginning of the seventies the Soviet Union has also been supporting freedom movements wherever the risks were not too great. The increasing interest of the Soviet Union in the Third World is further reflected in the expansion of the Soviet Navy, which is one of the strongest in the world today.

The opponents of the Soviet Union first began to have dealings with the Third World on a large scale in the early sixties. Threatened regimes could count on deliveries of arms, often free of charge, and on military training and education programmes, and where indirect support was inadequate, Washington would often intervene directly. Thus, in the sixties alone, the United States supported their Third World policy by military means on a good ninety occasions, even using their nuclear arsenal as a threat.

At the end of the Carter period and under President Reagan it was decided to strengthen US intervention potential (the rapid deployment force) and to speed up the nuclear arms programme. The major part of the extra sums voted for defence is destined for army units capable of intervening in the Third World.

According to Secretary of Defense Caspar Weinberger, attempts to strengthen the US nuclear arsenal are part of the same process: Moscow must be made to realize that the United States can escalate a conflict in the Third World more effectively than the

Soviet Union dares or is able to do. By threatening the territory of the Eastern Bloc and the submarines of the Warsaw Pact powers with a coordinated attack from the United States and from Western Europe, from the sea and from the air (if necessary to the point of total destruction), the United States hopes to force the Soviet Union to keep out of conflicts in the Third World in which United States' interests are involved, thus increasing US freedom of military action. And if the Soviet Union takes up the challenge and itself escalates the arms race, then there is a good chance that the Soviet economy will be weakened to the point where it is unable to aid its allies in the poor countries. The United States can afford a gigantic arms expenditure and arms race more easily than can the Soviet Union. In Chapter 9 we shall see that peace and disarmament will only be achieved if underdevelopment in the Third World is brought to an end.

## Liberation struggle and development

The argument presented in the liberation theory of Chapter 6 urges development in the interests of the oppressed. To achieve that, the oppressed must first strip the bourgeoisie of its political power. A socialist strategy is essential.

Many people in the former colonies who participated in their resistance struggle realized this perfectly well. But quite often, once the struggle was won and the resistance leaders achieved important social positions, their ideas changed. That was not so much a consequence of personal circumstances as of social forces. The role of political leaders after independence is mainly determined by the influence of national and international power groups. These are generally social classes.

In a situation controlled by the class system, the national bourgeoisie and foreign enterprises will come off best if their opponents are not strong. Powerful foreign companies usually play a crucial role, since they are able to bribe some of the national bourgeoisie into acting as their accomplices. The national bourgeoisie becomes a dependent bourgeoisie and, in return, collects a share of the profits foreign corporations make from the exploitation of their countrymen, writes the Guinean expert Aguibou Yansané.[53] If, at liberation, the position of the peasants and workers is strong enough, then another social structure is produced, another path followed – that of socialism.

The class situation at the moment of victory is a creation of developments during the colonial period and also of the nature and intensity of the liberation struggle. As far as the nature of that struggle is concerned, a distinction must be made between a people's war and a war of national liberation. A people's war, which is directed against internal oppressors, is based on the political organisation of the poverty-stricken peasants and other suppressed classes,[54] and leads to a quite different class situation at the moment of liberation than does a war of national liberation, waged mainly by the petty bourgeoisie against *foreign* oppressors.

The intensity with which the struggle is waged is another important factor, because a fierce struggle has a radicalising effect. According to Yansané, a bitter and protracted armed struggle sparks off revolutionary thinking in various groups of society,[55] a view that I share with him.

The petty bourgeoisie plays a key role in the process of transformation. It usually makes a great, sometimes the greatest, contribution to the liberation struggle and, if the revolution is victorious, is able to determine the future course. In that it can choose one of two sides, depending on the political tide. If there is a weak proletarian current, then it will join the bourgeoisie and foreign capitalist interests, with a good chance that it will be able to insinuate itself into the state apparatus and into state enterprises. It then becomes a bureaucratic bourgeoisie and serves its own interests. But if the oppressed peasants and workers are strong enough, wield enough organised power, and have a political consciousness hardened in the struggle, then a large section of the petty bourgeoisie will side with them, will play a leading part in the struggle and will be offered leading positions in the state machinery after victory. They will have become a revolutionary bureaucracy. In that case, their personal benefits will be smaller but they will still try to seize as large a slice of the cake as they can. Peasants and workers must be on their guard against this eventuality.

As a rule, the new bourgeoisie will eliminate the most blatant agents of foreign interests; sometimes it will expropriate the big landowners, nationalise such key utilities as water, gas and electricity, and of course transfer both the civil service and business into native control. In that respect, there is little difference between a nationalist bourgeois policy and a revolutionary policy. In the first case, however, there will be no emancipation of peasants and workers and little change in international economic relationships. A bourgeois regime will continue to export cash crops and minerals to the rich countries, and use the proceeds to import capital goods for investment projects that are of little benefit to the peasants and workers who produce the exports.[56] Such a policy does not preclude the use of socialist and anti-imperialist rhetoric to gain popular support.[57]

These general remarks will now be examined in the light of some concrete examples. In Iran, for instance, the clergy played a leading role in the Islamic revolution and also gained much influence on the post-revolutionary development of the country. On that subject, the Imam Khomenei said that, in Islam, politics and worship are inseparable so that the religious leaders are meant to play an important role in government, not by holding executive positions but by supervising the executive officers on behalf of the people. The position of these religious leaders in government is comparable to that of members of the Communist Party in socialist countries.[58]

In the African anti-colonial resistance movements, peasants and workers did make a contribution, but it was above all an intelligentsia made up of people with a greater or lesser degree of education (office clerks, trade-union leaders, teachers, students, academics) who took the leading role. Many members of this group had been unemployed, and those who had been in work had had no prospect of social advancement. They could hardly wait to take over the lucrative functions of the foreigners. The major demand of the nationalist parties who fought for independence was self-rule.

Once in power the nationalist parties made the promotion of national unity and economic development their top priority. The leaders also called for a return to the traditional values, but this they did not only to develop an African identity but also, and above all, to mask class contradictions. By and large it proved easy to keep the great majority in nationalist harness, but if necessary coercion was used to prevent the proletariat from organising. As a result the petty bourgeoisie, which had emerged even before independence, and the bourgeoisie were able to strengthen their hold on the country, to the advantage of rich planters, of merchants and other business people, of government employees and also of trade unionists. The armies, built up soon after independence, often seized political power from these heterogeneous groups but did not interfere with the economic power of the privileged. Though progress towards socialism was hardly to be expected from a bureaucratic bourgeoisie governed by the military, it must be said that there are some countries, above all in Africa, in which a bureaucratic bourgeoisie seems to be steering the country in a socialist direction. In the terminology of Soviet experts, these are countries with a socialist orientation,[59] countries in which the means of production are increasingly being nationalised and with a policy based on the interests of the workers and peasants. Agricultural cooperatives in the rural areas counteract the tendency towards stratification among the peasants, while the power of imperialist monopolies and of feudal elements is held in check. The Soviet experts take an even more favourable view of these countries if the growth of a Marxist–Leninist party is allowed or even encouraged. That, they say, is the case in Algeria, Benin, Congo, Angola, Mozambique and Ethiopia.

Tanzania, which barely witnessed a liberation struggle, evinced a strong urge towards Africanisation as a reaction to a colonial system that had been completely subservient to the British bourgeoisie. Moreover, because commerce had been predominantly in Asian hands, the development of the African petty bourgeoisie had been stunted. Now it was this very class which formed the nucleus of the resistance against the British, and which are gaining *uhuru* (independence) demanded a large say and eventually developed into a bureaucratic bourgeoisie antagonistic to the mass of the population.

In India the independence movement, although led by intellectuals, was heavily based on prosperous farmers and an urban commercial and industrial bourgeoisie. In 1947, the British handed over power to these groups, with the result that no policy of revolutionary change was introduced.[60]

During the Mexican revolution (1910 and successive years) the peasants played a significant part, but they were too badly organised to benefit fully from their contribution. Middle-class people took possession of the revolution, and because the condition of the poor showed some slight improvement, any protests they had were curtailed.[61] The revolutionary Mexican peasants lacked the intellectual leaders who could have drawn up a coherent economic and social programme, as the sociologist Daniel Chirot, of the University of Washington in Seattle has stressed.[62]

In Algeria, too, peasant resistance was an important factor in the struggle against the French oppressors. The peasants wanted to recover their land from the foreigners, who defended their interests ferociously. The result was a bitter people's war and the emergence, after independence, of a progressive regime that passed various measures in the interests of the peasant population. Immediately after liberation in 1962, Algerian peasants began to work land formerly French-owned under a self-management system and in 1961 the government decreed the break-up of large estates and their reorganisation into cooperatives.[63]

The stress on rural development was particularly strong in Mao's China, which is not surprising when one considers that the liberation struggle was mainly carried out by peasants.

According to Yansané, the fierce oppression practised in the Portuguese colonies inspired a radical approach. Even during the people's war, there were literacy campaigns in the liberated territories, a health service was set up, collective working of the land was initiated, and the population was encouraged to take collective decisions. After victory in 1974, all these measures were extended to the rest of the country. In Vietnam, too, innovations were introduced while the struggle was still proceedings: rural cooperatives and people's shops were set up as models for the future, we are told by Lewis Gann and Thomas Henriksen of the University of Sheffield.[64]

In some African countries where guerrilla warfare was waged, for instance in Kenya and Zimbabwe, it seemed impossible to liberate large territories and to build up socialist structures in them. As a result, a selfish bureaucracy has taken charge of Kenya, and in Zimbabwe, five years after liberation, no revolutionary party has been able to dismantle capitalism in favour of a socialist system. It must be admitted, however, that the government of the Marxist–Leninist Robert Mugabe is in a very difficult situation. It is bound by a treaty with the British which imposes restrictions and it took over an economy almost

entirely in European hands and with strong links with South
Africa. Meanwhile, Mugabe and his followers place their hopes
in a vast extension of education and medical services.

The transition from colonialism to socialism is a social process
and takes time. Leading this process is no simple matter.

# 8 Development Strategy: General Aspects

## Introduction

For the poor, a socialist strategy offers the best prospect. Its specific characteristics will be discussed in the last chapter; but first I must discuss the solutions implied in the theory I proffered in Chapter 6 in general terms.

Because some of the oppressed in the Third World believe that the kind of welfare state found in north-western Europe would solve their problems, the penultimate section of this chapter will be devoted to a capitalist strategy that promises to benefit everybody. We shall then go on briefly to examine the 'third path' often proposed by the military.

To begin with, however, I must introduce and define a number of basic concepts: socio-structural development strategy and autochthonous, social and integral development. Then I shall go on to discuss policy objectives (in the section *Problems and solutions*) and shall stress the need for a policy based on the vision of a better future. The path to that model future runs through a number of intermediate models, social structures that create the necessary conditions for the emergence of the society considered to be the final goal. In changing the prevailing situation, a political party (and later, after the party has come to power, the state) plays a central role. The first objective, which must be attained as quickly as possible, is to distribute the national income more fairly and to strengthen the physical and mental power of the poor by medical care and education. These are prerequisites of the mobilisation of the great majority of the people for increased production with the help of a better system of production, not least on the land. Cultural developments, too, must be fostered. This is an important objective because production must not be allowed to develop at the expense of cultural values. During the period 1932–50, that is what seemed to be happening in Turkey when the government mistakenly began to suppress the Islamic and Ottoman roots of the Turkish identity. According to Kemal Karpat,[1] this attempt caused numerous crises and ended in failure. And once the productive capacity and culture of a country have been invigorated, the country may well be able to improve its international standing as well, the more so if it joins an economic community.

## Socio-structural development strategy

A socio-structural development strategy involves society as a whole and aims at producing social changes, that is, at changing society in the sense that elements inhibiting the desired development are removed and elements fostering it are reinforced or added. That strategy must also be able to gain the active support of population groups able to contribute to the pursuit of the goal, and to remove those groups which threaten it and must therefore be stripped of power. That is precisely what happened in Cuba. One of the first acts of those who came to power in 1959 was the abolition of large estates and the consequent removal of the power bases of an influential group. There were other drastic changes as well; in particular, nearly all the means of production fell into the hands of the state.

The aim of a socio-structural development strategy is to change the direction of a more or less spontaneous development that is considered to be undesirable (see Figure 8.1).

The planner must first of all draw up a model of the current situation, i.e. the initial model of the planning process. A model is a carefully researched simplification of an actual or future situation which retains the essential aspects of that situation. What is an essential aspect is determined by the political and philosophical approach of the designer of the model, and is always connected with many other aspects. The aim of the strategy is to change the starting situation $X$ (reflected in the starting model) into a situation $Y$, which reflects the policy makers' image of the future. The process of transformation occurs

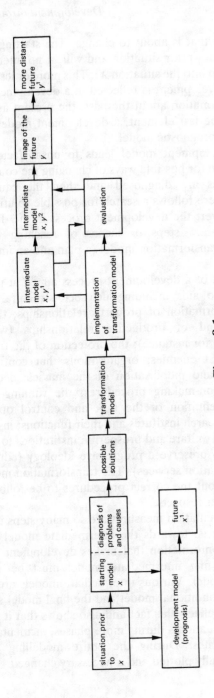

**Figure 8.1**

in a situation that is about to change. The starting situation has emerged from a prior situation and will, if no intervention takes place, develop into the situation $X^1$. This more or less spontaneous process of development is reflected in a development model that provides information about the past, the present and the future. Because of the last element, a development model may also be considered a prognostic model.

If the development model leads to unsatisfactory results, a search is made for possible ways of changing the course of events. The problems are diagnosed and then the causes of these problems. There follows a search for possible solutions, for steps that could divert the development process in the direction of $Y$. The various new steps or means of reaching the objective constitute a transformation model (a plan and an implementation strategy).

The leaders of a development process aimed at progress draw on an arsenal of aids, including such socio-structural interventions as the transformation of property relationships; the control of production and of productive relationships (workers' self-determination for instance); the protection of the transformation process against enemies; organisations that contribute to the development and mobilisation of the masses; decision-making bodies; decision-making procedures; the running of the state machinery; definition of the task and control of the military apparatus; research institutes and their functions; institutions that help to spread welfare and prosperity; institutions to influence the masses and to preserve a progressive ideology (education, mass media, information services). The transformation model contains indications about the correct procedures to be followed in these and many other respects.

The implementation measures are so many steps in the desired direction, that is, towards the intermediate model $X$, $Y^1$. As a rule, it is a conformation that makes development and progress possible; the first intermediate model must be considered a conditional model. Various intermediate models are conceivable between the conditional model and the final model of the future. The diagram reflects this fact and also shows that it goes hand in hand with evaluation – during more phases, incidentally, than the diagram indicates. During the entire modelling process, the course is carefully plotted and if necessary changed.

The diagram also shows a situation $Y^1$, for the strategists must allow for the fact that $Y$, once attained, may change into $Y^1$. If this consequence of $Y$ is to be avoided, then steps to avert the development $Y$-$Y^1$ must be taken at an early stage.

The image of the future has an important strategic function. It is a target model. Now, a target model is crucial to the strategists, because to take the correct steps he must have as concrete a picture of the future as possible. There is some resistance to the construction of models of the future on the ground that they are utopian, but that resistance is unjustified. If contemporary society is found to be systematically wanting, and if we wish to replace it with a better society, then we must of necessity have some idea of a better way of life. Our view of the future largely determines our thinking about society as it is and shows us how we must act to arrive at a better future.

I hope it is clear that it is not liberation scientists who make the crucial decisions during the various strategic phases. They cannot do so because they do not hold leading positions. All they can do is make a contribution to the discussion, dispense advice and try to exert some influence. In other words, they may influence policy decisions but they are not political leaders. The responsibility for policy decisions is rightly vested in others.

## Autochthonous, social and comprehensive development

The aim of autochthonous or independent development is to create a situation in which the resources of a particular country (or of a group of collaborating countries) are developed by the native population with their own means of production and in such a way that the national product is augmented. This type of development is something quite other than autarchy (a system or policy of complete economic self-sufficiency) for that system aims at the exclusion of the outside world. With autochthonous development, admittedly, people do as much as they can in and for their own country, but they nevertheless entertain all sorts of relationships with foreign countries, albeit these are better relationships than they maintained before, namely relationships between equals. Thus Cuba sells the largest proportion of its sugar on favourable conditions to the Soviet Union and obtains

products from that country at fair prices. This exchange
relationship is more favourable than that which capitalist Cuba
had with the United States in the past. Third World countries
have to make constant efforts to force the capitalist countries to
offer them better conditions.

The Kenyan political scientist, Ali Mazrui, has introduced a
concept that tallies with autochthonous development and has
called it indigenisation. It means, he tells us, the greater utilisation
in Africa of African personnel and African resources such as
hydroelectric power and indigenous technology and know-how.[2]

Autochthonous development is also an important learning
process. At the beginning, the indigenous population works less
efficiently than foreigners but learns from its mistakes and
failures. A North Korean industrial leader told a reporter from
*Time* magazine (7 May 1979) that not a single foreigner had had
any dealings with his factory. 'The quality is probably not perfect,'
said another Korean, referring to certain consumer goods, 'but
they are good enough for us because we made them ourselves.'

'Social development' raises the question of the distribution of
profits from production: its object is to distribute the national
product in such a way that the quality of life of the still backward
majority of the population is raised and greater economic equality
achieved.

If autochthonous and social development take place
simultaneously then there is a good chance that the autocentric
development process described by Samir Amin (see page 113)
will be started.

Underdevelopment is a problem with complex causes and can
only be solved by a comprehensive programme. Unfortunately,
however, most development plans have an economic bias. Usually
missing or neglected are such aspects as nutrition, national health,
child care, family planning, housing, education, culture, public
works, etc. A good and integrated programme must embrace
everything that makes development and progress possible. With
limited financial resources all these aspects can, of course, be
tackled in a modest way only.

**Problems and solutions**

As shown in Figure 8.2 the various problems and their causes must
be determined at the beginning of the development programme.

Change of the internal balance of power
by party and state

↓

Fairer distribution of national income

↓

Medical care and education

↓

Mobilisation of the population

Improvement in the ↙         ↘
productive process            Vitalisation of culture
(development of                       and
agriculture and                social provisions
industrialization)

↓                                    ↓

Improvement of international position

**Figure 8.2**

They have been described in brief in the theoretical section of
Chapter 6. The theory reflects the two main objects of the
development policy, namely to change the balance of power
inside the country and to achieve less one-sided economic
relations with the capitalist world economy.

As far as the internal balance of power is concerned, the
strategy must aim at the creation of a particular kind of society,
some aspects of which will be examined in the section entitled
*The picture of the future*.

In theory, the best way of eliminating subordinate dependence
on the rich foreign countries is a (gradual) disengagement from
the capitalist world economy, but in the section entitled
*Improvement of international relationships*, we shall see that such
disengagement cannot be fully achieved.

It is impossible to depict a development strategy in a simple
diagram because components of a social system are interrelated
and not simply in pairs: groups of components are connected with
other groups of components. Though the scheme shown in Fig.
8.2 does not, therefore, give a correct picture, it is nevertheless a

useful survey of what follows. Any one item listed is a precondition of any listed below it. Thus a fairer distribution of national income is a prerequisite of mobilising the population and such mobilisation, in its turn, is a prerequisite of improvements in the productive process.

## The picture of the future

Marxists often claim that it is unrealistic to contrast the capitalist system with an ideal of a better society. That is a mistaken point of view: the struggle against a bad system is fuelled by the desire for a better future and by thinking about it. Moreover, a conscious look at a better world, at a better country, is essential for framing and implementing a socio-structural development strategy. For that strategy must have an objective and avoid any steps that might divert it from that objective.

Policy-makers in the Third World who work for a better life for the poor peasants and workers naturally have a progressive picture of the future. Various models are currently being offered, so that the planner must make a choice, must form his own picture of the future he desires. That picture then becomes the basis of his policy, although it is quite possible that in due course the picture may have to be changed in the light of practical experience.

I shall now present my own view of a progressive picture of the future. It involves three well-known ideals: liberty, equality and fraternity. These ideals, which were first proclaimed jointly in France, are the basis of the *Universal Declaration of Human Rights*. 'All human beings are born free and equal in dignity and rights and must treat one another in a spirit of fraternity', we can read in the first article of that declaration.

The concept of freedom has two different meanings. There is freedom to do what you like (freedom to . . .) and there is freedom from subjection (freedom from . . .). Freedom from fear was one of the ideals President Roosevelt proclaimed shortly before and during the Second World War.

Freedom to do what one likes is something one feels is there when a choice exists between various possibilities of action open to all alike; in other words, when people believe they can shape their lives as much as possible to suit themselves.

The political scientist Arnold Brecht, who made a study of the values that according to twentieth-century social scientists should inspire state policy, found that the principle of justice was generally acknowledged. According to that principle, similar cases must be treated alike. Justice demands that all people are considered equal, that as a principle of state every man is worth exactly the same, is as important, as every other man.

Fraternity rests on the ethical principle 'thou shalt love thy neighbour'. Fraternity means that people who belong to a group stand up for that group, and in so doing have the feeling that they are standing up for their own interests. Fraternity implies a positive attitude toward one's fellow beings: in the family or among friends, at work or in society at large.

If liberty, equality (justice) and fraternity are brought into play in combination, they correct and complete one another. Thus, liberty is limited by equality for the sake of fraternity. Fraternity demands the kind of wisdom that restricts the pursuit of purely selfish goals.

Liberty must be confined because all citizens must enjoy the same degree of freedom; freedom must be fairly distributed. Restrictions on personal freedom may only be imposed in democratic ways, and only within a context that affects the whole society, for instance production or national defence. For the rest, the individual must be free to do what he thinks right, and must be allowed to develop his own personality to the full.

People must be allowed and encouraged to grow in all sorts of directions, except in the economic sphere where they must not be allowed to further their own interests at the expense of others and to accumulate capital. If economic self-interest rears its head, the authorities must make a vigorous response, and if necessary put a stop to it by force, for the basic economic principle of the new system is at stake. We see the same thing happening if free enterprise is threatened in a capitalist society. In that case, the bourgeoisie intervenes with armed force; in Spain under General Franco and in Chile under General Pinochet.

This discussion of the cultural elements of the progressive future deliberately preceded a discussion of its structure because a progressive society will not function smoothly unless the underlying values are shared by all or most of the people. That involves political consciousness together with the freedom from material anxieties. But there is also a converse relationship: it is partly thanks to the structure of society that a progressive consciousness can be maintained.

The progressive view of the future entails communal ownership of the means of production; a share in decision-making by all persons at all levels and in all sectors of society; a planned economy; government departments with a coordinated function and under the control of the people; the collectivisation of domestic work (and equal division of this work between men and women); and a refusal to continue treating the family as a privileged social form.

Government departments with a coordinating role remain necessary because there may be conflicts between individuals or groups of people, between town and country, between producers and consumers, between the common good (the general interest) and the interests of industry; between industrial managers and workers; between the executive and the public. I cannot therefore see the state wither away, as many communists hoped it would, but do believe that it is possible to aim at an elimination of the conflict between state and society following the creation of an overriding organ that reflects the feelings of the great majority and that thus serves and protects the general interest.

It is impossible to abolish all posts from which people can be dominated and from which influence can be exerted, but one can watch carefully that such influence is exerted in a spirit of leadership and not as a display of power. The emergence of self-seeking rulers can be prevented by various methods, the most important of which is workers' self-management, by vesting power in councils run by organised groups of industrial workers, of consumers and even of those in charge of leisure activities. Citizens will be able to defend a variety of interests at a variety of meetings.

Moreover, the citizen must have the power, at general, regional, district and municipal elections to choose what representatives he likes.

At my lectures at the University of Amsterdam I discovered that the idea of a picture of the future could not be explained often enough. I find this an astonishing fact, particularly when those whom I address are students of social science, for after all it is part of their job to think about the organisation of society. I am reproached for succumbing to romantic dreams, for lulling students with the consoling thought that there are easy and pleasant solutions to all the world's problems. I must demur. For seven chapters, I have tried to show how very badly off a large part of humanity is; I have confronted my readers with a very harsh reality. Why, then, should I not lead them on to a different path? What I write now springs logically from what went before: the problems themselves impose the search for solutions, reflections about measures that lead to a better future. And such measures cannot be formulated without a picture of a better society.

## The intermediate model

Because the implementation of a model of the future takes a great deal of time (or perhaps can never be achieved!) we must aim for an objective that represents a step in the right direction. That objective – in fact a complex of objectives – is the intermediate model.

The road to a democratic socialist system invariably passes through the intermediate stage of a fairly undemocratic form of state socialism, much as the road towards a highly developed form of capitalist system passes in the Third World through the stage of state capitalism. The names say it all: in both intermediate models the state plays a considerable role. In Chapter 9, we shall see that a socialist strategy involves a first, fairly long, phase during which the state wields a great deal of power. The same is true of capitalist development aiming for greater prosperity. Thus in South Korea the state plays a considerable role in a capitalist strategy that aims not only at growth but also at spreading the benefits. Here the Republic of Korea reflects what happened in Western Europe, where the authorities – during the emergence of capitalism – encouraged development by supporting private enterprise.

I must comment briefly at this point about the difference between state capitalism and state socialism. That difference hinges on the answer to the question of who profits from the efforts of the state. In a state capitalist system it is above all the bourgeoisie which plucks the fruits, while the proletariat is the chief beneficiary of state socialism.

## Party and state

Generally, it is only a system with a single political party that is able to put an end to the power of groups that exploit the majority of the population. However, that party must be a good party. Zambia and Tanzania both have a one-party system, but these parties are unsatisfactory. The party and its ideology (in Zambia humanism, and in Tanzania an African form of socialism) were meant to be cohesive forces in a country split by ethnic conflict. But the party introduced a different division, between a bureaucratic bourgeoisie out to feather its own nest and the great majority who are its victims.

Let me add quickly that Zambia and Tanzania deserve all the sympathy of those who support the liberation of the oppressed, because both countries have done a great deal for the liberation of the African people in neighbouring countries, and they continue to do so. But this fact must not blind us to the internal situation in these countries where there are still few signs of the spirit of liberation. After some twenty years of humanist and socialist rhetoric, there are still great differences in wealth, especially in Zambia, where sixty per cent of the population (the poorest) enjoy just twenty per cent of the national income.

For genuine development and progress a country needs a party that stands up exclusively for the interests of the oppressed peasants and workers and whose members must all be of a high standard, people who make sure that no one enriches himself at the expense of the masses. If the country is unable to produce a party of such incorruptible men and women, it will not enjoy real emancipation, true liberation. For the party guides and controls the footsteps of the state.

Allow me a slight digression on the state concept. The state is an organisation made up of a government and an apparatus of officials who wield power over society, the regulation of class relationships being a case in point. The state can impede the development of some classes and encourage that of others. In his *State and Revolution*, Lenin makes a remark that still holds good for most countries in the Third World, namely that the state is an instrument for the exploitation of the oppressed majority. After the revolution, however, the roles are reversed; according to Lenin, the state will then keep the bourgeoisie under control. That is necessary if the proletariat is to have any chance of progress. However, before it can exercise control, the state must provide the people with what information they need to appreciate that the authorities are steering the right course. The support of the population is largely determined by what sociologists call the legitimacy of state authority. If the people see a justification for the coercive measures, then most of them will submit.

## Spreading the national income

In order to achieve a better society, economic growth and a fairer distribution of income, of the means of production (land, etc), of education, social and medical provisions, and so on, are essential. According to the Polish economist Mieczyslaw Falkowski, who has summed up the views of development experts in socialist countries, economic growth is the central problem. However, he considers the redistribution of property and income a prerequisite of such growth. Without redistribution there can be no escape from stagnation.

Among development experts in the capitalist countries, too, there are some who give priority to an improvement of the situation of the great majority of the poor. This emerges, for instance, from the title of a report by the North American economist, Irma Adelman: *Redistribution before Growth*. The so-called basic needs strategy devised by the International Labour Office hinges on an increase in consumption: all mankind must enjoy a guaranteed minimum in basic necessities.[3] The Malaysian expert, Doh Joon-Chien, takes much the same view. He questions the relevance of a Western-orientated type of development to Asian countries, on the grounds that the poor are not its chief beneficiaries. He advocates an alternative approach that stresses People's Development (PD) and People's Administration (PA). The primary objective of PD is to achieve an acceptable minimum standard of living for every household, so that each can be productive and self-reliant. According to Doh, this does not exclude the execution of projects from which the separate households benefit indirectly. In order to realize the objective of PD the people themselves must administer their development efforts (PA).[4]

Doh's proposals cannot, in Samir Amin's view, be implemented in the framework of a market economy which is affected by price fluctuations on the world market. There must be disengagement from the worldwide accumulation of capital so that a strategy can be pursued directed at one's own country and, moreover, in the framework of a society rid of class conflicts. What is needed is a sytem that prevents social conflicts from getting out of hand. For conflicts are to a large extent inherent in the system Amin advocates, a system in which a modern sector with a high labour productivity and a traditional sector with a low labour productivity exist side by side without the workers in the more productive, modern sector drawing higher wages. It is essential to make sure that the whole available workforce participates actively in the work of reconstruction, that all earn the same amount and that overall wages increase proportionally to overall rises in national productivity. That is hardly possible, says Amin, without extensive public ownership of the means of production. But that must be attended by a large measure of control by the workers.[5]

## Medical care and education

The poor derive much benefit from medical care and education, because these provisions strengthen their physical and mental resources and help them to fight more resolutely for their own interests when the time comes. The Mugabe government (in Zimbabwe), as I said earlier, significantly expanded medical care and education as soon as it came to power.

Thus the Ministry of Health immediately began to tackle the reconstruction of the largely urban and therapy-biased health service that would ensure access by all citizens to at least some form of basic health care, including health education of a preventive character. Small, low-cost medical units were set up throughout the country, and manned by paramedical staff working in conjuction with, and supervising, village health workers. The first step, of course, was the training of these village workers. The training programme started in October 1980 with provisions for 900 students a year.

The Ministry of Education, in its turn, had to tackle the task of reconstructing the repressive education the country had inherited from the colonial period into a Zimbabwean education for freedom. Before 18 April 1980, when Southern Rhodesia passed away and Zimbabwe was born, only a few Africans were able to enjoy the benefits of education. Moreover, what little education they received was intended to turn them into useful and obedient servants of the ruling Europeans. It also alienated them from their roots in the countryside and from most of their fellow Africans. The new education, by contrast, links academic studies with productive labour, thus stressing the importance of the latter. The new approach is called 'education and production' and its primary objectives are the mental decolonisation of the people, the restoration of the dignity of the national culture and the destruction of the culture of subservience that has been taught to the few educated blacks. Secondly, the new form of education is meant to develop political consciousness in the students from an early stage. By the way in which school work and productive activities are organised, emphasis is placed on group work, and a cooperative spirit inculcated into the pupils.

Thus pupils studying woodwork and construction methods in class, also work on building sites. Theory and practice go hand in hand. Similarly, agricultural students grow vegetables, maize and chickens for their own consumption, with a surplus to sell. Again, instead of studying mathematics in the abstract, these students are taught mathematics in conjunction with their work on the land. It goes without saying that this type of education is also intended to enhance the country's productive strength.

In order to give the children of the poor a real chance to profit from education, education must be geared as much as possible to their way of life, and an attempt must be made to eliminate the handicaps that way of life imposes. When Zimbabwe became an independent country, school fees were abolished and the number of schools extended, and a great many more African children were able to enjoy the benefits of education.

## Mobilisation

The true meaning of mobilisation was demonstrated by Peter the Great in about 1700. He was determined to raise his country to the same level of development as Western Europe in record time, and to that end he mobilised all his forces. A kind of forced-labour system was introduced: for some ten years the workers were tied down to their factories and the peasants driven without mercy to produce as much as they could.

If a society or group deploys an especially large number of resources to attain social and economic objectives in record time, we speak of mobilisation. Amitai Etzioni, of Columbia University, has defined mobilisation as the process by which latent energy is made available for collective action.[6] As a result, the collectivity comes into possession of a considerably larger number of resources than it had before. Mobilisation also usually entails a psychological concentration of all forces. Those in charge of mobilisation try to increase solidarity and loyalty to the communal cause.

Etzioni has stressed that mobilisation is imposed from the top and that it has an elitist character.[7] Mobilisation depends on organisations, and these, too, strengthen the elitist element, for organisations are the instruments through which elites wield influence.

In a study of what political system is most likely to achieve considerable economic growth in a short time, the North American political scientist David Apter comes to the conclusion that a type of autocratic[8] system with a devoted and skilful group of leaders produces the best results, above all if the aim is the greatest possible distribution of incomes. He calls this the mobilisation system.[9] It is a system in which the leaders expect the people to deploy all their strength, to submit to the necessary disciplinary measures and to stand loyally behind them. Hard work is declared to be a virtue, as is the making of sacrifices for the sake of a better future. On the economic front, the immediate satisfaction of certain demands, above all for luxury articles, must be postponed. The population is, as it were, forced to save so that more can be invested. In a mobilisation system, life means hard work and a low level of consumption, and will to some extent be less pleasant, but then the circumstances are more or less the same for everyone; there are very few or no privileged people.

In the mobilisation system, the single political party has a mobilising task. To that end, the Neo-Destour Party in Tunisia set up local divisions which tried to foster political consciousness and engaged in many different projects.[10] Together with government departments, they were involved in the building of schools, campaigns for improving the soil and reafforestation, the fight against illiteracy, and so on.

The mobilisation of the population as a whole will only succeed if there is (1) an improvement in the lot of the poor (*inter alia* by means of such collective provisions as health care and education) that will enable them, physically and mentally, to make a full contribution to production; (2) an equal distribution of the available consumer goods; (3) the forging of ideological instruments to strengthen the resolution and motivation of the people; (4) a favourable outlook which encourages confidence that a better future lies in wait for all.

Poverty has led to the frustration of the great majority, so much so that the masses can only be mobilised by inspiring them with well-founded hopes in a better future.

One way of encouraging the right spirit is to involve the population in the decision-making process. In some cases, this participation is a sham. The party and the government in fact do what they like, although the people are indeed called together for public meetings in the streets and at their workplaces in order to make known their views of the proposed laws, which, at best, may lead to a few minor changes. Such methods can only be used as long as the masses are convinced that the leaders are protecting the interests of the people.

A mobilisation system has a temporary character. It is not possible to sustain the exertions needed for mobilisation, or the enthusiasm, for a long time. At a given moment, the mobilisation system must make way for more lasting social structures, and I shall now comment on the processes in the mobilisation system that force the leaders to introduce these more lasting structures. The processes concerned are all based on rigidification.

When the enthusiasm of the masses wanes, when the constant exertions weaken them, then the leaders will be inclined to use coercion in an attempt to reactivate the people. In that case, there is a good chance that resistance to mobilisation will increase, with the result that people in various positions will no longer be prepared to provide the government with the information it needs to pursue an effective policy. The subjects no longer dare to submit their complaints and suggestions to the authorities, which leads to unjust decisions, to the wastage of resources, and to further disappointments and frustrations among the people, who will exert themselves less and less. The mobilisation system is no longer able to attain its high objectives; its time is past.

In these general remarks about the mobilisation system I have made no comment on its objectives. That may seem unsatisfactory to some, but in my opinion it is not. Such descriptive concepts as 'mobilisation system' are useful in identifying social situations – no less so than, say, the pattern of poverty discussed in Chapter 1. Just as a geologist searching for minerals needs instruments (and knowledge) to probe for deposits, so the social scientist needs concepts to probe into human relationships. That does not, of course, mean that I think it is irrelevant to determine the aims of a mobilisation system, the less so as these aims can differ a great deal. In Cuba, for instance, mobilisation was aimed at increasing the welfare of the great majority of the people and at furthering the international struggle against imperialism, whereas the North American development expert Richard Behrendt advocates mobilisation in the interests of a quite different socio-economic system, namely the capitalist system.[11]

## Production

The progressive Cameroonian People's Union believes that the most urgent task is to improve agriculture so as to raise the peasants' level of consumption, and that the expansion of industry must be based mainly on the domestic peasant market.[12] Various experts agree with these views. An attractive aspect of agricultural development is that it can be largely achieved with native productive resources. Relatively little material has to be imported, and agricultural investments generally produce returns more quickly than do industrial investments.

Samir Amin, too, gives priority to agriculture in a strategy geared to the needs of one's own country, a strategy he calls national and popular self-sufficient development. According to him, industry must be primarily designed to reinforce the productivity of agriculture, supplying fertilizers, farm equipment, and so on, and to develop the infrastructure of rural areas (irrigation, transport, etc). Factories, will also supply the needs of the non-food consumption of both the rural and the urban areas and will do so on an egalitarian basis.[13] In China, that approach made possible the absorption into agriculture of nearly 100 million additional workers during the eighteen years from 1957 to 1975, while providing substantial growth and fairly equal living standards.[14] True, China has a large amount of hidden unemployment, inasmuch as communes and industrial concerns maintain a labour force that could often be reduced without affecting production. That approach, however, is implicit in a philosophy that grants every able-bodied citizen the right to work.

While heavy industry is not absent from a system of national and popular self-sufficient development, its role is confined to the support of light industry.

In the system I have just described, imports will be reduced but not completely eliminated. Essential capital goods (machines, technological equipment) and other essentials the country cannot, or cannot yet, produce, will have to be bought from foreign countries if there is enough money.

It is clear that Amin is dealing with an initial phase, although one that usually lasts a long time. It is during this phase that there is strong emphasis on agricultural development, but it is important realize that economic growth is mainly achieved through industrialisation. If we classify countries by per capita income and by sectors of the economy, we shall find that the higher the per capita income the more important the contribution of industry.

Samir Amin believes – in my opinion correctly – that industrialisation must be based on the best available technology so that there can be maximum productivity and enough economic surplus may be generated to release large funds for reinvestment.[15]

The prosperity of the rich countries is largely due to industrialisation, but it needs no explanation that this process caused a multitude of problems. The Third World must try to stave off these problems, but not by concentrating on intermediate technology as many Western experts have suggested. An example of so-called foreign aid on the basis of intermediate technology can be found in the Altiplano of Peru, round Cuzco and Puno, where young Dutch experts are busily looking for what they call local solutions to local problems (Andean solutions for the Andes). By that they mean new means of production, and new techniques attuned to the local scene and largely based on the use of local materials. These people believe that the production of tools, machines, mills, and so on in the Altiplano will give employment to many people, needs few new skills and hence little extra training. A basic principle of this approach is to improve the level of technology of a region while avoiding growing dependence by the region on the state. The idea seems a good one, but it must be remembered that the region remains relatively backward and underdeveloped.

The great prophet of intermediate technology is the British journalist, economist and entrepreneur, E.F. Schumacher. He championed small-scale factories that call for a relatively small investment per worker employed, speaking of £100 technology in the place of a modern £1000 technology.

However, Schumacher made two crucial mistakes. He failed to define the key problem of the poor correctly, and he overlooked social conflict. The primary need of Third World, he argued, is workplaces, literally millions of workplaces. 'For a poor man the chance to work is the greatest of all needs, and even poorly paid and relatively unproductive work is better than idleness.'[16] This, however, is a misapprehension of the main problem of the poor. Their greatest need is not for work but for money. They may occasionally be able to get some badly paid work, but their problem is precisely that the work is so badly paid.

Schumacher claimed that the poor can be helped with an intermediate technology. In fact, however, his strategy was aimed at placing intermediate technology in the hands of small entrepreneurs, not of the poor. The actual producers would be people with some capital for whom the poor would be working. Now what Schumacher did not see, or did not wish to see, was that small entrepreneurs are the biggest exploiters of the poor.

Those in favour of small-scale or intermediate technology often refer to the development policy adopted by China under Mao Tse-tung, and stress that the level of industrial and agricultural production was raised with relatively simple means. This, however, is a false comparison since the Chinese farmers and factory workers who applied these simple methods did not have to fear competition from large-scale capitalist companies. Moreover, the people themselves were the main beneficiaries of their improved efforts.

In theory, a fairly gradual pace of economic development is desirable because a sudden transition from the simple technology of ancient cultures to modern technology causes problems. There must be adequate time to help the old culture absorb the new, while preserving what is most precious in the past. Unfortunately, however, time is often short, the more so as, with a socialist strategy, violent resistance must be expected from some rich countries. There must therefore be a gain in strength as quickly as possible, above all through industrialisation.

**Peasant holdings**

Seeing that the poorest producers of all are peasant farmers, the development of small-scale agriculture enjoys high priority in any movement devoted to emancipation. Anyone studying the many rural programmes drawn up and implemented in capitalist Third World countries over the past few decades is likely to discover that peasants derived little if any benefit from them.

Some thirty years ago the international development 'jet set' – the people who hurry from one conference to the next – expected a great deal from *community development* as a means of encouraging the population to avail itself of the still untried possibilities of their own environment. The crux of the matter was that people should be helped to help themselves. Community development officials went into the villages to persuade villagers to form organisations, to study their own needs, and to pool their efforts. However, these schemes were not very successful: the poor themselves did not benefit from the community developments.

A serious mistake made by the advocates of community development was the assumption that a village in an underdeveloped country constitutes a community: a group of people with common interests. The power structure on a rural level was ignored. However, every 'community' includes persons wielding power, and it was they who took control of community development.

In academic circles there is another misconception, namely that exploited peasants can be helped by the setting up of *cooperatives*. However, detailed studies of attempts to do so in the Third World demonstrate that peasant farmers are unable to set up and maintain cooperatives for lack of money, and also because they are obstructed by their enemies. Only large farmers can benefit from this type of organisation.

The deleterious effects of large land ownership are, of course, well known. The solution is *land reform*. Unfortunately, however, in capitalist countries only a small section of the rural population benefits from land reforms, and if it does, then only by a little at a time. The Peruvian land reforms at the end of the sixties, for instance, affected no more than thirty per cent of peasant families, and it quickly appeared that the level of living of even those who had 'benefited' had hardly increased. India, too, introduced land reforms, but the economy remained under the control of big landowners and moneylenders who did not shrink from theft (the snatching of land), aggression (the infliction of mutilation) and even murder to retain their position.[17]

If land reform is confined to the allocation of parcels of land without provisions for successful farm management, it is bound to end in failure. The same is true of *agricultural colonisation*: peasant farmers left to their fate in the bush, where they are expected to open up the land and to make all sorts of other provisions by themselves, are bound to fail.

In the Third World there is no shortage of *agricultural extension* services. A wealth of information is being supplied and there is an abundance of talk. But few tangible results are achieved, other than the provision of well-paid posts for middle-class extension officers in an attempt to neutralise them politically.

Wherever farmers are given aid, only those with sufficient means of production can benefit from such aid. Studies of the effects of agricultural extension work have shown time and again that the larger a farm is, the greater the benefit it derives from this kind of service. In other words, agricultural extension widens the gap between the poor and those who are better off.

Agricultural extension services and agricultural research are substantially governed by the interests of academics. Many of those who work in agricultural research or in extension services are bent on making a career in the academic world. They publish the results of their research in professional journals, attend congresses and use a language which even agricultural field officers find difficult to understand. With a few notable exceptions, they are not interested in the fate of peasants.

Wherever ministries of agriculture give these academics a free hand, the position of the large and middle-sized farmers is strengthened. And that means that the position of the small farmers automatically worsens.

Readers may have gained the impression that I take too pessimistic a view of the situation. I can appreciate their reaction, for I know that people like to see progress being made in the solution of the vast problems that confront mankind. But forward-looking people of goodwill cannot expect me to tell them only what they would like to hear. I must stick to the facts, and these are beyond dispute: despite decades of so-called development aid, in spite of all the splendid-sounding development programmes, the lot of the poor, far from improving, has deteriorated.

The reason why the destitute, who constitute the majority in the capitalist Third World, fail to benefit significantly if at all from development aid is that they wield no power. This also applies to the development activities conducted under the label of 'The Green Revolution'. This *green revolution*, meant to prevent red revolutions, began with the breeding of high-yield plant varieties. Such plants need extra care and will only grow on well-irrigated land treated with fertilizers and insecticides. If these conditions are not met, the new seeds will not produce high yields. In other words, the plants are socially selective: they feel most at home on the land of the large farmers and on them they bestow additional benefits. The fruits of this 'revolution' have enabled large farmers to procure agricultural machinery and hence to reduce their labour force. As a result of this and of the increased supply of labour from the ranks of small farmers who have lost their land because of the green revolution, wages have fallen.

Should we therefore conclude that modern technology should be banned from the Third World? By no means! But it must be used correctly, that is, not in the interest of the rich or bureaucratic bourgeoisie, but in the interest of the poor. Whether that is possible depends on the social system into which the technology is introduced.

Since it has appeared that peasant farmers – who constitute a substantial section of the proletariat – derive little if any benefit from development programmes in capitalist systems, it makes sense to reflect on what a progressive government can do to promote small-scale farming and improve the living standard of the peasants. Reports on this matter dwell at length on improvements in production methods and conditions. The implicit argument is that if only the peasant farmers had better farm buildings and better insecticides, better equipment and better transport, if only they received better agricultural extension services, they would be better off. This is the usual approach of conservative reports, but it is a fallacious one, for it confuses cause and effect. A better way of arguing is the following: if peasant farmers were better off (would get better prices for their products) they would certainly put up better farm buildings and procure better means of transport, etc. This argument is more in accordance with the facts.

So-called development work based on the unsatisfactory theory I have outlined has been practised for decades now, but to no avail. There is an immense number of social welfare workers and extension officers who have gone into the villages, have delivered lectures on better farming methods, on the construction of farm buildings and so on, with little success. Further thought is required.

Imagine a large company which, like the peasant farmer in the Third World, works within a capitalist system, except that it makes radio and TV sets. Suppose that the market price of TV sets drops below cost price, or that the government prevents sales at a profitable price. You may then send as many officials, extension officers, prophets and faith healers to the ailing company as you like, but that company will cease operations, despite all the good advice, credit facilities and so on. A company does not make TV sets unless it can command a good price for the product, regardless of all kinds of well-intentioned community development workers.

Similarly, the only way to persuade poor farmers to work harder and produce more is to pay them a good price for their crops. If their income increases and their financial position improves, there is a good chance that they will welcome changes: a switch to other crops, credit facilities, better farming methods. Then they will feel able to take risks, and can afford to do so.

A government wishing to develop small-scale farming should therefore first make sure that farmers earn more money. Next, very simple but essential measures can be taken that do not force farmers to run new risks, but do promise considerable improvements. Cases in point are the allocation of more land and better irrigation. But improvements can only be expected if the farmers are granted enough political power and influence to ensure that they themselves, not others, are the chief beneficiaries of their extra exertions.[18]

In the section that now follows we shall be looking at a number of non-economic means for attaining progressive political objectives.

## The vitalisation of culture

As a reaction to cultural domination by the United States, some countries have chosen to protect their own culture from foreign infiltration and to reduce their dependence on information sources from the United States. This trend is detectable in Canada, where there has been special legislation to curb media imports from the powerful neighbour, and also in Australia and in Europe.

In the Third World, too, there have been similar reactions. In Peru, the military government (1968–80) banned the screening of television series and cartoons from the United States and the importation of twenty-four leading US magazines, on the grounds that these imports corroded the intellectual, moral and patriotic fibre of the nation, and threatened the historic and cultural heritage of the country. The military government was determined to root out cultural colonialism and to develop a Peruvian cultural identity.

In various parts of the Third World indigenous culture survives because the mass media do not reach many people. Amilcar Cabral found that this was particularly true of Africa, so much so that the liberation struggle in Guinea-Bissau was rooted in the African identity of the people. Consequently, a progressive government could aim at fostering a richer, popular, national culture. That approach, according to Cabral, does not mean an uncritical attitude to indigenous culture; on the contrary, as greater progress is made there is a gradual elimination of vestiges of the tribal or feudal mentality and the rejection of social and religious taboos incompatible with the rational and national character of the liberation movement.[19] The British Africanist, Basil Davidson, will undoubtedly agree with this analysis, for he contends that the basic problem for Africans is to find their own way of revolutionising the structures of the past.[20]

The new rulers in Iran were faced with a similar problem. In their country, imperialist forces had managed to turn the universities into institutions that seduced the students with Western cultural values and failed to give them the kind of education that met the needs of the people and of the country. That, at least, is the view of the Imam Khomeini who, while not rejecting modern science, contended in a speech to students in Teheran that an Islamic university must be autonomous, that is, independent of the West as well as of the East.[21]

I have been reproached for paying too little attention in my search for solutions for the Third World to autonomous cultures in that part of the world. That accusation is based on a misunderstanding. I take it so much for granted that a nation should solve its problems in accordance with its own character and culture that I do not find it necessary to keep stressing the point. I agree with Sékou Touré that culture reflects not only the way in which a society is organised but also what aims it has set itself. Accordingly, he believes that leaders who have the people's mandate to guide them are also charged with the defence of their cultural heritage.[22]

In some countries, the search for a cultural identity is impeded by deep-seated ethnic or religious differences. In that case, the aim must be to foster unanimity in diversity. In Surinam, where cultural differences between various sections of the population groups are very great, many people are opposed to integration because they are afraid that the various separate groups would lose their cultural identity or have it seriously impaired. In such circumstances I feel that it would be far better to use another concept, to speak of, say, conglomeration rather than of integration. 'Conglomeration' is borrowed from geology and refers to the combination of unequal parts. When applied to social relationships, it refers to a process by which people or groups that used to look upon one another as wholly or largely different (for instance, in religious or cultural respects) are coming to realize that they nevertheless agree on many issues. This concept does not imply that the parts which combine lose their own characteristics. A conglomerate consists, by definition, of parts that differ from one another but nevertheless form a whole.

## Improvement of international relationships

While political and economic relationships are being improved at home, collaboration with other countries must be increasingly based on the elimination of the country's subordinate and dependent position *vis-à-vis* the rich foreign countries.

In theory, the best result can be expected from cutting relations with the capitalist world economy to the minimum and having closer commercial ties with the socialist countries. This is not an unmixed blessing but it happens to be a fact that the United States, and the European right as well, look mainly after the interests of the entrepreneurial class, while the Soviet Union and the international left side mainly with the working class. In practice, however, most of the countries concerned have their hands tied. In some cases, the United States will prevent them from drawing closer to the socialist worlds, if necessary by force. And other countries cannot allow themselves this 'de-linking' or 'disengagement' because they are much too closely tied to the capitalist world economy. This is, for instance, true of the Netherlands Antilles with their oil refineries and offshore activities.

But even if they are free to join the socialist camp, some poor countries may not be welcome in the socialist family. This family is called the CMEA, the Council of Mutual Economic Assistance. In conversations with officials of various Soviet embassies in Africa, it became clear to me that the Soviet Union is playing for time. 'The African countries are not sufficiently developed economically and politically to join the socialist community,' various officials told me. 'In the circumstances, no *mutual* assistance is possible as yet.'

The CMEA was founded in 1949 by the Soviet Union and the East European countries, and was later joined by Mongolia (1962), Cuba (1972) and Vietnam (1978). These three developing countries have been given a great deal of aid by their more highly developed partners, but I gained the impression that the family is not to be extended for the time being. A booklet about the CMEA does give the information that Angola, Mozambique and Ethiopia will be participating in the work of the CMEA as observers, but what that means was left rather vague.[23] In any case, the aid these countries receive does not seem to be adequate, or Mozambique and Angola would not have been forced to sign a form of non-aggression treaty with South Africa and to limit their support of the African National Congress, the South African liberation movement. When I asked for information on this subject, I was told that the South African government had considerable powers to weaken these neighbours and to destabilise them. Implicitly those interviewed thus admitted that the Soviet Union is unable to stem the undermining activities of South Africa. The reason, the Soviet officials admitted, was the arms race that was being foisted on them by the North Americans.

The Third World countries will thus have to rely largely on their own strength to improve their position within the world system of the rich, and it is obvious that they will be the more successful the more they can combine forces. UNCTAD has for some time been urging them to do just that. The problem is also mentioned in the Annual Report for 1983 where we can read that by opening their markets to one another, the poor countries can improve their productive structure and raise the level of their real per capita income.[24] In fact, trade between the poor countries is already growing. Thus if trade in mineral fuels is excluded, the figures show that intra-trade in other products grew from less than 20 per cent of world trade in 1970 to nearly 32 per cent in 1981,[25] partly as a result of widespread protectionist measures in the North against manufacturers from the South.[26]

By pooling their efforts, the poor countries can enjoy a kind of division of labour, that is, share out various economic tasks amongst themselves. Thus if one country produces tractors for the whole alliance, another will produce artificial fertilizers and insecticides, a third consumer goods, and so on. The chances of success will be greater if the countries involved have a similar social and economic system, and greatest if that system is a socialist one.

To reduce dependence on the rich West, the poor countries

will first have to strengthen their own economies, especially by encouraging autochthonous development. That means that greater use must be made of the country's own productive forces and that the means of production will increasingly be owned by nationals, either privately or collectively.

For the protection of a country's own industries it is essential to limit the import of those products that can drive local manufacturers out of the market by being more competitive. This is a policy that the United States, too, adopted in the early days. Thus Elenga M'buyinga tells us that at the end of the Civil War, when US industry was still in an embryonic state, General Grant stated quite unequivocally that when America had got all she could get out of protection she too would embrace free trade.[27] G.A. Amin contends that a period of self-imposed isolation is needed to arrive at balanced economic development, and he points to the successes that Japan, the Soviet Union and China have enjoyed as a result.[28] But, as I said earlier, I myself do not advocate total isolation, but as much self-reliance as possible. This problem is closely related to the size of the country and the nature of the economy.

During the development of an economy that is as independent as possible, it is advisable to make use of local and foreign private enterprises, with the proviso that foreign companies must have limitations placed upon them so that local workers obtain the highest possible reward for their skills.

To prevent the poor South from turning its back on the rich North, progressive experts in the North have been advocating an international division of labour: certain industries will be given a chance to develop in the poor countries while being run down in the rich. This process is called restructuring or redeployment in the international jargon, but it is clear that the North has little interest in it. Thus the editor of the French business journal *L'Expansion* writes that he is incensed that 'Tunisian entrepreneurs should make our trousers and Japanese yards our ships'. 'And soon,' he adds, 'South Korea will be making our cars, Iran our ethylene and Brazil our aluminium.'

Political friends of this French editor are in a stronger position at international conferences on North–South relationships than those fairly progressive experts who want to accommodate the poor countries. The result is that these conferences lead to nothing, as we know from Jan Pronk, formerly Dutch Minister of Development Cooperation. Pronk has attended many such conferences on behalf of his country, and his conclusion is that nothing of any value has been done. 'The rich countries simply follow a policy of divide-and-rule, as a result of which any country that is of strategic importance to them is given some money. In the commercial field nothing at all has been achieved', he said in an interview he gave to a Dutch paper. A case in point is the failure of attempts to achieve agreement between the producers and consumers of cacao. The United States, Great Britain and West Germany opposed such an agreement because, as consumers, they suffered less from fluctuations of the cacao market than did the producers in the poor countries.[29]

A favourable subject discussed time and again by the international development establishment is the so-called New International Economic Order (NIEO), which is intended to achieve better economic relationships between poor countries and industrialised countries. Many governments in the poor countries are in favour of this idea, but their pleas go unheard, according to someone with a great deal of experience: Don Mills, former Jamaican representative at the United Nations.[30]

Progressive-liberal experts from the rich countries who favour NIEO believe that in principle all labour-intensive production should be confined to the Third World because the wages there are low. As a result, a number of people in the Third World will be given work – poorly paid work, to be sure.

The observations of experts from the rich countries (which strike me as being somewhat dishonest) make a covert, and sometimes overt, appeal for what they so elegantly call 'free and fair international trade'. What they think fair – it may be read between the lines of their reports – is that the products of foreign investors in the Third World should have free access to the markets of the rich countries. In this way, admittedly, development is encouraged, but not autochthonous development. For the latter to take place, the balance of power inside the poor countries must first be changed and a united front of progressive countries must be formed to fight jointly for a better international system. If that happens, then there may well appear an economic order from which the poor in the Third World will benefit. As it is, the so-called improvements called for by capitalist experts will only benefit the ruling class in the Third World. There is no need for a NIEO: what is needed is a NIEO-P; a new international economic order for the poor.

An economic struggle waged by a united front of poor countries contains risks, especially if it should be necessary to boycott the rich countries and to deprive them (temporarily) of essential raw materials. If that happens, the United States, as champion of the 'free world' may well react with war. This danger can to some extent be mitigated by forging links with capitalist companies in the rich countries. Libya, which makes a considerable contribution to the struggle against imperialism, is relatively less vulnerable to North American reprisals because many North American concerns have subsidiaries in that country. Needless to say, Libya does not encourage their presence for reasons of self-protection alone: Third World countries with a vigorous approach to development are unable – especially in the initial phase – to dispense with foreigners. They will cordially welcome those with skills as well as those with a well-filled purse. But they must first have become strong enough to keep the reins in their own hands so as to be in a position to decree that a large proportion of the foreign profits will be reinvested in their country, as well as to reach agreement with foreign enterprises that their subsidiaries will eventually be taken over, whether privately or by the state. At an early stage the foreign concerns must also be made to hand on knowledge and skills to the native population and to begin to train local experts. In order to achieve all this the governments concerned must become shareholders in the foreign companies in order to exert some influence and retain some control.

There can be no question of a quick withdrawal from the capitalist world system – the poor countries will continue to be part of that system, albeit with a militant attitude. Their participation is an oppositional participation; the ultimate aim is still to change an exclusive *economic* world order into a *social* order, and that order will not be a capitalist one but an order in which the exploitation of man by man will have ceased – on the international no less than on the national plane.

## Capitalist strategy

We have seen in the preceding pages in broad outline how development in the interests of the downtrodden can be furthered, and it has already been argued that such development must follow a socialist path. But let us digress for a moment, and see what a capitalist strategy has to offer. This is all the more important in that many of the oppressed in the poor countries would like their country to adopt a system that has brought prosperity to so many in north-western Europe: the capitalist welfare state. What appeals to these people is not merely the high standard of living in Europe, but also the great political influence of organised workers, the mainspring of so much social legislation.

Characteristic of the capitalist welfare state is the balance of the two most important social forces: the employers whose social task it is to produce the goods society needs and if necessary to expand production; and groups of organised citizens (trade unionists chief amongst them) who ensure that the population has the highest possible purchasing power to buy the manufactured goods.

People in the Third World who have placed their hopes in a capitalist welfare state will be disappointed to learn that the chances of having that sort of system in their part of the world are not very great. The European welfare states owe their existence in part to the exploitation of colonies and neocolonies, and where can a Third World country anxious to follow the European example nowadays engage in such plunder? Moreover, it seems almost impossible through planning, that is by government intervention, to achieve equilibrium between the leading partners in the productive system. To do that, the state will first have to help build a powerful workers' movement able to offset the power of the employers. Very high demands will be made on such a movement. It must not confine itself to the defence of the organised workers but must also stand up for the non-organised workers and for the unemployed. Unfortunately, however, a system that leaves a great deal of power in the hands of the employers will prevent the government from building a powerful workers' movement – the bosses are unlikely to do much to help limit the power of their own class.

In Europe, the balance between the interests of the workers

and of the employers is a consequence of spontaneous social forces that led in the right direction. The workers drew their strength from the class struggle, above all in trade unions, but also by uniting in political parties that championed the interests of the oppressed classes.

## The third path: the armed forces

A third path is alleged to run between the highways of capitalism and socialism, and is said to offer a chance of avoiding the unpleasant aspects of the two main routes. The implicit assumption is that there are three paths only, but that assumption is false. Even a cursory examination of development literature will show that there are many more paths. Thus there are various forms of socialism and all sorts of capitalist strategies, while Libya and Iran follow Islamic paths.

In fact the strategy discussed in the preceding section can also be considered a 'third path', because a strategy that grants a great deal of influence to the workers and involves far-reaching social provisions in a capitalist system is not a purely capitalist path. And we must indeed distinguish between an unrestrained and a restricted form of capitalism. Unrestrained capitalism was characteristic of nineteenth-century Europe; moreover in the poverty-and-wealth systems of the Third World, too, the power of capitalist companies is almost unlimited. The power of capitalism is much more restricted in the capitalist welfare states, and for that reason these states must also be considered a middle path between capitalism and socialism; this is the social democratic solution.

An example of the social democratic path was provided by the military administration that came to power in Peru in 1968. The new president, General Velasco, declared that his government pursued neither Marxist nor capitalist objectives which meant, in practice, that the means of production remained predominantly in the hands of private enterprise but that the state exerted a great deal of power.

The Peruvian generals based their system of government on theories of a type that appeal to many Catholic philosophers and political scientists in Southern Europe and Latin America.

Alfred Stepan of Yale University has described this approach as the organic-statist tradition of political thought. (Statism is a theory that stresses the interests of the state.)

The basis of the organic-statist approach is the belief that man's nature is such that he can only flourish in a social context. In other words, social institutions, including government departments, must be counted among institutions demanded by human nature. The state, accordingly, plays a positive role: it performs an ethical task, that of turning people into good citizens. Now that task is so important that the state (and hence the community) must be deemed to be more important than the individual. However, not only the state but many other organisations (such as the family or a voluntary association) serve the general interest.

This political approach is the basis of the papal encyclical *Rerum Novarum* published in 1891. It rejects Marxism on the grounds that the idea of the class struggle runs counter to the organic-statist ideal of the harmonious community. The liberal state and classical capitalism, too, are rejected as being systems that increase class conflicts. Forty years later, in 1931, the same ideas were repeated in the encyclical *Quadragesimo Anno*. Once again, the importance of the state is emphasised, but the power of the state must be limited by two principles: the principle of the common good and the principle of subsidiarity. The state must do nothing that runs counter to the common interest, and must not encroach upon areas reserved for important elements in society: the individual, the family and private organisations (to which Catholics like to refer as 'associations'). Each of these components has a territory of its own from which the state must keep out. In these territories the state can only play a subordinate, a subsidiary, role; it must not interfere in what the individual, the family, etc, are best suited to do by themselves.

Now, the question arises which social units, which 'associations', fulfil a useful role in society. And who decides? The state itself must do so and on 'objective' grounds, that is, in accordance with natural law. Only those organisations are lawful which have received a concession from the state (concession theory of associations), and these privileged organisations must perform their tasks in such a way that, as it were, they form part of the state machinery which, after all, promotes the welfare of all.

According to the organic-statist theory, the state wields great power on the economic plane, but delegates much of that power to organisations, including those industries in which power is shared between workers and employers. It follows that labour and capital (workers and managers) must collaborate harmoniously.

Stepan disagrees with this interpretation; he believes that in practice the workers are granted less freedom and the employers more elbow room than the theoretical model allows.[31] The result is the emergence of authoritarian and corporatist capitalist regimes as were found in fascist Italy and Portugal. In these countries the workers (together with the employers) were organised industry by industry separately, and were not allowed to join national, let alone international, unions.

It cannot be denied that state capitalism on the Peruvian model, or based on the papal encyclicals, could, in theory, lead to the emergence of a capitalist welfare state. In Peru, there was a declared intention to strengthen workers' organisations and to develop industries based on workers' self-management, as well as to increase the say of workers in private industries. But it all stayed theoretical in the main: the newly established services did not function well. It became increasingly clear that the declared intentions had only been for show and that the authorities favoured private enterprise.

The Nigerian army, which on 31 December 1983 overthrew, that is imprisoned, the politicians elected by the people, based their system on a philosophy that strongly resembles that of the Peruvian generals. When they seized power, they solemnly declared that they were moved by patriotic ideals. To them, they declared, the national interest came before doing anything else. No one social group or class would have preferential treatment, and they firmly believed that employers and workers must engage in a continuous dialogue to arrive at a full understanding of each other's point of view and hence to achieve industrial harmony. In Ghana, the military adopt much the same stance. They tell the population that nationalism helped the highly developed nations to build up the institutions to which they owe their welfare and prosperity, and that trade unions must collaborate with the government as a reliable partner instead of looking exclusively after the interests of their members.

In Nigeria, the army tries to shore up its authority with appeals to an African rather than a Christian tradition. They seek the support of kings and chiefs, of traditional rulers who are no longer part of the official administrative machinery but are still highly respected by the people.

As I pointed out in Chapter 4, when discussing social structures, the military belongs predominantly to middle-class groups who care little for poor peasants or workers. They are inclined to make common cause with kings, chieftains and politicians, or else with cardinals and bishops who have a hold over the masses and know how to discipline them.

# 9 Socialist Strategies

## Introduction

A large number of writers in capitalist countries feel called upon to emphasise the unpleasant aspects of the socialist system. Some of them merely wish to say that socialism is not *for them*. That is something with which I can sympathise but for the purposes of this book that approach is irrelevant. I am concerned with a solution to the problems of the oppressed majority in the Third World. What ambitions people in privileged positions in the rich countries have for their own society is irrelevant here.

My approach towards socialism differs from the usual one put forward in Europe. Both left and right in that part of the world judge socialism in terms of good and evil. While defenders vie with one another to show that life in a socialist system is good for the great majority, or at least much better than it used to be under capitalism, opponents argue that under socialism life is bad, and that there are few signs of any real progress. The right refers mockingly to a socialist utopia. But I view socialism from quite a different angle. For me it is a militant system aimed at the destruction of imperialism and designed to pave the way for a better life for all mankind. This is something I cannot stress enough. Many development models have been put forward, but most were conceived for individual countries, national units. When I advocate the creation of socialist systems throughout the Third World I am thinking of a worldwide development model. I shall return to this point at the end of the book.

Creating a national basis for socialist development means making immediate provisions to improve the position of the great majority, and also offering them the prospect of a better society in the future. Both for the internal task (the improvement of the lot of the poor) and also for the external task (the defeat of imperialism), production and productivity must be raised significantly in a short time, to which end sacrifices will have to be made. It follows that any country which takes the socialist path faces a host of difficulties. It will be drawn into a fight against powerful forces, a fight that may last a long time and impose a great many hardships. There will be disappointments and setbacks. Socialism offers its followers no utopia; indeed, the first phase of the socialist process, a phase that can be very long, is anything but utopian. It is an arduous phase of reconstruction. Moreover, socialism has limited objectives; it does not offer solutions for all human problems, nor does it help to eradicate all social conflicts from the world. Socialism introduces essential changes in economic relationships, in the confident belief that this will have a favourable effect on other human relationships (ethnic and racial relationships, for instance), but it does not aim to establish ideal relationships (in accordance with whatever criterion), for to attempt that would be irrational. Still, a nation following the socialist path is engaged in a lofty task that brings great satisfaction and promotes a feeling of self-respect.

**Practice and theory**

The road to socialism is marked out by a combination of internal and foreign political and economic factors. This is reflected by the experiences of Cuba, the Soviet Union and China.

Prerevolutionary Cuba had a rigid structure with little hope of social advancement, and a stagnant economy. In the thirty years preceding the revolution there was no progress at all. True, exports grew, but the real value of these exports, i.e. what the Cubans could buy abroad, remained the same and unemployment increased ominously. The combined cause of the immutable class barriers and of economic stagnation was large estate ownership. The large plantations were inefficient; the economy was characterised by the under-use of people and land. In these circumstances it was not surprising that the large estate owners were expropriated: barely four months after the *guerrilleros* had come to power, the agricultural reform law was promulgated on yesterday's battlefield, the Sierra Maestra. The time of the *latifundia* was past. Later, industrial concerns, too, were nationalised. That would, perhaps, have been the end of the reforms, but Cuba was driven further along the socialist road by the hostile attitude of the United States.

In the Soviet Union and China, too, internal and external factors were responsible for the course of events. The foreign threat took different forms in these two countries and was interpreted differently, and there were also great (socio)-geographical differences between them. Thus at the time the Soviet Union was founded, US, British, French and German troops were encamped on her soil, and a few years later the country was again threatened, this time by the growing might of Germany and Japan. These threats were responsible for the introduction of a rigorous system of state socialism, for a strong emphasis on heavy industry, the construction of railways, and so on. The harsh regime associated with these measures undoubtedly caused a great deal of hardship but – in my view – it also made possible the victory over the Germans. For the oppressed in the Third World, too, this fact is not without significance, since without the power of the Soviet Union their situation would be altogether hopeless. In China, by contrast, the foreign threat was less serious, and the Chinese, moreover, felt confident that they could trap any invader in the vast Chinese hinterland, fight him with guerrilla detachments and eventually drive him out. For China, accordingly, heavy industry had a less high priority.

The Soviet Union comprises large, thinly-populated areas that were exceptionally well-suited to mechanised agriculture. Moreover, the Soviet Union has much more arable land per head of population than China, so that she was in a much better position to adopt an 'agriculture must serve industry' approach.[1] In China, by contrast, the agricultural regions were densely populated and communications bad, which imposed a policy of decentralised and labour-intensive development. Chinese agriculture and industry were developed simultaneously (walking on two legs) and, what is more, by manpower rather than with machines or other capital goods.

In view of the marked differences in the way that a socialist alternative was first developed and then implemented in practice, it seems obvious that socialist theory must be geared to cope with a variety of circumstances. In all parts of the world, accordingly, the idea of a country's own path to socialism is being put forward.

That does not mean that experiences elsewhere are of no value at all; if it did, the rest of this chapter need not have been written. One has to learn from the experiences of others, but the suggestions I make in the sections that follow and the information I give may or may not be applicable depending on local circumstances.

Lenin was one of the first to insist on the need to adapt revolutionary theory to revolutionary practice. It was a central point of Lenin's teaching that a socialist mode of production may be introduced provided the political situation is favourable, and that there is no need to wait for capitalism to fall apart in the wake of its internal contradictions.

China has shown that a socialist system can, if necessary, change course. In recent times, a determined attempt has been made to increase the country's productive potential as quickly as possible. Now, that potential has been growing ever since 1949, when the People's Republic was proclaimed. Even in the stormy years of the Cultural Revolution, agriculture did well: the production of grain could at least keep step with the population increase, and in other sectors, too, production increased. Thus, steel output rose by about ten per cent and petroleum production, too, increased. For some time now, heavy industry has been in a position to produce tractors, lorries, motor cars, steam and diesel engines, steamships, electrical instruments, computers, equipment for oil extraction and refining, aeroplanes, etc.[2]

In order to deter potential aggressors China has built up a nuclear force, yet she may still not feel secure, which would explain why she is tackling the modernisation of her system of production with so much energy. The Chinese government is also trying to stimulate production by increasing the purchasing power of the people. It does so by giving the workers in town and country a chance of earning higher incomes. The political power of the workers is increased, as a result and so are the chances of industries' planning their own schedules which – with special effort – can lead to a further rise in incomes. Enterprises can compete against one another and be rewarded for their efficiency and profitability.[3] In rural China, the per capita income was doubled over some five years and, what is more important, the peasants were allowed to buy what they liked with the extra money. In order to meet the increased demand, light industry was boosted, while the improved harvests enabled townsfolk and factory workers to buy a larger variety of foodstuffs in larger quantities. At the beginning of the 1980s, agricultural production rose by an average of 8.4 per cent per annum, while the output of light industry increased by an average of 9.9 per cent.

Greater decentralisation of the economic system reduced the power of the bureaucracy and of the Communist Party. Thus planning authorities were prohibited from making detailed provisions for the various industries. However, it would be quite wrong to assume that China has exchanged a planned economy for one based largely on competition and market forces. China is still a planned and regulated economy in which market relations among collective enterprises are encouraged, but only within the framework of government control.[4]

Critics of the present-day system fear a damaging impact on the socialist values of equality, self-sacrifice, collectivism and mass participation.[5] Pessimists expect that the position of one social stratum – the technocrats, professional administrators, economic managers, scientists, technicians and educators – will be strengthened, and that these people will pursue their own interests.[6] While this may, of course, happen, it seems more likely that the Party, if it considers the time ripe to do so, can and will put a stop to any such elitist tendencies. According to Jack Gray of the Institute of Development Studies, the University of Sussex, there is no need to doubt China's commitment to the limitation of income differentials.

The new strategy calls for closer ties with the capitalist world for the express purpose of gaining access to foreign capital and technology.[7]

**Ends and means**

The socialist path has clear advantages. On ethical grounds alone, there are reasons for choosing a socialist development strategy because in so doing we commit ourselves to the creation of the kind of society that makes possible better human relationships than does the capitalist system, which is based on egoism and competition for material objects. But there are other arguments, too, in favour of a socialist strategy. For such a strategy is based on an ideology that provides solid foundations for the struggle against imperialism, offers an explanation of the unfavourable situation of the great masses and serves the interests of the great majority.

A strategy devoted to development and progress must have the following objectives:

- to provide the prerequisites of rapid development, such as education and medical care, and improvements in the fields of nutrition, clothing and housing, as quickly as possible;
- to ensure the balanced, large-scale, development of the country's forces of production;
- to turn the prevailing social values in a socialist direction;
- to effect the complete emancipation of women;
- to abolish class distinctions and establish a political system in which power lies with the people;
- to end all disadvantageous economic relationships with the rich, powerful capitalist world.

A balanced development must be based on a system of production that makes adequate provision to meet every citizen's needs. To achieve that, there must be economic growth; the production of consumer as well as of capital goods must be expanded. Such expansion requires a great deal of investment, which means that everyone will have to save, i.e. will have to live frugally for a considerable time. People will tolerate the hardships involved if they see that there is social equality, that social contrasts have been reduced and that there is no personal enrichment by some at the expense of the rest.

A further condition of a successful mobilisation for rapid development is the provision of good educational services, good housing, and so on, as well as of leisure facilities. All these inspire enthusiasm in the population and benefit the economy. In an address to Cuban peasants, Fidel Castro reminded his audience of the social provisions the Cuban revolution had brought them: they now had a system of social security and there was work for everyone. A very large number of hospitals had been built in the countryside and medical services vastly expanded. Education, too, had been brought to hundreds of thousands of children of peasants and agricultural workers who could now attend secondary schools, institutes of higher education and universities.[8]

Without changing the prevailing values of most citizens, it is hardly possible to employ a socialist strategy. Some of the new values have been discussed in Chapter 8 under *The picture of the future*; in the section on culture included in the present chapter, we shall have more to say on this subject.

The abolition of class distinctions means that when the proceeds of the productive process are distributed there will be no one to receive a disproportionate share. For that to happen, the rank-and-file must have a say in all decision-making bodies. That implies freedom of expression and above all freedom from fear: people voicing their opinion must run no danger of being arrested or punished. Self-administration, by workers in industry and the inhabitants of a region or district, is an important means of preventing people with more ability or more education from dominating the rest.

The government must take steps to expand the state sector of the economy and to control foreign investors as much as possible, but it should not act precipitately in this field. Nor is it essential to vest all the means of production suddenly in the people or in the state on behalf of the people. Some sectors of the economy can be left in private hands for a considerable time. A socialist government will have to make changes enough without having to interfere in concerns that run smoothly or to bother with matters that are of secondary importance to a socialist society. Although much agricultural produce will have to be produced by large, mechanised state farms, it would be quite wrong to abolish small agricultural holdings. The same is true of petty trade. Many people have strong emotional bonds with small industries, and despite all the objections that can be raised against these industries, it is a fact that many people are employed by them and that they make a useful contribution to the life of the community. They may be expected to disappear in the long run, when better forms of production and distribution emerge and when the children of petty entrepreneurs have come to prefer other work, so that there are no successors to the old owners. Admittedly, limitations will have to be placed on the number of workers employed in these small concerns, with the result that the private sector will mainly be confined to family-run businesses. The wages of the workers will have to satisfy the legal provisions.

So much for a general overview of the ends and means of

socialist policy. In the sections that follow they will be elaborated and completed. At the end of this chapter I hope to be able to show that people in the rich countries, too, will benefit from a prosperous Third World, that an increase in the purchasing power of the poor will benefit the whole of mankind.

## Two socialist structures

The socialist reconstruction of society is one phase in a process that differs from country to country. But generally speaking, the process of change can be divided into the following phases:

- The capitalist mode of production, in which the bourgeoisie is the ruling class and dominates the state.
- The abolition of the capitalist mode of production which begins with state supervision of the most powerful capitalist concerns and other institutions hostile to the people, whereupon, by increases in taxation, government revenue is boosted and the means and levers of production, beginning with banking, gradually nationalised. During this transitional period, the interests of the people are represented by the state and the people themselves do not have a great deal of say.
- The state-socialist phase, in which private enterprise has been largely (but not yet completely) abolished and the people still have very little say, even though the government now defends the interests of the formerly oppressed and exploited majority. The socialist mobilisation system is a sub-phase of the state-socialist phase.
- The democratic-socialist phase, in which the power of the state is significantly reduced and the decision-making powers are increasingly vested in the people, who elect various councils, including industrial ones.

I have not numbered these phases, lest I give the impression that this is the normal or desirable sequence. I must also point out that some phases can be omitted altogether (Mongolia, for instance, changed from a feudal to a socialist society without an intermediate capitalist phase), or appear in a different sequence (in the Soviet Union, state socialism was preceded by a democratic-socialist phase).

I shall now look more closely at two of these phases, namely the state-socialist and the democratic-socialist phases. The first is often imposed by necessity: the socialists may have come to power in difficult circumstances, the development of productive forces may have made little progress as yet or have suffered a setback in the wake of a crisis or a revolutionary struggle. It will sometimes take years before the economy can return to the pre-revolutionary level. In such cases, state socialism as defined below will lead to the best results.

| STATE SOCIALISM | DEMOCRATIC SOCIALISM |
| --- | --- |
| A socialist government controls production (in the interests of the people). | The government implements the decisions of the people's representative on the national level. |
| Official bodies have a great deal of influence. | Official bodies do not have a great deal of influence. |
| Separate industries and separate branches are run by managers supported by staffs of experts. | An intermediate body representing industries and organised peasants tempers the decision-making powers of the separate industries. |
| Rank-and-file peasants and workers have a say over the course of events but no real power. | Rank-and-file peasants and workers have real power at the industrial level. |

Under state socialism, the state plays a crucial role in developing the economy; it not only plays a leading part but also exerts a decisive influence on investments (in the state sector and to some extent in the private sector as well). As a result, it is able to set up industries and businesses that will only pay in the long run. Almost the entire economy is, so to speak, run like a great hierarchically organised company.

If we make democratic socialism our standard or comparison then, clearly, state socialism has unpleasant features: peasants and workers alike remain alienated from the means of production. Much the same happens during the first phases of capitalist development, when the great majority of the population has no influence either. The difference, however, is that in a socialist system the prosperity of the great majority comes first.

The lack of democracy at the beginning of socialist development is regrettable, but in view of the extremely difficult situation in which the young socialist regime finds itself there is often no alternative. Experts from capitalist countries have admitted that state socialism has certain advantages. Thus the economist Wilhelm Breuer says that the centralised Cuban system has facilitated the distribution of scarce resources and has also fostered variety in agriculture.[9] But what is good for quick growth during the mobilisation phase may be bad during a later phase, when the productive system has grown more complex. Serious mistakes may be made and stagnation may set in once the central planning authorities are no longer able to gauge what is happening on the ground. This explains why the Amsterdam sociologist Michael Masuch found so many flaws in the complex East European economics. He criticises East European planning authorities for basing their decision-making models on an unjustified simplification of the economic reality. Moreover, to gather information they have to rely on all sorts of officials, above all in industry, who are interested in producing such figures as will result in the state setting them low production targets. This benefits them inasmuch as if they exceed these targets they are given a premium.

Because it is impossible to plan with sufficient precision, there are delivery holdups during various phases of the productive process, so much so that the Soviet Union loses twenty-five per cent of the total labour time as a result. (It should be remembered, however, that there are such losses in the capitalist system as well and for the same reasons.) Masuch also believes that the overcentralised decision-making power found in Eastern Europe inhibits changes, not least in the technological sphere. The planning chiefs are unable to judge what basic technological innovations are needed and the industrial base itself is averse to change, not least because change leads to much confusion and hence endangers the fulfilment of the current plan.[10] It is important for governments of socialist Third World countries to realize that such problems may arise at a given moment, but as long as these countries are in a state of emergency they cannot avoid steering a centralised course with the hierarchic relationship that course entails.

The stasis, or at least the rigidity of a state-socialist system is usually foreshadowed: the disadvantages outweigh the advantages and social tensions lead to a drop in production and productivity. Exasperation intermingled with fear of the bureaucracy causes the country to slow down. The rank-and-file grows aloof, the distance between the nation and its leaders increases, and less information flows from the bottom to the top, increasing the likelihood of further mistakes.

The situation becomes even more serious when groups of people holding power are unable to resist the temptation to feather their own nests: a kind of class conflict creeps into the socialist system. The leading groups become isolated and the enthusiasm of the people dwindles, and with it productivity. As a result, the earlier expectations of an increase in consumer goods are frustrated.

During the early 1970s Fidel Castro was to some extent able to stifle such tendencies in Cuba. At the start of the revolution, the state machine was a faithful executor of the decisions of the charismatic group round Castro. Unfortunately, the bureaucracy grew ever more powerful in the wake of the many nationalisation decrees and the extention of social provisions. Castro and his group of revolutionaries were in danger of being left behind. To offset what was called *burocratismo*, the masses were given greater say in the official machine and in the party.[11] In general, if the national situation allows it, the best solution is to grant greater autonomy to individual concerns and greater say to the workers in them, which means development in the democratic-socialist direction.

The transition from a state-socialist to a democratic-socialist system will not be smooth in many cases. This process takes place in a situation in which the rich capitalist countries, and the United States above all, will try to destablise the socialist system by all conceivable means. Thus the United States has been boycotting Cuba for the past twenty years, much as they oppose other countries that encourage autochthonous development, even threatening them with destruction.

However, internal factors, too, can impede the transition.

There is a good chance that the leaders of the state-socialist system, above all if they have degenerated into autocrats, will not themselves steer a more democratic course. In that case, the people will have to exert pressure and perhaps even revolt. In that struggle, too, the liberation scientist has a role to play: he will choose the side of the people when he finds the time is ripe.

Workers' and peasants' self-management is an essential feature of the democratic-socialist system and must be enshrined in a constitution that is vigorously upheld. It must guarantee feel employment and prevent particular industries or the workers in them from taking advantage of their privileged economic position. Should that happen, we have a capitalist system with the means of production in the hands of workers' collectives. Even with decentralisation, production in a socialist system must to some extent remain a centrally guided process. Guidance from above is the responsibility of the people's representatives who formulate the national objectives and encourage their implementation by a balanced credit, wages, prices and taxation system.

Citizens in a socialist society enjoying a maximum of democracy will be able to form organisations to counteract the concentration of power in the administrative machinery and in industry. However, they will not be entitled to set up organisations that protect group interests at the expense of the community. A maximum of democracy implies that the power of the party and of party members is severely restricted, and as the power of the government is increasingly reduced so the party ceases to be the pivot of the socialist system.

A democratic-socialist system can only work satisfactorily if the country is not beset with very grave problems, if the workers make a decent living, if there is freedom of organisation, the press, and permission to strike, and if the masses are not afraid of the police.

So much for my account of the two types of socialist system. They are two models that, though based on real considerations, cannot be found anywhere in the pure form I have described. Existing socialist systems are located somewhere between these two or may even be less pleasant than the state-socialist system if there is an excess of state coercion.

## Party and state

In the socialist system, the party is considered to control the departments of state in the interests of the proletariat. The party brings together the most active and politically conscious workers and their leaders: idealistic and committed men and women who are not motivated by self-interest and who can provide leadership and sound advice in various social bodies and organisations and at work. This fosters the unity of policy and action, for it is the party that charts the correct course towards a better future and that keeps the ship of state on this course. It should do so by persuasion, of course, but there is always the danger that it may abuse its position and become an autocrat instead of a guide. To prevent that from happening, the party members must be in as close a contact as possible with the people and, at meetings and other gatherings, listen to what the people have to say instead of manipulating them. If it is a good party, it will function as a representative of the people.

While it is still impossible to hold proper elections to choose people's representatives (because of economic and military tensions), the people must be inspired with confidence in the integrity of the party leaders. This is no complete guarantee, but, alas, there is no alternative. When they choose a socialist system, the people run risks (sometimes very great risks, as we saw in Kampuchea), but they have no alternative if they want liberation. During the struggle for freedom the people come to know their leaders and will repudiate them if they lack confidence in them. As a rule, the progressive leaders in the Third World are serious men and women who have fought for the oppressed for years and have run great risks in so doing. They almost invariably have their hearts in the right place.

Nevertheless a socialist system needs safeguards if it wants to make sure that its leaders do not stray. Independent accountants must check the industrial figures and report to management, factory committees and trade-union associations. Elsewhere, too, checks are needed to prevent the government and party machine from degenerating into a bureaucracy that treats the population unfairly, looks to its own advantages and impedes development.

We saw that the state may be forced to limit the decision-making power of the people, but that is only acceptable for short

212 Development through Liberation

periods, while the revolution continues to be under serious threat, not least from internal enemies who resent the loss of their entrenched privileges. People who were rich and influential in the capitalist system are, as a rule, not only energetic, powerful and intelligent, but also quite unyielding and not prepared to be pushed into a corner. Quite often they also buttress their resistance by philosophical and ethical principles which they consider so important that they are prepared to sacrifice everything for them, even their lives. The revolution will have to defend itself against them, but the revolutionaries can be expected to have some understanding of their enemies and, even should it be necessary to imprison them, to treat them humanely. The fight against counter-revolutionaries must be confined to the most dangerous enemies of the revolution. These do not include people who resist with words only. Above all, the revolution must make certain that ordinary citizens do not feel threatened by it and become alienated from it. However, the degree of freedom to be allowed is, of course, closely related to the magnitude of the internal and external threat to the revolution.

To keep the minority of counter-revolutionaries in check, the freedom of the press will have to be curtailed, at least in the transitional phase. Opponents of socialism consider this a proof of weakness, and they are right. A weak people must be protected against ideologies that shore up capitalist interests, and the party must also prevent anyone from inflaming the spirit of resistance of counter-revolutionaries.

As the chances of a counter-revolution decrease and the development of the productive forces progresses, the power of the state should be decreased and that of the organised people increased.

**People's power**

Peasants' and workers' self-management with due regard being paid to the national interest is the most important organisation principle of the socialist system of production. If the peasants and workers have no power over the use of the means of production and cannot have a say in the spending of the surplus value of labour, the principle of communal ownership of the means of production has little meaning.

In their organisations and at their workplaces, the peasants and workers will elect representatives to councils with great powers, including the fixing of wages. Wage levels should, however, also be discussed by similar industrial concerns, and above all by those in the same region.

Concerns in the same industry form industrial unions that hold a half-way position between the separate industries and the ministry bearing ultimate responsibility for the branch of protection concerned. They have a coordinating task, can launch scientific investigations and generally fix wage scales that hold for the entire branch of industry. However, care must be taken to prevent the autonomy of an industry turning into group egoism. The profits from industry have a social character; in principle they belong to all the inhabitants of the country. What is produced and who profits from it cannot be decided exclusively on the shop floor; there must be a balance between the interests of the producers and those of the customers, albeit the two groups largely overlap. Moreover, funds must be withdrawn from the production sector for provisions considered of general importance by the people's representatives: defence, art, and a host of other spheres. To satisfy all interests in the fullest possible way, the people must be organised not only as producers but also as consumers and inhabitants of various geographic units (municipalities and provinces).

Only if there is democracy at many levels of society is there a chance that workers' self-management will prove generally beneficial. Only a chance, that is, because democracy at all levels is a necessary but not a sufficient condition. Investigations shows that industrial democracy only works in the absence of too many intra-industrial and extra-industrial tensions. In Yugoslavia, for instance, autocratic forms of organisation appeared in democratised industries when these industries experienced economic difficulties.

The idea of peasant self-management may seem paradoxical because peasants in the strict sense of the word are not workers but independent producers. However the idea can be applied to situations in which peasants are part of a collective or in which peasant communes are subject to government regulations. In that case, peasant self-management means that peasants wish to have some say in solving the problems of their own village communities. They were granted this in Maoist China, where village communes are in charge of production (agricultural and otherwise), the construction of irrigation works and of roads, the acquisition and maintenance of equipment, transport and education. As a result, the involvement of the central authorities in the life of the countryside was confined to political control, mainly by the party, and to the attempt to gear local production more or less to the national objectives.

People's power at a regional level can also be found in Mozambique, where the revolution, even at an early stage, that is, during the resistance struggle against the Portuguese, went hand in hand with a large measure of popular power: *Poder popular*. People's committees in liberated regions were given the task of examining and if possible solving local problems. One of their guiding principles was that solutions to national problems cannot be found if there are groups with conflicting interests, that the prosperity of every citizen can only be realized if the whole society does well, and that a local community can only prosper if the whole country prospers. At general meetings, industrial rallies, local gatherings, the people of Mozambique come together, discuss their problems and choose delegates to an executive committee.[12]

With this example I wish merely to focus attention on a form of popular democracy and do not claim that in Mozambique all power has been vested in the people. It is, however, of interest, it seems to me, that such political structures should be found in a Third World country, because they have a mobilising function and enable the people to concentrate more power in their own hands.[13]

## The emancipation of women

Political parties aiming for a socialist society usually advocate the emancipation of women. Once they have seized power, they make sure that the material position of women is improved, though in many cases they allow the continuation of a division of labour, as a result of which women receive lower wages and do less rewarding work. In socialist Vietnam, for instance, women now account for fifty per cent of the workforce, but according to a representative of the Northern Women's League they continue to be dissatisfied in three respects: their self-image (women still see themselves as inferiors), their participation in the political and administrative machinery and their inequality in the family. The last two complaints are still voiced even in Cuba. As for the self-image of Cuban women, Margaret Randall found that they come a long way since the days before the revolution when they suffered from lack of education, objectivisation, subservience, and other forms of exploitation. However, after twenty years of socialist revolution their societal position must still be considered a secondary one. Women's representation on the Central Committee of the party, on the State Council, on the Council of Ministers, is not yet what it should be, reports Randall. And the same is true of lower government organs.[14]

As far as equality within the family is concerned, Cuba has an excellent law which not only prescribes equality for all in their work-places (equal work, equal wages) but also in the home: husband and wife must share household chores between them. However, there is still a large gap here between theory and practice. There will only be real equality once women participate fully in the work process outside the home and men share fully in the housework.

Organisation helps to increase the power and influence of women, and in Cuba an important emancipatory role has been reserved for the Federation of Cuban Women. The fact that the ability to organise is a powerful tool in the emancipation of women was also seen in China: it was above all in regions where women, on Mao's advice, had formed women's groups that they benefited from the land reforms and were able to seize land on which they could earn an independent income.[15]

It is clear that for women socialism is but one step on the road to complete emancipation, because the emancipation of women does not follow automatically upon the triumph of socialism. For that very reason, there must be a separate socialist women's movement which makes its voice heard even before the victory of socialism.[16]

## Medical care and education

In its first year, the Cuban revolution began to organise and improve the health service. Statistics collated by Dr Vicente Navarro, a US authority, show that two-thirds of all hospital beds available in 1969 were added after the revolution. The number of nurses almost doubled during the same ten-year period. There is no country in Latin America that can boast anything comparable. And it was all accomplished under difficult circumstances: nearly half Cuba's physicians left the country when the *guerrilleros* won their last battle.[17] The doctors decamped because they could earn much more money abroad than in the country of their birth.

The improved physical strength of the people is reflected in their achievements on the sports field. During the Pan-American Games in Venezuela a few years ago, the Cubans collected 79 medals while the Canadians and Brazilians collected only 18 and 14 respectively. The United States came first with 137 medals, which was to be expected since with her 230 million inhabitants the US has a much greater potential than Cuba with her ten million.

It gave the Cubans great satisfaction to see the 'yanquis' defeated in so many sections, but it was not only they who cheered: whenever Cuba was ranged against the USA, encouraging shouts of 'Cuba! Cuba!' reverberated through the sports halls and across the stadia. The Venezuelan public backed the Cubans because they knew that this small country was the champion of the struggle against North American imperialism, a struggle Cuba does not wage in the field of sport alone. The physical strength of her people, improved by medical care and education, enables Cuba to withstand the armed might of the United States and to prevent any further attempts at conquest. Moreover, it also allows Cuba to aid progressive countries in the Third World militarily and in other ways.

The extension and improvement of Cuban education served several ends, and especially the training of cadres to ensure industrial and agricultural expansion and to raise the political consciousness of the population. This last aspect was strongly emphasised during the literacy campaign of 1961. Young people from the towns with a middle-class background were brought face to face with the poor living standards of the rural population while working side by side with the peasants. The hope was that, as a result, political consciousness would be raised all round. Political training is thus greatly enhanced by the combination of study and productive work, a lesson that – as we saw – has not been lost on Zimbabwe as well. In Maoist China, too, much attention is paid to this fusion. Thus students at the Tsing-hau Polytechnic College in Peking are engaged on research projects at the request of various industrial concerns.

In China, education was largely supervised by workers and peasants, in contrast to what happens in capitalist countries, where middle-class people dominate school administration and parents' committees, and big business is strongly represented on university governing bodies.

While education and the mass media help to train socialist men and women, they also learn by being directly involved in the running of the social system. A socialist system must, accordingly, ensure that there are structures which further the training and emergence of a new political consciousness.

In China, speakers and writers keep emphasising the view that manual labour deserves great honour and respect, but matters are not left at that: intellectual workers are given a chance and encouraged to do manual work. And in Cuba, too, there were (and are) a number of opportunities to do voluntary labour on behalf of the community at large.

## Socialist mobilisation

A relatively short period of socialist development has the character of a mobilisation system, a subject to which I have referred in Chapter 8, so that here I can confine myself to the specific features of the socialist mobilisation system.

In addition to developing the forces of production, a socialist mobilisation system also aims to raise the level of political consciousness. This is of great importance, particularly at the beginning when people have to work hard for low wages. To persuade them to do so inevitably calls for some moral pressure and coercion. However, these measures will have to be limited to a minimum; instead socialists will concentrate on the development of a political consciousness that urges people on without the need for outside pressure. In Cuba it was above all Che Guevara who advocated moral stimulation, because he found that it fosters the development of socialist consciousness and behaviour. He hoped that the revolution would prepare Cubans to work for progress out of a sense of social responsibility alone.

We saw in Chapter 8 that one of the first conditions for the success of a mobilisation system is that improvements should be made, and be seen to be made right away. Now, this is precisely what happened in Cuba: wages rose while rents and prices fell and tenants were given the opportunity to become permanent owners of their homes. Theatres were built, libraries were opened, sportsfields were laid out and holiday tours organised. Beaches previously reserved for rich Cubans and North Americans were opened up to all. Beggars and bootblacks disappeared from the city. At the same time, the people were given the opportunity to translate their enthusiasm into deeds; a host of voluntary work campaigns, great and small, were organised.

A great national effort, in which much was at stake, was the sugar campaign of 1969–70, when the government aimed at a harvest of ten million tons of sugar. '*Todos listos para los 10 millones*', '*10 VAN*' ('All ready for the ten million', 'The ten will come') were two popular slogans summoning the population to make extra exertions during 'the great agrarian offensive, in the year of the crucial effort'.

In the circumstances, with the sugar cane being cut by clerks and other outsiders, the harvest became a matter of honour, a patriotic struggle, and this was reflected in the slogans and chants, all of them reminiscent of the days of the guerrilla struggle prior to the revolt of 1959. Thus people who worked with tireless devotion were given the title of *guerrillero* of labour. The fight against Spanish domination, too, served as an example of sacrificial patriotism. New fronts were opened up, victories were won and defeats suffered by 'red brigades of sugar workers'.[18]

The Cuban campaigns helped to raise the workers' level of consciousness but their immediate aim was to help strengthen the forces of production so as to increase output as quickly as possible. In fact there is an interaction between these two elements: a politically conscious nation makes a greater contribution to production, and increased production raises morale and raises the level of political consciousness.

We saw in Chapter 8 that organisations are required to mobilise people. In socialist systems, organisations devoted to change play a particularly important role. Thus soon after they seized power, the Cuban revolutionaries established a special body charged with looking after the confiscated plantations, with drawing up an agricultural plan and with implementing it. This body was called INRA, the National Institute for Agrarian Reform. In addition, many other organisations, and especially mass organisations, arose that involved the population in all sorts of ways in the revolutionary process: the Federation of Cuban Women, the Young Communist League, the Confederation of Cuban Workers, the National Federation of Sugar Workers, the National Association of Small Farmers, the National Union of Workers in Education and Science, the Federation of University Students, and numerous Committees for the Defence of the Revolution. Though the main task of these committees was to keep an eye on counter-revolutionaries, they did much more than that, engaging in many forms of social reconstruction, organising voluntary work and leading various campaigns. And they continue to do so. Following the threat of the invasion of Cuba by the Reagan administration, committees were set up to strengthen the country's defences and to guard the coast. The fight against *dengue*, or break-bone fever, an infectious disease which according to the Cuban authorities was brought to Cuba by their North American enemies, also involved a number of committees.

The most important organisation in a socialist mobilisation system is the political party. Its members are expected to be totally committed to the success of the revolution and to the persuasion of their compatriots.

In the section devoted to mobilisation systems (pp. 178ff.) I tried to show how these systems can grow rigid and hence forfeit their usefulness. Socialist Cuba, too, showed such a hardening process, both in 1968 and later, when too much emphasis was placed on reaching the enormous sugar production targets. A great deal of power was concentrated in the hands of the government, which meant that the influence of the mass organisations was reduced. The decision-making structure of the social system became more authoritarian. This process agrees with David Apter's analysis of mobilisation systems: the leaders pursue objectives that have ceased to be realistic, as a result of which resources are wasted. To stifle resistance against this process, more coercion will have to be used and the masses will have to be manipulated even more than before: ideological conformity is imposed by force. Leo Huberman and Paul Sweezy saw the severe punishments meted out in 1968 to Aníbal Escalante and some other communist members of the pre-revolutionary guard as a warning to all Cubans not to oppose the government.[19]

At the time, many socialists were anxious about these hardening tendencies, but the sociologists among them must have realized that society is a constantly changing whole and that some social phenomena are of a temporary nature. It was obvious that the strengthening of the authoritarian tendencies was a by-product of the sugar campaign and the failure to reach the unrealistic targets quickly resulted in the emergence of new, more democratic processes.[20]

Sociological laws are not natural laws, but the chances that the processes described by Apter will appear are very great indeed. Though hardening is an almost unavoidable phase of the mobilisation system it is certainly not beyond repair.

## Production

That the capitalist system of production leads to unbalanced growth and a division of incomes in the poor countries, and to great differences between urban and rural areas, between industry and agriculture and between intellectual and manual labour is the conclusion of J.B.W. Kuitenbrouwer of the International Institute of Social Studies in The Hague. He contends that only by deliberate planning of the economy and intervention in the way society is organised can the needs of the entire population be met.[21] Now this is precisely what the socialist mode of production concerns itself with: it replaces production by private enterprise with a planned economy controlled by the state. This process goes hand in hand with an attempt to achieve quick economic growth to ensure the fairest possible distribution of incomes and to build up the armed forces.

Production is largely concentrated in industries that are the collective property of groups or of the whole nation, but in a transitional phase private enterprise, too, can be allowed to continue.

During the nationalisation of industries, the state will turn its attention first to banks and key industries, i.e. industries on which many other industries depend. In Algeria, the nationalisation programme began with the banks, the mines, the oil and the heavy metal industries. Foreign trade, that is imports and exports, are also placed under state supervision in a socialist system. If the business community refuses to join in the construction of a better system of production then the businesses concerned will be expropriated as well. But all businesses will first be given a chance to collaborate and, what is more, on fair terms.

During the first years of a socialist government and economy, problems with highly-skilled employees often appear. Dyed-in-the-wool managerial and senior clerical staff of the old capitalist enterprises tend to leave the country, and though the government may actually be pleased to see such people go, it does well to keep a cool head and attempt to restrain those with special abilities. Cuba suffered badly from the mass emigration of entrepreneurs and conservative academics, but the revolutionary government of Angola tried to prevent such an exodus. Even so, many, particularly Portuguese, business and industrial experts left, whereupon the government tried to persuade them to return to Angola and to help reopen those enterprises that had had to close after their departure.[22]

The Angolan government realized that in other respects, too, it could not dispense with the services of foreigners. It accepts a great deal of help from the socialist countries but it also maintains relations with capitalist companies. In particular, it has signed contracts with companies from Italy, France and the United States covering the extraction of oil, and a British-Belgian-Angolan mining consortium has taken charge of diamond prospecting.

Both agriculture and industry will have to be developed, but at a rate that, naturally, depends on the economic and also on the foreign political situation of the country. In the long run, however, industrialisation is imperative; in its absence, no satisfactory living standard can be reached. Moreover, industrial might is needed to protect the socialist system from potential foreign enemies.

During the 1921 revolution, the People's Republic of Mongolia inherited an economic system that revolved almost entirely round nomadic shepherds, people who had been badly indebted to Chinese landowners. The revolution put an end to the power of the feudal lords and of the Buddhist priests (lamas) and set up a trading company to buy goods from the shepherds and to export them, but also to import goods from abroad. The profits were used to finance industrialisation. The Soviet Union helped with funds and technical expertise. In the end, the Mongolians were able to process their own raw materials, especially leather, wool, wood, lime and iron. In Darkhan, in the middle of the steppes, one of many new industrial centres was opened to produce fuels, electricity, building materials and food. In 1970, industry accounted for more than 20 per cent of the national income and for 30 per cent of all exports. Forty per cent of the population no longer work in the agricultural sector.[23]

The Democratic People's Republic of Korea also made tremendous strides. In the war of 1950–53, US forces and their allies were responsible for large-scale devastation: they covered the country with a carpet of bombs, with the result that millions of people, soldiers and civilians, were killed or wounded, and no city, village, factory, school, hospital or pagoda remained intact. When reconstruction could begin, heavy industry had to be given priority, and especially machine construction, metal casting, chemicals and energy, in the hope that this emphasis would lead to the production of enough capital goods for the subsequent development of light industry, agriculture and defence production.[24]

The economic development of North Korea is based on the idea of *Juche* which stresses independence and self-sufficiency. This implies relying as much as possible on domestic resources and domestic technology.[25]

To achieve their objectives, the North Koreans called for the help of the socialist countries. The Soviet Union, for instance, supplied enough material to equip forty factories and also sent a large number of technical advisers. The results were not slow in coming: ten years after the armistice, North Korea was more or less economically independent and able to generate further industrial growth with its own technical and financial resources. From 1964 to 1973, industrial production rose by 13 per cent a year. The country has an extensive machine industry which meets 95 per cent of North Korea's own needs for machinery and exports machinery to twenty-five countries.[26] Approximately 60 per cent of the population work in non-agrarian occupations and about 60 per cent of the national income is provided by industry. Ninety per cent of all industry is state property and 10 per cent is owned by cooperatives.[27] In the agricultural field, too, North Korea has scored many successes. Mechanisation, electrification and the use of chemical fertilizers have, according to the North Korean authorities, led to an appreciable rise in grain production. In about 1974, the country was fully able to feed itself.[28] N.K. Chandra, of the Indian Institute of Management, concluded that the performance of North Korea is not much inferior to that of South Korea, but the former is self-reliant, has an egalitarian income distribution and commands the support of most Koreans in exile.[29]

Agriculture can be developed in various ways, to some extent determined by socio-geographic factors. If circumstances allow, socialists must try to introduce modern agricultural methods that produce the highest possible yield per unit of labour and invested capital. Cuba, which has a great deal of land suited to agriculture and is not overpopulated, aims for the kind of development characteristic of Australia and New Zealand: a technically advanced agriculture and an industry geared mainly to processing agricultural produce. Cuba's ideal is a completely mechanised sugar industry, which Fidel Castro continued to extol in addresses he gave at the time that the Cuban people were wearing themselves out in the sugar fields. The time will come, Castro explained, when all the work on a big sugar cooperative will be controlled by someone at a switchboard in an air-conditioned office right in the middle of the sugar fields. With a single touch of a button he or she will cause a whole phalanx of remote-controlled harvesting machines to move into the field and cut the cane in battle formation.

An important aspect of a production system is the manner in which the workers are treated. A socialist labour system is based on three principles. The first is that all workers must be given employment. In a land of workers everyone must indeed be a worker, that is, play a part in the production process. If it should unexpectedly become impossible to use everyone, then the available work will have to be shared out. In a socialist society there must be no outcasts. A second principle is that manual labour is held in high regard. And finally, work must be turned into a vocation, become an end in itself, for the benefit of the whole community. That means that apart from the material mainsprings there are ethical motives to do the work as well as possible. As I have stressed, ethical motives were emphasised by Che Guevara when he held an influential position in Cuba. He was bitterly opposed to all systems that reinforced the materialism and egoism of individuals and groups. He therefore opposed the use of material rewards to increase labour productivity, for with them Cuba would be straying from the socialist path.

In the early years of the Soviet Union, people were given as many chances as possible to work voluntarily on projects of national, regional or local importance. In everyday work, too, an appeal was made to ethical ideals. Members of 'labour shock troops' were given high honours and also more tangible rewards such as theatre tickets and free excursions. In the factory canteens, workers who had exceeded their norms would find bunches of flowers on their tables.

Another system to boost output is so-called socialist emulation, by which work is treated much as a sport in which honour and glory may be gained. Thus during the construction of a dam on the Dnieper, two teams starting from opposite banks competed with each other to complete the work first. But one of the rules of these contests is that the winners must help the losers; factories that are better organised and economically stronger are expected to support weaker enterprises.

## Culture

Raising the self-confidence of the people is a task of paramount importance and demands of them great familiarity with their own history and culture as well as a halt to the spread of the culture of the imperialist powers.

Socialist culture involves the ideal of a 'new man' who fits into a socialist society. The new man will be free of the intellectual distortions that beset his or her forefathers and led to race discrimination, the subordination of women and a dislike for manual labour, among other things. The new man may be expected to be far less swayed by self-interest and material considerations than his capitalist counterpart, and to have more idealism and a greater sense of social responsibility. Socialists work for a society that offers everyone the chance to develop as much as possible in accordance with his or her own personality without harming others in doing so. The more talented will be encouraged to play a part in raising the social and cultural level of the masses.

One great benefit of socialism is that its ideals may foster solidarity among a culturally or ethnically divided people: appeals to comradeship and equality may find a ready ear among people of different religious faiths, of different ethnic origins. These ideals can spur the population to make common cause enthusiastically without sacrificing their cultural and ethnic heritage.

Art and science, too, are actively encouraged by revolutionary governments. In Cuba, state support and the liberation from capitalism released a great wave of creative forces. Before the revolution the country was awash with the cheapest aspects of North American culture such as Westerns, pornography and racism, and what genuine cultural contributions the United States or the Cubans themselves made to Cuban culture were modest in scale. But now Cuba can boast a flourishing cultural life. Illiterates learned to read, and all over Cuba access to books is easier than ever before: according to the authorities, the number of books published in Cuba since the victory of the revolution has increased tenfold. Travelling libraries bring literature to all parts of the country, and other forms of culture, too, are encouraged everywhere: poetry, theatre, ballet. Castro asked the Cuban prima ballerina, Alicia Alonso, to form a national ballet company, which today is among the best in the world. An indigenous film industry has also been highly successful: it focuses attention on the history of the country, *inter alia* for the purpose of strengthening the self-esteem of the Cuban people.[30] Cuban literature, too, has blossomed.

In the past, Havana alone had something to offer in the cultural sphere. Before the revolution, Cuba had just one philharmonic orchestra, which only gave concerts in Havana. Today there are three big national orchestras that play throughout the country.

The influence of the revolution reaches far beyond the 'green cayman', as the poet Nicolás Guillén has called his country because of its shape and vegetation. Three months after the revolution triumphed, the Casa de las Américas was founded, a centre for writers and other artists from the whole of Latin America. Its annual prizes are held in high esteem.

## Improvement of international relationships

A socialist government follows an anti-imperialist foreign policy, making common cause with all who fight imperialism in all parts of the world. These fighters for freedom are the liberation movements in the Third World and the progressive forces in the highly-developed countries, capitalist as well as socialist. The government of Cuba has enshrined this policy in its constitution, where we can read that the republic supports the principles of proletarian internationalism and of militant solidarity among nations.[31] It recognises the legitimacy of national wars of liberation and of armed struggle against every form of aggression and every attempt at conquest. It considers it a legitimate right and also an international duty to offer help to the victims of aggression and to all people who fight for their liberation.

Cuba has translated these sentiments into practice and has done so in an impressive manner. More than 100 000 Cubans have been engaged in military missions and in peaceful development work abroad. During the years 1978 to 1979, for instance, some ten to eleven thousand Cuban civilians were at work all over Africa putting up buildings, repairing bridges destroyed by military action, working on agricultural projects, in animal husbandry, on fishing projects, on medical and educational programmes, etc.[32] Agibou Yansané holds that by helping to resist foreign aggression in Angola, Ethiopia and other African countries Cuba is becoming a world power.[33] Nor have the Cubans confined their activities to the African continent. In Nicaragua, for instance, two thousand Cuban teachers, more than two hundred doctors, countless medical assistants, building workers and agricultural experts are providing help and support.[34]

It goes without saying that the international liberation movement must take account of the international balance of power. It is easy to provoke a landing by US marines, but much more difficult to give no cause for such landings while steering a socialist course. The governments of the rich countries must be assured – a poor country that follows a socialist path needs good diplomats – that their interests are not being threatened, indeed that capitalist enterprises remain welcome under certain conditions. For a long time to come, the poor countries will still have to supply the highly developed countries with raw materials while continuing to rely on the rich countries for many things, technical expertise included. The presence of quite a few capitalist enterprises will prove indispensable during the development phase, for the expansion of production is something in which they excel. It needs no stressing that these enterprises will not be expected to work for nothing; however, they will have no political influence.

Without doubt, socialist Third World countries will try to play Western Europe and the United States off against the Soviet Union, but that is what capitalist Third World countries do as well. Thus Egypt in former times and Ghana today market their products in the Soviet Union in an attempt to strengthen their position *vis-à-vis* capitalist buyers. Deliveries to the Soviet Union and other developed socialist countries have a stabilising effect on world markets, and sometimes help to raise prices. The Soviet Union helps the poor countries by buying their exports at well above the market price (and by selling them below cost price). Cuba, in particular, derived considerable advantage from signing contracts to supply the Soviet Union with sugar at prices fixed for many years in advance, for one of the major problems of a poor country is the wide fluctuation in price of their exports.

The Soviet Union has provided free, and often considerable, development aid to countries following the socialist path (Cuba, North Korea, Vietnam, Mongolia and others), above all helping to speed up the process of industrialisation in these countries. The policy of speeding industrialisation is also applied in countries that have to pay for Soviet aid. In Africa, for instance, the Soviet Union supports many agricultural, infrastructural and other non-industrial projects, though the stress is on industry, and particularly on heavy industry, which is considered the basis of economic independence. Seventy per cent of the aid given by socialist countries goes to state-owned industrial concerns. Examples are the iron and steel industries in Algeria and Nigeria, the bauxite industry in Guinea, an atomic power station in Libya and hydroelectric power stations in Ethiopia and Angola. According to a Soviet official in an article written for the North American *Foreign Affairs* magazine, 40 per cent of the pig iron and 30 per cent of the steel produced in Africa and Asia comes from plants built with Soviet aid.[35]

Training local supervisors to manage these plants is another part of Soviet aid. The Soviet Union also gives military aid to socialist countries, in the case of Cuba free of charge, and in other cases at below cost. It is largely thanks to these contributions by the Soviet Union and other socialist countries that socialist systems have been able to emerge in the Third World and that they can maintain themselves.

**Foreign enterprise**

Foreign enterprise can assuredly benefit from the emergence of socialist regimes; indeed, experience has shown that they can do very good business with socialist governments. When Cheddi Jagan, a Marxist, was prime minister of Guyana, he negotiated numerous contracts with foreign industrial companies, which were given the right to set up local subsidiaries and to run them for a specified period. At the end of that period, by which time the foreign companies would have recovered their costs and made a decent profit, the industries were to become state property. Something similar happened in the Soviet Union, where shortly after the revolution, entire factories, expert staff, equipment and all, were imported. And this still happens today in the Soviet Union, just as it does in China. The government of Zimbabwe, too, has no objection to doing business with 'capitalists'. Prime Minister Mugabe confirmed this during an address he gave in the elegant Plaza Hotel in New York in which he welcomed US investors. Admittedly, he made some conditions: some state supervision would have to be accepted, trade unions allowed, decent wages paid and part of the profits invested in Zimbabwe.[36]

In the Third World, no less than in the First, it is important to force capitalist enterprises to change with the times and to appreciate the advantages of helping to raise the living standard of the great majority of the people in the Third World. At the moment their policy is largely guided by blind economic laws that direct them to establish themselves in countries with low wages and then to exploit the people. If they wish to make large profits and expand they have, indeed, no alternative at the moment, but if the balance of power in the world should change, these very enterprises will be able to play a useful role as development companies (with, of course, every chance of making a profit). Such a change in the balance of power is essential and will also benefit the rich capitalist countries. This view is shared by the US sociologist, Daniel Chirot, who believes that large companies and the bureaucratic elites in his country must realize that the further exploitation of the resources of the poor countries is not desirable and in the long run not even profitable.[37]

The change in the balance of power that will force capitalist enterprises to change tack must also take place in the rich countries, but it is only to be expected that changes in the Third World will tip the balance. The greater the number of poor countries that develop in an autochthonous way, that is, follow one socialist path or another, the more capitalist companies will be forced to change their policy and to become dispensers of development aid. Unquestionably, foreigners will initially suffer losses through social disruption, nationalisation, increased taxes, and so on, but thereafter the political and social stability and the economic growth of the socialist countries will offer foreign capital many new possibilities.

## World-wide prospects

We may take it that capitalism will be able to surmount its current crisis, which is not just a temporary slump but has fundamental (structural) causes. To that end, incisive changes on an international scale are necessary, for instance the emergence of authochthonous developments in the Third World which lead to an increase in international purchasing power and hence to the kind of growth that has brought so much prosperity to the rich countries.

As we saw in Chapter 5, production in the rich countries is stimulated by the high wage levels organised workers are able to wrest from the employers. High wages mean good markets for industrial products. In the rich countries there is a fairly favourable distribution between what workers (and other consumers) receive and what companies keep back for investment. The same situation can also arise in the international arena, but that will take time. Socialist systems will first have to spring up throughout the Third World. They will have to start by disengaging themselves as much as possible from the international capitalist economy, and it is not until later – when they have developed sufficiently – that they will be able to play their full part in the world economy under more favourable conditions. If this happens on a large scale, then there is every prospect of welfare for the whole of mankind, which will only be regretted by those in highly privileged positions today.

While the Third World proletariat takes the lead in the fight against imperialism, the labour movement in the rich countries will also have to play its part in hastening the process described above, and that in the workers' own interests as well. This calls for a shift in policy from the national to the international sphere, not least because the balance between labour and capital in the rich world is disturbed. The reason for this is that capital available for investment is used more and more for the acquisition of machinery that renders human labour redundant. While productivity increases, the number of workers decreases; moreover manufacturing work is increasingly being done in the poor countries, i.e. in countries paying low wages. Both factors contribute to unemployment in the rich countries. The transformations of the forces of production (through labour-saving machinery) do not go hand in hand with a change in productive relationships. Economic power remains in the hands of a small group of industrialists, while the state is increasingly at a loss how to protect the interests of the workers. The rich countries can still control the social consequences of technological expansion to some extent, but the time does not seem far off when mass unemployment will force people to think about solutions to their problems more seriously than they now do. Quite obviously, their thoughts will then turn to changes in the balance of power between capital and labour on an international scale and to increases in the purchasing power of the great majority of mankind. Working for these objectives will seem more promising than the path workers and employers pursue today. Chasing after the short-term interests of workers (by trade unions and some political parties) or employers (by the other political parties) must make way for a system that defends the general interest: the interest of the great majority throughout the world.

The defensive strategy currently in use by organised labour – job security and social security – is doomed to failure because of increasing automation and the exodus of industries to the Third World. Far greater prospects are offered by a world strategy based on international solidarity and opposition to the three powers that now dominate the world: multinational corporations, finance capital and the dependent bourgeoisie of the Third World. All three will only be prepared to replace a system based on self-interest with a more equitable one under the threat of force.

Once the peasants and workers of all countries are united in international organisation, then it should be possible to reconstruct the world economy into an instrument for the benefit of all mankind and into a guarantee of world peace.

# Notes and References

## Introduction

1. Kruijer (1973).
2. Onoge (1979, p.64).

## 1 Poverty

1. De Jesus (1960).
2. By 'North America' I shall be referring exclusively to the United States – in deference to the many Latin Americans who object to those who reserve the term 'America' for the United States.
3. I am thinking particularly of the studies of Mexico and Puerto Rico by the North American anthropologist, Oscar Lewis, whose 'culture of poverty' has many similarities to my 'pattern of poverty' (see note 6). I myself have made studies of poverty in Peru, Jamaica and Surinam.
4. In Surinam, one section of the poor, namely the 'East Indians', were involved in a successful emancipation struggle that inspired them with hope in a better future. As a reaction, the 'African' inhabitants made common cause as well. The Javanese who were largely indifferent to the emancipation of the 'East Indians' and who did little for their own emancipation (in 1969), were the most frustrated population group at the time.
5. Papanek (1975, pp.24ff) has shown that the income of the poor went up following their drift to the towns. Most of those who moved had had some education and an appreciable number had even been to secondary schools. Papanek comments (on p.2) on the absence of 'marginal and very low-income groups'.
6. Lewis's books contain few case histories. His *Five Families* gives a mere five; in another book (1961) he discusses one family in greater detail; and in yet another (1964) he deals with the life of a Mexican peasant family as told by three of its members. Finally, one large volume (1968) is devoted to a Puerto Rican family spread over five households. Not surprisingly, some writers doubt that so few people can paint a reliable picture of the life of the poor at large (Valentine 1971, p.195).

7. From a report by the Deputies of the General Diaconal Working Committee of the Reformed Churches in the Netherlands, 1975.
8. Ogundipe-Leslie (1984, pp.83ff).
9. Njoku (1980, p.51).
10. Fröbel (1977, p.529).
11. Rural Development and Women, etc. (1982, p.14).
12. Kruijer (1968).
13. Bromley and Gerry (1979, pp.12ff).
14. Banfield (1958, p.71).
15. Gutkind (1975, p.30).
16. Pechuël-Loesche (1907, p.21).
17. This proverb is meant as a warning that fame is exceedingly short-lived (information by H. U. E. Thoden van Velzen).
18. Rodgers (1976, pp.272ff).
19. Gutkind (1975, p.11).
20. Keur and Keur (1960, pp.245ff).
21. Desai (1961, pp.510ff).
22. *The New York Review of Books*, 19 March (1981, pp.38ff).
23. Young (1981, p.112). Kate Young is attached to the Institute of Development Studies, University of Essex, England.
24. This, roughly, is Merton's definition (1957) of anomie. My view of reactions to frustration is fairly close to Merton's description of 'deviant behaviour'.
25. Rural Development and Women, etc (1982, p.25).
26. Burns (1978).
27. Reynaud (1962, p.167).
28. Gaitskell (1959).
29. Hydén (1974, p.16).
30. Huizer (1963).
31. Gutkind (1975, p.15).
32. Shanin (1970, p.23).
33. Lloyd (1979, p.203).
34. Collin-Delavaud (1978, p.31).
35. Cronje (1979, p.77).
36. Breman (1979, p.733).
37. This emerges from a report by the NAR (National Advisory Board for Development Cooperation of the Netherlands Ministry of Development Cooperation).
38. Profiles (1979, p.1).
39. Profiles (1979, p.44).
40. Ahluwalia (1974, p.19).

## 2 Liberation Science

1. Kruijer (1973).
2. Mukherji (1985, p.280).

3. We distinguish between general and working definitions. The latter tell us what data must be collected to discover the characteristics entailed in the general definitions. A working hypothesis must be framed in operational terms (that is, based on observable phenomena).
4. Even if the progressive forces are weak, they can act in a dialectical spirit, particularly by helping to sharpen contradictions.
5. Galtung (1977).
6. I have consulted Horton and Leslie (1955), Smigel (1971) and Timms (1967) among many others.
7. Mills (1963, pp.525ff).
8. Fei and Chang (1945, p.17).
9. Lukes (1979, p.678) says that any given interpretation or conception of power is 'inextricably tied to further assumptions which are methodological and epistemological, but also moral and political . . .'
10. One concept is more abstract than another if it has a smaller number of characteristics and covers a larger number of objects. In my view, most definitions of power are much too broad and general.
11. Senior (1958, p.66).
12. Siy (1982, p.155).
13. Bartlema and Kortenray (1977, p.4).
14. Utrecht (1973).
15. The exaggerated emphasis of class contradictions and the denial of ethnic and religious differences are just as mistaken. In my book on Surinam (Kruijer 1973) I have tried to avoid this trap.
16. NAR, see note 37 to Chapter 1.
17. Freire (1972).
18. Stavenhagen (1971). De Schutter, a Dutchman attached to CREFAL (Mexico), also speaks of 'investigación participativa'.
19. Tarp (1982, p.33).
20. Hoogvelt (1982, pp.211ff).

## 3   The Poverty-and-Wealth System

1. Sharma (1985, pp.83ff).
2. Ahmad (1977, p.128).
3. Kruijer (1975).
4. Lefort (1978, p.52).

## 4   The National Poverty-and-Wealth System

1. Coquery-Vidrovitch (1980, p.33) found this to be the case in Africa. Cf. Harwood (1979, pp.11ff).
2. Wolf, too, gives a political definition. According to him, peasants produce crops, etc., the surpluses (that is, a proportion of the

earnings or profits) from which are handed over to a dominant group who use these surpluses to raise their own standard of living or distribute them amongst those social groups that supply them with goods and services (Wolf 1996, pp.3ff).

3. Jazani (1980, pp.100ff).
4. Streefkerk (1985, pp.245ff). Streefkerk, a social anthropologist, is associated with the University of Amsterdam.
5. Onimode (1982, pp.125ff).
6. Babu (1981, p.4).
7. Kiamenga (1980, p.79).
8. Selbourne (1979, p.20) Arief and Sasono (1981).
9. Douglass (1984, pp.97 and 69).
10. Hoogvelt (1978, p.4).
11. Surplus value is the amount an employer gains from a worker's labour. Assume an employer supplies the worker with raw materials, electricity, etc. (including support by non-productive workers) to the tune of £10, and that he can sell the finished product for £15. If he pays the workers £3, then the surplus value is £2.
12. Van Gelder (1984, p.10).
13. Kruijer (1973, p.163).
14. Streefkerk (1985, p.249).
15. Onimode (1982, p.199).
16. Tibi (1973, pp.78ff).
17. Finer (1975).
18. Onimode (1982, pp.125ff) Cabral (1974, p.245) Babu (1981, pp.2ff).
19. Babu (1981, p.3).
20. Jazani (1980, pp.78ff).
21. Frank (1972, p.5).
22. Mamdani (1983, p.103).
23. Arief and Sasono (1981, p.165).
24. Nelson (1950, p.160).
25. Onimode (1982, pp.223ff).
26. Mies (1982).
27. Pambou (1982, pp.147ff).
28. Scott (1976, p.239).
29. Similar ideas can be found in Kielstra (1975, pp.168ff).
30. Gutiérrez (1973, pp.11ff).
31. 'They provide harmless channels for the dispersal of individual discontent' 'Thus, in a complex and subtle manner, radical, reformation or avant-garde groups may serve as a third line of defense against actual social change' (La Pierre 1965, p.358).

## 5 The International Poverty-and-Wealth System

1. Information provided by the president of the Movement of Non-Aligned Countries (*Granma*, Resumen Semanal, May 10, 1981, p.6).

2. By my definition, the Soviet occupation of Afghanistan was not an imperialist act but one of military and political domination.
3. Arief and Sasono (1981, p.155).
4. Survey of Current Business (1980).
5. World Development (1985, p.2).
6. Officially, the IMF exists to promote international monetary cooperation and the expansion of international trade.
7. These are called no-tariff barriers (NTBs). They refer to 'voluntary' export restraints, orderly marketing arrangements, antidumping measures, countervailing duties, safeguard codes, and so on (Salvatore 1985, pp.1ff).
8. Because of the growing tendency of industrialised states to regulate the market, the modern system has been given the paradoxical name of 'managed free trade'.
9. World Development, etc., (1985, p.23).
10. Hoogvelt (1978, p.82), quoting McMichael *et al.* (1974, p.99).
11. Ho (1984, p.138).
12. Bairoch (1977, pp.197ff).
13. Amin (1976, p.144).
14. If the reader feels this is too improbable a situation, he might prefer to think of a North American drinking coffee. The argument is precisely the same. The production figures that follow are taken from Andreae (1971). On the table printed on p.203 of his article we can see that Thai peasants (with from 0.75 to 4.00 ha of land) invest from 600 to 1200 hours of labour per hectare, while large-scale rice growers in California and Arkansas put in 20–30 hours of labour per hectare. The respective yields in Thailand and the USA are 1.68 and 4.96 tons per hectare.
15. The brain-drain is offset to some extent by the education and training the rich countries provide, free of charge or at very low fees, for students from the Third World.
16. Amin (1984, p.vii).
17. Shoup and Minter (1977, pp.117–76).
18. Barongo (1980, p.39) Barongo is a political scientist from Uganda. Andrew Webster (1984, p.79) points out that neocolonialism was first examined in detail by Nkrumah, President of Ghana in the early 1960s.
19. Umozurike (1979, p.127).
20. Trade Act Development Report (1983, p.52). Also referred to by Nayyar (1983) of the Indian Institute of Management in Calcutta.
21. De Castro (1984, pp.15ff).
22. Hoogvelt (1984, p.57).
23. Hoogvelt (1978, p.4).
24. Hoogvelt (1982, p.3).
25. Vernon (1974, quoted in Lall 1983, p.41).
26. Amin (1976).
27. Jo (1976, pp.90ff).
28. Kim (1980, p.4).

29. Kim (1980, p.1).
30. Senghaas (1983, p.8).
31. *Time*, 11 November 1978.
32. Pronk (1972).
33. Babu (1981, p.45).
34. Trade and Development Report (1983, p.105).
35. M'buyinga (1982, p.186).
36. Organisation of Economic Cooperation and Development, Paris; European Monetary System; International Monetary Fund, Washington. The World Bank in Washington is officially known as the International Bank for Reconstruction and Development.
37. Clairmonte and Cavanagh (1984, p.271) point out that the new technologies introduced into the Third World by the big transnational corporations are responsible for the rapid spread of western consumption patterns and style of life and implicitly suggest the desirability of a capitalist economic and social order.
38. Dominguez and Huntington (1984, p.4). In 1979, more than 53 500 US and Canadian overseas (Protestant) missionaries were working with agencies that grossed nearly $1.2 billion dollars in income. These figures do not include 30 300 Mormons and 100 Jehovah's Witnesses (ibid, 1984, p.3).

## 6 Liberation Theory

1. Rostow (1960).
2. Mariátegui (1928).
3. This summary of the two types of theory is taken from Hoogvelt (1982).

## 7 The Liberation Struggle

1. Barrett (1979, p.32).
2. Barrett (1979, p.xiii).
3. During the First Conference of the Peoples of Asia, Africa and Latin America held in Havana on 3–14 January, 1966.
4. Frank (1980, p.424).
5. M'buyinga (1982, p.5).
6. Kende (1978).
7. Kende (1978).
8. Scott (1976, p.4).
9. Scott (1976, p.229).
10. Shanin (1970) presents a similar view.
11. Pomeroy (1970, p.262).
12. Carrier (1976, p.126).

13. The liberation struggle in Guinea-Bissau was supported by urban intellectuals and semi-intellectuals, as well as by dockers and urban youth without skills or fixed employment (Chaliand 1977, p.76).

14. Skocpol (1982, p.159).

15. Scott (1977, p.291).

16. Kruyt and Vellinga (1975, pp.287ff).

17. Zeitlin (1967).

18. Zeitlin (1967, p.97).

19. Smilg Benario (1928 and 1929).

20. Mowoe (1980, p.154).

21. *Time*, 16 March 1962.

22. Thomas (1971, p.1477).

23. Though it may be ideologically mistaken to stress the ethnic origins of Cuban soldiers, centuries of oppression by white rulers persuade one to do so. It is equally mistaken to give the impression that the Cuban army consists of exclusively of blacks. This fact is nevertheless stressed because the myth created round Cuban intervention hinges on it, helps to expand political consciousness, and hence reinforces the liberation struggle.

24. Laïdi (1979, p.96).

25. Rural Development and Women in Asia (1982, p.38).

26. Njoku (1980, p.6).

27. Mba (1982, p.91).

28. Reddock (1984, pp.673ff).

29. Rowbotham (1975, pp.233–244).

30. Basil Davidson, quoted by Njoku (1980, p.6).

31. Bujra (1978, p.41).

32. Mba (1982, pp.234 and 301).

33. Fanon (1961).

34. Freire (1972).

35. Drysdale and Myers (1975, p.262).

36. From the 'Social, Political and Ethical Declaration' of Siqueiros and his group, published in 1922 (Siqueiros 1975).

37. Hussain (1985, pp.204ff).

38. Chaliand (1977, p.46).

39. Udechuku (1978, pp.119ff).

40. Skubiszewski (1968, p.816).

41. Hyams (1975, p.186).

42. Laqueur (1977, p.79).

43. Hyams (1975, p.171).

44. In the text, I have set out the tactical principles, but I have to admit that matters sometimes turn out differently in practice: groups of workers can successfully oppose the wishes of the party leadership. Spontaneity cannot be entirely prevented and may have favourable results.

45. Klare (1972, p.44) defines counter-insurgency as the military, paramilitary, political, economic, psychological and civil actions launched by a government to suppress revolutionary uprisings.

46. Barnet (1972, pp.76–95).
47. Klare (1981, pp.36ff).
48. Wolpin (1972, pp.61ff).
49. Eckhardt and Young (1977, p.71).
50. Hilsman (1962, pp.455ff).
51. Rostow (1962, p.470).
52. Rostow (1962, p.470).
53. Yansané (1980, p.289).
54. Chaliand (1978, p.37).
55. Yansané (1980, p.27).
56. Yansané (1980, p.28).
57. Chaliand (1977, p.28).
58. Islam and Revolution (1981, pp.341f). For the important role of the religious leaders, see Hussain (1985, pp.204ff).
59. Cf. Gromyko (1983[a] and 1983[b]) (Gromyko is director of the Africa Institute of the Soviet Academy of Sciences.)
60. Chirot (1977, p.144).
61. Chirot (1977, p.139) reports that illiteracy decreased within forty years from 77 per cent to 43 per cent; during the same period the proportion of poor people dropped from 57 per cent to 39 per cent.
62. Chirot (1977, pp.137ff).
63. Kurian (1979, p.46).
64. Gann and Henriksen (1981, p.119).

## 8 Development Strategy: General Aspects

1. Karpat (1985, p.6).
2. Mazrui (1983, p.144).
3. Employment, Growth and Basic Needs (1977).
4. Doh Joon-Chien (1980, pp.128ff).
5. Amin (1984, pp.xx and xviii).
6. Etzioni (1968, p.388).
7. Etzioni (1968, pp.389 and 406).
8. I prefer the term 'pseudo-autocratic' because it makes all the difference whether an autocrat serves his own interests and that of a small group or if he heeds the interests of the great majority. In the last case, 'pseudo-autocracy' strikes me as being the more correct description.
9. Less suited to stimulating national exertion is another system distinguished by Apter, namely the reconciliation system. It involves compromises between various groups of interest; private initiative plays an important role in it and as a consequence political as well as economic power is more widely spread (Apter 1965).
10. Tunisia could also boast various other organisations interested in social change, including particularly the General Union of Tunisian Workers, the National Union of Tunisian Peasants, the National

Union of Tunisian Women, the General Union of Tunisian Students, the Tunisian Scout Movement, all of them with links to the Neo-Destour Party (Halpern, 1963, p.299).

11. Behrendt (1965, p.537).
12. M'buyinga (1982. p.170).
13. Amin (1984, p.xviii).
14. Amin (1984, p.xxi).
15. Amin (1976, p.230).
16. Schumacher (1974, p.169).
17. Desai (1961, pp.683 and 486).
18. Bharadwaj (1985, p.20) mentions a scheme to help peasant farmers in Uttar Pradesh which was used by well-to-do farmers to gain credit and other concessions under false pretences. Peasant farmers who joined the scheme were caught in a debt trap and became pawns in the hands of those who bought and paid for the milk the peasants produced. Kandoke (1985, p.189) contends that the decline of agriculture in Zaire will only be halted when the peasants gain political power.
19. Cabral (1974, p.246).
20. Davidson, quoted in Gutkind and Waterman (1977, pp.262ff).
21. Islam and Revolution (1981, p.295).
22. Sékou Touré (1979, pp.439 and 441).
23. Sinyakov (1984).
24. Trade and Development Report (1983, p.43).
25. Trade and Development Report (1983, p.105).
26. Lall (1985, p.1).
27. M'buyinga (1982, p.170).
28. Amin (1983, pp.58ff).
29. Kem (1985, p.189).
30. Mills (1978, p.66).
31. Stepan (1978, p.45).

## 9  Socialist Strategies

1. Hoogvelt (1978, p.164).
2. Carrier (1976, p.145).
3. Van Ness and Raichur (1983, pp.2ff).
4. Gray (see Gray and White) (1982, p.299).
5. White (see Gray and White) (1982).
6. White (see Gray and White) (1982, pp.9ff).
7. Van Ness and Raichur (1983, pp.2ff).
8. *Granma*, Resumen Semanal, 31 May 1981.
9. Breuer (1973, p.79).
10. Masuch (1981, pp.170–82).
11. Valdés (1976, pp.25ff).
12. Davidson (1980, pp.79–81).

13. For the People's Democracy of Libya, see Wright (n.d.) and El Fathaly and Palmer (1980).
14. Randall (1981, pp.45ff).
15. Croll (1978, p.59).
16. Rowbotham (1975, p.247).
17. Matthews (1975, p.361).
18. This enormous campaign ended in a fiasco. The target of ten million tons of sugar was not attained and the economy was dislocated as a result of the one-sided concentration on just one crop.
19. Huberman and Sweezy (1969, p.215).
20. In May 1970, Castro advocated greater say for the trade union movement and shortly after his address a beginning was made with *Poder Popular* – People's Power.
21. Kuitenbrouwer (1975, p.32).
22. *Time*, 23 October 1978.
23. Carrier (1976, pp.106ff).
24. Srivastava (1982, p.95).
25. Suh (1983, p.167).
26. Carrier (1976, p.169).
27. Kurian (1979, p.778).
28. Ky-Hyuk Pak (1983).
29. Chandra (1983, p.41).
30. Matthews (1975, pp.334ff).
31. Mestiri (1980, p.68).
32. Moreira and Bissio (1979, pp.6ff) give a journalistic view of this work.
33. Yansané (1980, p.29).
34. Fidel Castro in an address reprinted in *Granma*, Resumen Semanal, 1 November 1981, pp.4ff.
35. Trofimenko (1981, p.1033).
36. *Time*, 8 November 1980, p.38.
37. Chirot (1977, pp.249 and 252).

# Bibliography

Adelman, Irma (1977) *Redistribution before Growth: A Strategy for Developing Countries* (The Hague: Institute of Social Studies, 25th Anniversary Conference, 16–20 December).

Ahluwalia, Montek S. (1974) 'Income Inequality: Some Dimensions of the Problem', Chenery, Hillis *et al.* (1974), pp.3ff.

Ahmad, Saghir (1977) *Class and Power in a Punjab Village* (New York: Monthly Review Press).

Amin, G. A. (1983) 'Economic and Cultural Dependence', in Talal Asad and Roger Owen (eds), *Sociology of 'Developing Societies': The Middle East* (London: Macmillan) pp.54ff.

Amin, Samir (1976) *Unequal Development* (New York: Monthly Review Press).

Amin, Samir (1984) 'Introduction', in *Human Resources, Employment and Development, vol. 5, Developing Countries* (London: International Economic Association) pp.viiff.

Andreae, Bernd (1971) 'Formen des Reisanbaus im Internationalen Vergleich', *Zeitschrift für Ausländische Landwirtschaft* (July–September) pp.194ff.

Apter, David (1965) *The Politics of Modernization* (Chicago: University of Chicago Press).

Arief, Sritua and Adi Sasono (1981) *Indonesia: Dependency and Underdevelopment* (Kuala Lumpur: Meta).

Babu, Abdul Rahman Mohamed (1981) *African Socialism or Socialist Africa?* (London: Zed Press).

Bairoch, Paul (1977) *The Economic Development of the Third World Since 1900* (London: Methuen & Co. Ltd.).

Banfield, Edward C. (1958) *The Moral Basis of a Backward Society* (Glencoe: The Free Press).

Barnet, Richard J. (1972) *Intervention and Revolution* (New York, The World Publishing Company).

Barongo, Yolamu R. (1980) *Neocolonialism and African Politics* (New York: Ventage Press).

Barrett, Leonard E. (1979) *The Rastafarians* (London: Heinemann).

Bartlema, Rob and Johan Kortenray (1977) 'De Gedrevenheid van een Bescheiden Revolutionair (The Impulsion of a Modest Revolutionary)', *Folia Civitatis* (weekly of the University of Amsterdam), (24 December) pp.3ff.

242

Behrendt, Richard F. (1965) *Soziale Strategie für Entwicklungsländer* (Frankfurt am Main: Fischer Verlag).

Bharadwaj, Krishna (1985) 'A View on Commercialisation in Indian Agriculture and the Development of Capitalism', *The Journal of Peasant Studies*, vol. 12, no. 4 pp.8ff.

Brecht, Arnold (1961) *Politische Theorie* (Tübingen: Mohr).

Breman, J. (1979) 'Ruraal Beleid in India (Rural Policy in India)', *Internationale Spectator (The Hague)*, December) pp.726ff.

Breuer, Wilhelm M. (1973) *Sozialismus in Kuba: Zur Politischen Ökonomie* (Köln: Pahl-Rugenstein Verlag).

Bromley, Ray and Chris Gerry (1979) *Casual Work and Poverty in Third World Cities* (Chichester: Wiley).

Bujra, Janet M. (1978) 'Female Solidarity & the Sexual Division of Labour', in Caplan and Bujra.

Burns, John F. (1978) 'Apartheid Veroorzaakt Omvangrijke Misdaad (Apartheid Causes Wide-Scale Criminality)', *Volkskrant* (a Dutch newspaper), (1 August) p.8.

Cabral, Amilcar (1974) 'The Role of Culture in the Struggle for Independence', *The Ecologist*, vol. 4, no. 7, pp.244ff.

Caplan, Patricia and J. M. Bujra (1978) *Women United, Women Divided* (London: Tavistock).

Carrier, Fred J. (1976) *The Third World Revolution* (Amsterdam: Grüner).

Chalian, Gérard (1977) *Revolution in the Third World* (Hassocks, Sussex: The Harvester Press).

Chandra, N. K. (1983) 'The Concept of Development in the Context of the New International Economic Order', in *The New International Economic Order: Problems and Perspectives* (New Delhi: Indian Council of Social Science Research).

Chenery, Hollis *et al.* (1974) *Redistribution with Growth* (London: Oxford University Press).

Chirot, Daniel (1977) *Social Change in the Twentieth Century* (New York: Harcourt Brace Jovanovich).

Clairmonte, Frederick F. and John H. Cavanagh (1984) 'Transnational Corporations and Services, the Final Frontier', *Trade and Development, an UNCTAD Review*, no. 5, pp.1ff.

Collin-Delavaud, Claude (1978) 'L'Evolution du Régime Militarie Péruvien (1975–77)', *Problèmes d'Amerique Latine*, (February) pp.9ff.

Coquery-Vidrovitch, Catherine (1980) 'Les Paysans Africains: Permanences et Mutations', *Sociétés Paysannes du Tiers Monde*, pp.25ff.

Croll, Elisabeth (1978) 'Rural China: From Segregation to Solidarity', in Caplan and Bujra, pp.46ff.

Cronje, Gillian and S. Cronje (1979) *The Workers of Namibia* (London: International Defence and Aid Fund for Southern Africa).

Davidson, Basil (1980) 'The Revolution of People's Power: Notes on Mozambique', *Monthly Review*, pp.75ff.

Debray, Jules Régis, (1967) *Révolution dans la Révolution?* (Paris: Maspero).

Debray, Régis (1977) *La Critique des Armes* (Paris: Le Seuil).

De Castro, Juan *et al.* (1984) 'Changes in International Economic Relations in the Last Two Decades', *Trade and Development, an UNCTAD Review*, no. 5, pp.1ff.

De Jesus, Carolina Maria (1960) *Quarto de Despejo: Diario de una Favelada* (São Paulo: De Azeve do Ltda.).

Desai, A. R. (1961) *Rural Sociology in India*, 4th ed. (Bombay: The Indian Society of Agricultural Economics).

De Schutter, Anton (1981) *Investigación Participativa* (Pátzcuaro, Mexico: CREFAL).

Doh Joon-Chien (1980) *Eastern Intellectuals and Western Solutions: Follower Syndrome in Asia* (New Delhi: Vikas Publishing House).

Dominguez, Enrique and Deborah Huntington (1984), 'The Salvation Brokers: Conservative Evangelicals in Central America', *Nacla, Report on the Americas*, XVIII, no. 1.

Douglass, Mike (1984) *Regional Integration on the Capitalist Periphery: The Central Plains of Thailand* (The Hague: Institute of Social Studies).

Drysdale, Robert S. and Robert G. Myers (1975) 'Continuity and Change: Peruvian Education', in Abraham F. Lowenthal (ed.), *The Peruvian Experiment* (New Jersey: Princeton University Press) pp.254ff.

Eckhardt, W. and C. Young (1977) *Governments under Fire* (New Haven: HRAF Press).

El Fathaly, Omar I. and Monte Palmer (1980) *Political Development and Social Change in Libya* (Massachusetts: Lexington Books).

*Employment, Growth and Basic Needs: A One-World Problem* (1977) (Geneva: International Labour Office).

Etzioni, Amitai (1968) *The Active Society* (London: Collier-Macmillan).

Falkowski, Mieczyslaw (1968) *Les Problèmes de la Croissance du Tiers Monde* (Paris: Payot).

Fanon, Frantz (1961) *Les Damnés de la Terre* (Paris: Maspero).

Fei, Hsiao-tung and Chih-i Chang (1945) *Earth Bound China* (Chicago: University of Chicago Press).

Figueroa, Adolfo (1984) *Capitalist Development and the Peasant Economy in Peru* (Cambridge: Cambridge University Press).

Finer, S. E. (1975) *The Man on Horseback: The Role of the Military in Politics* (London: Pall Mall Press).

Frank, André Gunder (1972) *Lumpenbourgeoisie: Lumpendevelopment* (New York: Monthly Review Press).

Frank, André Gunder (1980) 'L'Ennemi Immédiat', in Michael Lowy, *Le Marxisme en Amérique Latine de 1909 à nos Jours* (Paris: Maspero) pp.423ff.

Freire Paulo (1972) *Pedagogy of the Oppressed* (New York: Herder and Herder).

Fröbel, Folker *et al.* (1977) *die Neue Internationale Arbeitsteilung,*

*Strukturelle Arbeitslosigkeit in den Industrieländern und die Industrialisierung der Entwicklungsländer* (Hamburg: Rohwolt Verlag).

Gaitskell, Arthur (1959) *Gezira: A Story of Development in the Sudan* (London: Faber and Faber).

Galtung, Johan (1970) 'Feudal Systems, Structural Violence and the Structural Theory of Revolutions', *Proceedings of the International Peace Research Institute*, Third General Conference, part I (Oslo) pp.110ff.

Galtung, Johan (1977) *Methodology and Ideology*, vol. I (Copenhagen: Christian Ejlers).

Galtung, Johan (1978) 'Eine Strukturelle Theorie des Imperialismus', in Dieter Senghaas (ed.), *Imperialismus und Strukturelle Gewalt* (Frankfurt am Main: Suhrkamp Verlag).

Gann, Lewis H. and Thomas H. Henriksen (1981) *The Struggle for Zimbabwe* (New York: Praeger).

Gray, Jack and Gordon White (1982) *China's New Development Strategy* (London: Academic Press).

Gromyko, Anatoly (1983a) *Africa – Progress, Problems, Prospects* (Moscow: Progress Publishers).

Gromyko, Anatoly (ed.) (1983b) *The October Revolution and Africa* (Moscow: Progress Publishers).

Guevara, Ernesto Che (1961) *La Guerra de Guerrilla* (Havana).

Gutiérrez, Gustavo (1973) *A Theology of Liberation* (New York: Maryknoll).

Gutkind, Peter C. W. (1975) 'The View from Below: Political Consciousness of the Urban Poor in Ibadan', *Cahiers d'Etudes Africaines* pp.5ff.

Gutkind, Peter C. W. and Peter Waterman (eds) (1977) *African Social Studies: A Radical Reader* (London: Heinemann).

Halpern, Manfred (1963) *The Politics of Social Change in the Middle East and North Africa* (Princeton: Princeton University Press).

Harwood, Richard R. (1979) *Small Farm Development* (Boulder: Westview Press).

Hilsman, Roger (1962) 'Internal War: The New Communist Tactic', in F. M. Osanka (ed.), *Modern Guerrilla Warfare* (New York: Free Press).

Ho dac Tuong (1984) 'Developing Countries Fast Growing Exporters of Manufactures', *Trade and Development, an UNCTAD Review* pp.121ff.

Hoogvelt, Ankie M. M. (1978) *The Sociology of Developing Societies*, 2nd ed. (London: Macmillan).

Hoogvelt, Ankie M. M. (1982) *The Third World in Global Development* (London: Macmillan).

Horton, Paul B. and Gerald R. Leslie (1955) *The Sociology of Social Problems* (New York: Appleton-Century-Crofts).

Huberman, Leo and Paul M. Sweezy (1969) *Socialism in Cuba* (New York: Monthly Review Press).

Huizer, Gerrit (1963) 'Some Observations in a Central American Village', *América Indígena*, XXIII, no. 3 (July) pp.211ff.

Huizer, Gerrit and Bruce Mannheim (eds) (1979) *The Politics of Anthropology: From Colonialism and Sexism Toward a View from Below* (The Hague: Mouton).

Hussain, Asaf (1985) *Islamic Iran: Revolution and Counter-Revolution* (London: Frances Pinter).

Hyams, Edward (1975) *Terrorists and Terrorism* (London: J. M. Dent & Sons Ltd.).

Hydén, Göran (1974) *Political Development in Rural Tanzania* (Nairobi: East African Publishing House).

*Islam and Revolution: Writings and Declarations of Iman Khomeini* (1981) (Berkeley: Mizan Press).

Jazani, Bizhan (1980) *Capitalism and Revolution in Iran* (London: Zed Press).

Jo Sung-Hwan (1976) *The Impact of Multinational Firms on Employment and Incomes: The Case of South Korea* (Geneva: International Labour Office).

Kameir, El-Wathig and Ibrahim Kursany (1985) *Corruption as a 'Fifth' Factor of Production in the Sudan* (Uppsala: The Scandinavian Institute of African Studies).

Kankode, Mukadi (1985) *Approches d'Analyse Economique des Projets Agricoles de Développement Rural dans les Pays en Voie de Développement: le Cas du Zaïre* (Brussels: Les Cahiers du Cedaf).

Karpat, Kemal H. (1985) 'Introduction, Opening Remarks', *Central Asian Survey*, vol. 3, no. 3 (special issue 'Focus on Central Asian Identity') pp.3ff.

Kem, Maurice C. (1985) *Der Weltmarkt für Kakao unter Besonderer Berücksichtigung der Position Nigerias* (Frankfurt am Main: Peter Lang).

Kende, Istvan (1978) 'Wars of Ten Years (1967–1976)', *Journal of Peace Research*, vol. XV, no. 3 pp.227ff.

Keur, John Y. and Dorothy L. Keur (1960) *Windward Children: a Study in Human Ecology of the Three Dutch Windward Islands in the Caribbean* (Assen: Royal Van Gorcum).

Kiamenga, François (1980) 'Un Village au Zaïre: Makuta', *Société's Paysannes du Tiers Monde*, pp.67ff.

Kielstra, Nicolaas Onno (1975) *Ecology and Community in Iran* (Amsterdam: Ph.D. dissertation University of Amsterdam).

Kim, Phyllis (1980) 'Saemaul Agriculture', *Ampo: Japan-Asia Quarterly Review*, vol. 12, no. 1 and 3, pp.2ff. and 56ff.

Klare, M. T. (1972) *War without End: American Planning for the Next Vietnams* (New York: Vintage Books).

Klare, M. T. (1981) *Supplying Repression: U.S. Support for Authoritarian Regimes Abroad* (Washington: Institute for Policy Studies).

Kruijer, G. J. (1968) *Jamaica's Social Problems: a Report Indicating a Way Out* (The Hague: Directorate for International Technical Assistance, Ministry of Foreign Affairs of the Netherlands).

Kruijer, G. J. (1969) *Sociological Report on the Christiana Area: A*

*Sociologist's Contribution to Extension Work in Rural Jamaica*, 3rd ed. (Kingston: The Agricultural Information Service).

Kruijer, G. J. (1973) *Suriname: Neokolonie in Rijksverband* (Surinam: Neocolony within the Realm of the Netherlands Kingdom) (Meppel: Boom).

Kruijer, G. J. (1975) 'Aspectos Sociológicos' in *Rehabilitación de la Industria del Té en El Perú* (The Hague: Ministry of Foreign Affairs, Directorate of International Technical Assistance).

Kruyt, Dirk and Menno Vellinga (1975) *Arbeidsrelaties en Multinationale Onderneming: de Cerro de Pasco Corporation Peru (1902–1973)* (Labour Relations and Multinational Corporation) (Utrecht: Sociological Institute, University of Utrecht).

Kuitenbrouwer, J. B. W. (1975) *Towards Self-Reliant Integrated Development* (The Hague: Institute of Sociale Studies).

Kurian, George Thomas (1979) *Encyclopedia of the Third World* (London: Mansell).

Ky-Hyuk Pak (1983) 'Agricultural Policy and Development in North Korea', in Robert E. Scalapino and Jun-Yop Kim (eds), *North Korea Today: Strategic and Domestic Issues* (Berkeley: University of California).

Laïdi, Zaki (1979) 'Les Grandes Puissances et l'Afrique', *Cahiers du C.H.E.A.M.*, no. 7 (Paris).

Lall, Sanjaya (1983) *The Multinational Corporation* (London: Macmillan).

Lall, Sanjaya (1985) 'Trade Between Developing Countries', *Trade and Development, an UNCTAD Review*, no. 6 pp.1ff.

La Pierre, Richard T. (1965) *Social Change* (New York: McGraw-Hill).

Laqueur, Walter (1977) *Terrorism* (Boston: Little, Brown and Company).

Leacock, Eleanor Burke (ed.) (1971) *The Culture of Poverty* (New York: Simon and Schuster).

Lefort, René (1978) 'Guermano Galatu: Paysan Ethiopien', *Le Nouvel Observateur*, (11 March) pp.51ff.

Lehberger, Kurt (1983) *Die Arbeits- und Lebensbedingungen in Südkorea in der Phase der Exportorientierten Industrialisierung (1965–1980)* (Saarbrücken: Breitenbach Publishers).

Lewis, Oscar (1962) *Five Families* (New York: Science Editions Inc.).

Lewis, Oscar (1961) *The Children of Sánchez* (New York: Random House).

Lewis, Oscar (1964) *Pedro Martínez* (New York: Random House).

Lewis, Oscar (1968) *La Vida* (London: Panther Modern Society).

Lloyd, Peter (1974) *Slums of Hope? Shanty Towns of the Third World* (Harmondsworth: Penguin Books).

Lukes, Steven (1979) 'On the Relativity of Power', *Amsterdams Sociologisch Tijdschrift* (University of Amsterdam: March) pp.677ff.

Mamdani, Mahmood (1983) *Imperialism and Fascism in Uganda* (Nairobi: Heinemann).

Mannheim, Karl (1940) *Man and Society in an Age of Reconstruction* (London: Kegan Paul, Trench, Trubner & Co.).

Mariátegui, José Carlos (1972) *7 Ensayos de Interpretación de la Realidad Peruana* (Lima: Biblioteca Amauta, 1st ed. 1928).

Masuch, Michael (1981) *Kritiek der Planung* (Darmstadt and Neuwied: Luchterhand).

Matthews, Herbert L. (1975) *Revolution in Cuba* (New York: Charles Scribner's Sons).

Mazrui, Ali A. (1981) *The African Condition* (London: Heinemann).

Mazrui, Ali A. (1983) 'Exit Visa from the World System: Dilemmas of Cultural and Economic Disengagement', in Altaf Gauhar (ed.), *Third World Strategy: Economic and Political Cohesion in the South* (New York: Praeger Studies) pp.134ff.

Mba, Nina Emma (1982) *Nigerian Women Mobilised* (Berkeley: University of California Institute of International Studies).

M'buyinga, Elenga (1982) *Pan Africanism or Neo-Colonialism? The Bankruptcy of the O.A.U.* (London: Zed Press).

McMichael, P. *et al.* (1974) 'Industry in the Third World', *New Left Review*, (May–June).

Merton, Robert K. (1957) *Social Theory and Social Structure* (Glencoe: The Free Press).

Mestiri, Ezzedine (1980) *Les Cubains et l'Afrique* (Paris: Editions Karthala).

Mies, Maria (1982) *The Lace makers of Narsapur: Indian Housewives Produce for the World Market* (London: Zed Press).

Mills, C. Wright (1963) *Power, Politics and People* (New York: Ballantine Books).

Mills, Don (1973) 'The North-South Dialogue: Background and Present Position', in Antony J. Dolan and Jan van Ettinger (eds), *Partners in Tomorrow: Strategies for a New International Order* (New York: A Sunrise Book E. P. Dutton) pp.61ff.

Moreira, Neiva and Beatriz Bissio (1979) 'The Cubans in Africa', *Third World 1* (Mexico) pp.6ff.

Mowoe, Isaac James (ed.) (1980) *The Performance of Soldiers as Governors: African Politics and the African Military* (Washington: University Press of America).

Mukherji, Shekhar (1985) 'The Syndrome of Poverty and Wage Labour Circulation: the Indian Scene', in R. Mansell Prothero and Murray Chapman (eds), *Circulation in Third World Countries* (London: Routledge & Kegan Paul) pp.279ff.

Nayyar, Delpak (1983) 'South—South Trade: Trends, Problems and Prospects', in Chandra *The New International Economic Order: Problems and Perspectives*.

Nelson, Lowry (1950) *Rural Cuba* (Minneapolis: University of Minnesota Press).

Njoku, John E. Eberegbulam (1980) *The World of the African Woman* (London: The Scarecrow Press).

Ogundipe-Leslie, Molara (1984) 'African Women, Culture and Another Development', *Journal of African Marxists*, (February) pp.77ff.

Onimode, Bade (1982) *Imperialism and Underdevelopment in Nigeria* (London: Zed Press).

Onoge, Omafume F. (1979) 'The Counterrevolutionary Tradition in African Studies: the Case of Applied Anthropology', in Huizer and Mannheim, *The Politics of Anthropology*, pp.45ff.

Pambou Tchivounda, Guillaume (1982) *Essai sur l'Etat Africain Postcolonial* (Paris: Librairie Générale de Droit et de Jurisprudence).

Papanek, Gustav F. (1975) 'The Poor of Jakarta', *Economic Development and Cultural Change*, pp.1ff.

Pechuël-Loesche, E. (1907) *Volkskunde von Loango* (Stuttgart: Verlag von Strecker & Schröder).

Pomeroy, William J. (ed.) (1970) *Guerrilla Warfare and Marxism* (New York: International Publishers).

*Profiles of Rural Poverty* (1979) (Geneva: International Labour Office).

Pronk, J. P. (1972) 'Geen Vierde UNCTAD Meer! (No More Fourth UNCTAD!)', Pronk interviewed by Max Arian, *De Groene Amsterdammer* (an Amsterdam weekly), (6/12 June) p.3.

Randall, Margaret (1931) *Women in Cuba: Twenty Years Later* (New York: Smyrna Press).

Reddock, Rhoda Elizabeth (1984) *Women, Labour and Struggle in 20th Century Trinidad and Tobago: 1898–1960* (The Hague: Institute of Social Studies).

Reynaud, P. L. (1962) *Economie Généralisée et Seuils de Croissance: Etude de la Psychologie Economique du Développement* (Paris: Centre Universitaire des Hautes Etudes Européennes de l'Université de Strasbourg).

Rodgers, G. B. (1976) 'A Conceptualisation of Poverty in Rural India', *World Development*, (April) pp.261ff.

Rodney, Walter (1972) *How Europe Underdeveloped Africa* (London: Bogle-l'Ouverture Publication).

Rostow, W. W. (1960) *The Stages of Economic Growth* (Cambridge: University Press).

Rostow, Walt W. (1962) 'Countering Guerrilla Attack', in Hilsman, *Modern Guerrilla Warfare*.

Rowbotham, Sheila (1975) *Women, Resistance and Revolution* (New York: Vintage).

*Rural Development and Women in Asia* (1982) ILO Tripartite Asian Regional Seminar, Mahabaleshwar, Makarshtra, India (Geneva: International Labour Office).

Salvatore, Dominick (1985) 'The New Protectionism and the Threat to World Welfare: Editor's Introduction', *Journal of Policy Modeling* vol. 7, no. 1 pp.1ff.

Schumacher, E. F. (1974) *Small is Beautiful* (London: Abacus).

Scott, James (1976) *The Moral Economy of the Peasant* (New Haven: Yale University Press).

Scott, James (1977) 'Hegemony and the Peasantry', *Politics and Society*, vol. 7, no. 23 pp.267ff.

Sékou Touré, Ahmed (1979) *Africa on the Move* (London: Panaf Books).

Selbourne, David (1979) 'State and Ideology in India', *Monthly Review*, vol. 31, no. 7 pp.25ff.

Senghaas, Dieter (1983) 'Introduction', in Lehberger *Die Arbeits- und Lebensbedingungen in Süd Korea*.

Senior, Clarence (1958) *Land Reform and Democracy* (Gainesville: University of Florida Press).

Shanin, Teodor (1970) 'Class and Revolution', *Journal of Contemporary Asia*, vol. 1, no. 2 pp.22ff.

Sharma, Miriam (1985) 'Caste, Class, and Gender: Production and Reproduction in North India', *The Journal of Peasant Studies*, vol. 12, no. 4 pp.57ff.

Shoup, Laurance H. and William Minter (1977) *Imperial Brain Trust: The Council on Foreign Relations and United States Foreign Policy* (New York: Monthly Review Press).

Sinyakov, Yuri (1984) *Council for Mutual Economic Assistance* (Moscow: Novosti Press).

Siqueiros, David Alfaro (1975) *Art and Revolution* (London: Lawrence and Wishart).

Siy Jr., Robert Y. (1982) *Community Resource Management: Lessons from the Zanjera* (Quezon City: University of the Philippines Press).

Skocpol, Theda (1982) 'What Makes Peasants Revolutionary?', in Robert P. Weller and Scott E. Guggenheim (eds), *Power and Protest in the Countryside* (Durham N.C.: Duke Press Policy Studies).

Skubiszewski, K. (1968) 'Use of Force by States, Collective Security, Law of War and Neutrality', in Max Sørensen (ed.), *Manual of Public International Law* (London: Macmillan) pp.739ff.

Smigel, Erwin O. (1971) *Handbook on the Study of Social Problems* (Chicago: Rand McNally).

Smilg-Benario, Michael (1928) *Der Zusammenbruch der Zarenmonarchie* (Zürich: Amalthea Verlag).

Smilg-Benario, Michael (1929) *Von Kerenski zu Lenin: die Geschichte Der Zweiten Russischen Revolution* (Zürich: Amalthea Verlag).

Srivastava, M. P. (1982) *The Korean Conflict: Search for Unification* (New Delhi: Prentice Hall of India).

Stavenhagen, Rodolfo (1971) 'Decolonializing Applied Social Science', *Human Organization*, vol. 30, no. 4 pp.333ff.

Stavenhagen, Rodolfo (1981) *Between Underdevelopment and Revolution: a Latin American Perspective* (New Delhi: Abhinav).

Stepan, Alfred (1978) *The State and Society* (New Jersey: Princeton University Press).

Streefkerk, Hein (1985) *Industrial Transition in Rural India: Artisans, Traders and Tribals in South Gujarat* (Bombay: Popular Prakadhan).

Suh, Sang-Chul (1983) 'North Korean Industrial Policy and Trade', in Ky-Hyuk Pak, *North Korea Today*, 1983, pp.197ff.

*Survey of Current Business* (1980) (United States Department of Commerce, Bureau of Economic Analysis, August).

Thomas, Hugh (1971) *Cuba or the Pursuit of Freedom* (London: Eyre & Spottiswoode).

Tibi, Bassam (1973) *Militär und Sozialismus in der Dritten Welt* (Frankfurt am Main: Suhrkamp).

Timms, Noel (1967) *A Sociological Approach to Social Problems* (London: Routledge and Kegan Paul).

*Trade and Development Report 1983*, Report by the Secretariat of the UNCTAD (New York: United Nations).

Trofimenko, Henry (1981) 'The Third World and the US–Soviet Competition: a Soviet View', *Foreign Affairs* (summer) pp.1021ff.

Udechuku, E. C. (1978) *Liberation of Dependent Peoples in International Law*, 2nd ed. (London: African Publications Bureau).

Umozurike, U. O. (1979) *International Law and Colonialism in Africa* (Enugu, Nigeria: Nwamife Publishers).

Utrecht, Ernst (1973) 'American Sociologists on Indonesia', *Journal of Contemporary Asia*, vol. 3, no. 1.

Valdés, Nelson P. (1976) 'Revolution and Institutionalization in Cuba', *Cuban Studies*, vol. 6, no. 1.

Valentine, Charles A., (1971) 'The "Culture of Poverty": its Scientific Implications for Action', in Leacock *The Culture of Poverty*.

Van Gelder, Paul Jan (1984) *Werken onder de Boom: Dynamiek en Informele Sector, de Situatie in Groot-Paramaribo, Suriname* (Working under the Tree: Dynamics and Informal Sector, the Situation in Greater-Paramaribo, Surinam) (University of Amsterdam: Ph.D. dissertation).

Van Ness, Peter and Satish Raichur (1983) 'Dilemmas of Socialist Development: an Analysis of Strategic Lines in China, 1949–1981', *Bulletin of Concerned Asian Scholars*, vol. 15, no. 1 (January/February) pp.2ff.

Vargas Llosa, Mario (1967) *Los Cachorros* (Lima: Biblioteca Peruana)

Von Wiese, Leopold (1933) *System der Allgemeinen Soziologie als Lehre von den Sozialen Prozessen und den Sozialen Gebilden der Menschen (Beziehungslehre)* (München: Von Duncker & Humboldt).

Webster, Andrew (1984) *Introduction to the Sociology of Development* (London: Macmillan).

Wolf, Eric R. (1966) *Peasants* (Englewood Cliffs: Prentice Hall).

Wolpin, M. D. (1972) *Military Aid and Counterrevolution in the Third World* (Lexington, Mass.: Lexington Books).

*World Development Report 1985* (Oxford: Oxford University Press).

Wright, John (1932) *Libya: a Modern History* (London: Croom Helm).

Yansané, Aguibou Y. (1980) 'Decolonization, Dependency, and Development in Africa: the Theory Revisited', in Aguibou Y. Yansané (ed.), *Decolonization and Dependency* (London: Greenwood Press) pp.3ff.

Yansané, Aguibou Y. (1980) 'Conclusion', in Yansané *Decolonization and Dependency*, pp.287ff.

Young, Kate (1981) 'Vrouwen, Mannen en de Migratie in Mexico

(Women, Men and the Migration in Mexico)', *Socialisties-Feministiese Teksten*, no. 5 (Amsterdam) pp.91ff.

Zeitlin, Maurice (1967) *Revolutionary Politics and the Cuban Working Class* (Princeton: Princeton University Press).

# Index